THE SIGNING OF THE DECLARATION
OF INDEPENDENCE

Painted by Arthur E. Becher

THE MARCH OF DEMOCRACY

A

HISTORY OF THE UNITED STATES

By

James Truslow Adams

Volume I

THE RISE OF THE UNION

NEW YORK

CHARLES SCRIBNER'S SONS

PREFACE

THE history of the United States, as contrasted with that of the other great nations of the present day, is brief. It is only about three centuries since the first feeble beginnings of white settlement on our shores laid the foundations for the vast expansion to follow whereas the stories of most European nations carry us far backward beyond the days of the Roman Empire into the deepening mists and darkness of unrecorded time. Yet if we are the youngest of the great peoples, our history is neither simple, short, nor unimportant.

The prime historical concern of the citizen of any country is to know the past, the ideals, the great events and the great men of his own land, but the importance of American history transcends the merely local. Our national life, brief as it has been, has been lived in the period of greatest and swiftest change which the world has ever known. Between the days of the early seventeenth century and those of our own generation lies a deeper gulf than separates our colonial beginnings from the days of Cæsar. America has not only felt those changes, but has been one of the leaders in bringing them to pass. To understand the whole world in this critical period in which we live, we must have a clear idea of the part which America has played.

If the history of every modern nation is complex, our own is peculiarly so. Our race is not yet homogeneous, being still in the making, and contains elements from almost every other race in the world. The swarming to our shores of the tens of millions of immigrants since the first arrivals constitutes the vastest shift of population the world has ever known. Moreover, our history is not that of a simple unified State. For more than half of the period it covers, we have to follow the threads of the story in thirteen different commonwealths in relation to powers across the sea, and in addition we have to consider not only the forty-eight individual States which make up our Federal Union but the history of the partially diverse aims, ideals, and ways of life in at least the three different sections of North, South, and West. In addition, modern history no longer deals only with kings and wars but with the entire range of human interest, and its field is now as wide as it is diversified.

It is obviously impossible to compress our whole story into one "history" which shall tell everything which all readers of different sections and different personal interests might care to know, but the author of the present work has tried to tell in a readable and accurate narrative those facts regarding all phases of our past which are essential for the intelligent citizen both of our own country and the world. Of Southern ancestry but of Northern birth and upbringing, keenly alive to the importance and interest of the West, seeing the nation in perspective and as a whole from frequent residences abroad, he has been conscious of no sectional bias but only of being an American. He now offers his work to all his fellow-citizens in the hope that they may find in it a reasonably full, accurate, and fair account of our great past which may help in the effort which we should all make to create a still greater America in the future.

JAMES TRUSLOW ADAMS.

WASHINGTON, D. C.

CONTENTS

CHAPTER   PAGE

I. DISCOVERY AND SETTLEMENT   I
Columbus Discovers America. The Puritans. The Virginia Charters. The Pilgrims Land and Found Plymouth. John Winthrop Is Elected First Governor.

II. THE COLONIAL SYSTEM TAKES FORM   33
New England Makes Progress. The Dutch and the Quakers. The New Country Becomes the Hope of Many Races. Administration in New England.

III. THE DUEL WITH FRANCE   64
The Three Main Currents of Events. War Between France and England in America. The Beginnings of Conflict with England.

IV. AMERICAN LIFE IN 1763   90
Our Early Social and Economic Life. Our Early Houses and the Arts. Education and Religion. Other Forces at Work.

V. THE INSOLUBLE PROBLEM OF THE NEW EMPIRE   123
The Indian Problem. The Storm Breaks. The Difference in Political Ideas. Ferment in New England. The First Continental Congress and the First Conflict at Lexington.

VI. THE REVOLUTION   167
The First Battles of the Revolution. Washington Takes Command. Some of Washington's Difficulties. A Book Is Published. The Declaration of Independence. Washington's Movements. Burgoyne Is Defeated. The Plot of Benedict Arnold. Cornwallis Surrenders.

CONTENTS

CHAPTER   PAGE

VII.   THE FEDERAL UNION FORMED   218

The Rise in Prices. Difficulties for Our Commerce. Our
New Frontier. Conflict Between Conservatives and Radicals. The Constitutional Convention. The Constitution.
The Constitution Is Ratified: Washington Is Chosen President.

VIII. THE NEW NATION GETS UNDER WAY   261

Washington Is Inaugurated. Hamilton and Jefferson. Our
National Finances. Our Troubles with France and Eng-
land. Washington Declines to Be a Candidate. Adams Is
Chosen President.

ILLUSTRATIONS

The Signing of the Declaration of Independence   Frontispiece

PAGE

The Kensington Stone   facing page   4

The Arrival of the Englishmen in Virginia   facing page   5

Champlain's Map of Plymouth Harbor   facing page   5

King James I Charter   16

The *Mayflower* Compact   24

Part of the First Page of the Manuscript of Bradford's *History of Plymouth Plantation*   27

The Old Ship Church, Hingham, Massachusetts, Begun in 1681   facing page   36

Old Meeting-house, Sandown, New Hampshire, Built in 1774   facing page   36

An Old Print of the College of William and Mary in Virginia Showing It as It Was About 1732   facing page   37

The Wren Building as It Is Today   facing page   37

Reprint of the Original Tract on the Conversion of Indians, Written by Roger Williams in 1643   39

William Penn's Meeting-house at Chester and a Letter from Penn to the Indians   facing page   40

Harvard College, Cambridge   facing page   41

Bowen's View of Yale College, 1786   facing page   41

New England Punishment   43

xi

ILLUSTRATIONS

PAGE

Title-page of the First Edition of Anne Bradstreet's Poems   45

Map Showing Early Settlements in the English Colonies   49

A Broadside of 1689 Calling Upon Andros to Surrender His Powers and Person   61

Title-page of a Letter Denouncing Leisler and His Followers   62

The Oath of Allegiance to King William and Queen Mary   65

Map Showing French Settlements in North America   69

Facsimile of a Map in Colden's *History of the Five Nations*   81

Indian Trade—A Facsimile of a Broadside   82

Map Showing English and Spanish Possessions   88

An Advertisement for a Runaway Slave, 1752   91

An Advertisement of Cargoes in Vessels Out of Virginia   91

The Gibbs House, Charleston, South Carolina, Built in 1752   facing page 92

In the Vieux Carré, the Old French and Spanish Part of New Orleans   facing page 92

Joseph Cabot House, Salem, Built in 1748   facing page 93

Van Courtlandt Mansion, New York, Built in 1748   facing page 93

An Advertisement of a Sale of a Shipment of Liquor, Capers, and Anchovies, 1752   96

Advertisement of the Brigantine *Jane* Carrying Passengers and Freight, 1748   98

Two Interiors Preserved in the Boston Museum of Fine Arts   facing page 100

Santa Barbara Mission, California, 1787–1800   facing page 101

St. Michael's Church, Charleston, South Carolina, Built in 1742   facing page 101

San Xavier Del Bac, Tucson, Arizona   facing page 101

ILLUSTRATIONS

PAGE

Tavern Keeper's Advertisement, 1752   103

Isaac Royall and His Family   facing page   104

Announcement of the First Appearance of the Hallams in America
                                                     facing page   104

Mrs. Hallam as "Marianne" in "The Dramatist"   facing page   104

Nassau Hall and the President's House, Princeton, 1764
                                                     facing page   105

George Whitefield Preaching   facing page   105

A Protest of the Quakers of Philadelphia Against the Appearance
  of David Douglass and His Players in 1759   105

The Earliest Building of the Boston Latin School   106

Advertisement of an Opening for a "Tutor of Good Character" in
  the Symes's Free School in Elizabeth City County   107

A Page from Jonathan Edwards's *Freedom of the Will*   111

Advertisement for Sale of Negroes on Board the *Bance-Island* at
  Charleston   120

The Beginning and Ending of Two Letters from *Dickinson's Letters of a Farmer,* Published in London in 1768   145

British Troops Landing at Boston in 1768   facing page   146

The Able Doctor or America Swallowing the Bitter Draught
                                                     facing page   147

A Broadside Condemning Tea-Drinking Ladies   153

Map Showing General Battleground of the Revolution and the
  Line Established by the Quebec Act, 1774   159

The Selection of Delegates from New York to the First Continental Congress   161

A Broadside of 1775 Denouncing Patrick Henry and His Followers   163

How the News of Lexington and Concord Was Received by the
  Other Colonies   164

ILLUSTRATIONS

PAGE

The Fight on Lexington Common   facing page   168

The Battle of Bunker Hill   facing page   169

A Recruiting Poster   facing page   174

Handbill Sent Among the British Troops on Bunker Hill
    facing page   174

The Evacuation of Charleston by the British, December, 1782
    facing page   175

Two Favorite Songs, Made on the Evacuation of the Town of
Boston   182

The Title-page of Paine's *Common Sense*   185

Title-page of the *Articles of Confederation and Perpetual Union
between the States*   189

Facsimile of Washington's Oath of Allegiance   198

Map of the United States After the Treaty of 1783   215

Map Showing Land Claims of the Thirteen States   229

The Triumphal Arch Which Greeted Washington on His Entry
into Trenton on April 21, 1789   263

Obverse (turned) and Reverse of Twelve-Shilling Note of the
Colony of New Jersey, March 25, 1776   facing page   272

Paper Money Issued by Congress in 1779   facing page   272

A Pennsylvania Loan Office Certificate   facing page   273

A Third Bill of Exchange   facing page   273

A Cartoon Comparing American and French **Liberty in** 1789   281

The Burning of John Jay in Effigy   290

Congressional Pugilists   300

Announcement of Washington's Death   305

ILLUSTRATIONS

END OF VOLUME

GREAT SCENES AND PERSONAGES
OF OUR HISTORY

George Washington, our first President

Benjamin Franklin, author, inventor, diplomat, and great American

Alexander Hamilton, founder of our financial system

James Madison, fourth President, an author, and a defender of the Constitution

James Monroe, fifth President and last of the Virginia dynasty

Andrew Jackson, "Old Hickory," our first backwoodsman in the White House

Abraham Lincoln, unequalled in his love for his people, unsurpassed in their esteem and idealization of him

Grover Cleveland, the only President to be defeated, then re-elected

Theodore Roosevelt, our most versatile President in accomplishments and in interests

Woodrow Wilson, our great leader in the World War, expressing most forcibly the hopes and ideals of our country

Stone Street Looking Toward Whitehall, New Amsterdam, 1659

The Expulsion of the Quakers from Massachusetts, 1660

A Model of the Overshot Water Wheel in the John Winthrop Mill, New London, Connecticut

ILLUSTRATIONS

The Surrender of Fort William Henry to Montcalm in 1757

The Burning of the *Prudent* and Capture of the *Bienfaisant* in Louisbourgh Harbour, 1758

Abercrombie's Army Embarking at the Head of Lake George in an Expedition Against Ticonderoga, July, 1758

The College of Philadelphia Before the Revolution

Bruton Parish Church, Virginia

The Parlor of the Powell House in Philadelphia

A Dining Room of the Early Republican Period of Washington and Baltimore

The Evening Mail—Travel by Stagecoach on the Boston Post Road

Otis Protesting the Writs of Assistance

Paul Revere

Winter at Valley Forge

Hamilton Surrendering to George Rogers Clark at Vincennes

Benjamin Franklin and Richard Oswald, British Representative, Discussing the Treaty of Peace at Paris

The Signing of the Constitution in Independence Hall, Philadelphia, 1787

Washington Arriving at the Battery, New York, Prior to His Inauguration

Washington Taking the Oath of Office as First President of the United States

Settlers from Connecticut Entering the Western Reserve

Daniel Boone Leading a Group of Pioneers Through the Cumberland Gap

VOLUME I

THE RISE OF THE UNION

CHAPTER I

DISCOVERY AND SETTLEMENT

NOTHING is known with any certainty as to the origin of human life on the American continent. The history of the race which has been called "Indian," owing to the mistake of Columbus which we shall note presently, is shrouded in the mist of inference. The earliest ancestors of the barbarians whom the white men found inhabiting the more temperate and tropical regions of the New World may have come from Asia by way of the islands in Behring Strait or even across a land bridge which may have existed in earlier geologic ages.

Nothing, however, can be determined with the evidence yet at hand, and in any case these primitive "Americans" have little to do with the America of today. Unlike the original Britons, whose blood became intermingled with that of the successive invading hordes of Saxons, Danes, and Normans, the Indians never mixed their blood with that of the English settlers who were to become dominant in North America. The history and present culture of Mexico cannot be understood without ample consideration of Indian influence, but those of the

I

present United States need take little heed of the aborigines. They have, indeed, left their traces.

A good many words of Indian origin are embedded in our vocabulary and we owe to the savages a large number of our most beautiful and interesting place-names. The earliest white settlers were greatly helped by the Indian's knowledge of woodcraft, by the use of important foods, notably Indian corn or maize, known to the natives, and by other items in the Indian culture. But such influences were comparatively slight as compared with those of races elsewhere who have really fused their blood, language, and culture with those of the conquering race.

The white man himself, for the most part, regarded the Indian merely as forming the same sort of obstacle to his own advance and success as was offered by the wild animals or the hindrances of climate and topography. Indeed, until very recently, we have treated them as we have treated all other forces opposing our steady advance across the continent and our subduing of it as quickly as possible to our own wants. The record of our dealings with the first owners of our soil is one in which, except for isolated instances, we can take no pride, and which has left a bloody stain on the pages recording almost every decade of our history.

That history, unlike the records of the great powers of the Old World, begins with marked abruptness. In Europe, race gives place to race, and civilization to civilization, and in tracing them back the authentic record merges into myth and legend. It is true that our roots lie deep in the past of the European nations from which came the multitudes of immigrants who, with their descendants, have peopled the United States. Nevertheless, the passage overseas combined with our later breaking of all political ties and our failure to assimilate and mingle with any native population has served to delimit our history within a comparatively short period of recorded time.

Many of our institutions, like our language, come to us from England, and we must take account of influences from the many ancestral lands whence our people are descended, but as generally understood and accepted by us, our history begins with the first discoveries and settlements along our coasts, little more than four centuries ago at most.

Nearly five hundred years before that beginning, Europeans may indeed have landed on our shores. Almost as little is definitely known, however, of the possible explorations of the Norsemen within the present limits of the United States as of the origin of the Indians whom they may have encountered. About 982 Erik Thorwaldson, sailing from Norway, discovered Greenland, and a colony was later planted there. His son, Leif Erikson, and others discovered lands farther west, and efforts have been made to locate their landings all the way from Labrador to Long Island Sound but nothing can be ascertained with certainty as to the localities suggested by the very uncertain data given in the old Sagas.

Some remains, formerly believed to have dated from their time, such as the old mill at Newport, have long since been proved to belong to later periods, and learned discussions over such inscriptions as those on the Dighton Rock have proved nothing. One of the most interesting of these relics, and one which seems to have some real claim to authenticity, is the "Kensington Stone" found in the roots of a tree at Kensington, Douglas County, Minnesota, in 1898. The runic inscription on it indicates that the point where it was found marks the southern limit of an expedition of Norsemen who came overland from Hudson's Bay in 1362; and the summing up of the evidence in 1932 would seem to give this record the best claim, which, however, is only a claim, to being the earliest monument by white men within our limits. These Norse voyages and explorations, wherever they may have been made, were without further influence on history and apparently had nothing to do with the later and authentic discoveries.

These latter were occasioned by reasons quite dissimilar to the more or less adventurous spirit which led Leif and possibly others to voyage westward from the little colony in Greenland.

The European world of the fifteenth century, descended from Greece and Rome, was hemmed in on all sides by impassable barriers of sea and desert or by the bar-

THE KENSINGTON STONE
Courtesy of the Minnesota Historical Society, St. Paul, Minnesota.

THE ARRIVAL OF THE ENGLISHMEN IN VIRGINIA

*From a drawing by John White of Raleigh's First Colony, 1585, in De Bry's
"Grand Voyages," Frankfort, 1590.*

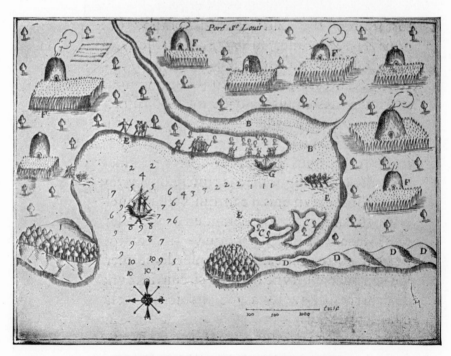

CHAMPLAIN'S MAP OF PLYMOUTH HARBOR

From Champlain's "Voyages," 1613, in the Lenox Collection, New York Public Library.

barian hordes which were beginning to press in on it from the East. This outer barbarian world was practically as little known geographically as it had been in the days of the Roman Empire. It was a world, however, with which Europe, as always, had commercial relations, the greatest and most lucrative trade being with the mysterious "East." From China, the Spice Islands, India, and many lands, the spices, pearls, jewels, rugs, silks, and other commodities of which Europe had need found their way by trade routes hidden from the knowledge of European merchants. These routes had their western termini in ports of the Mediterranean, encircling its eastern end from Constantinople to Alexandria.

In the fourteenth, fifteenth, and early sixteenth centuries, the warlike hordes of the Ottoman Turks spread out from their centre in Asia Minor. Steadily pursuing their conquests, they passed the Bosphorus and captured Constantinople in 1453, and had overrun Egypt by 1522. All the termini of Europe's greatest trade routes thus fell into their hands. The process had been gradual, and the Turks did not prohibit all trade, but in the long period of conquest, the disturbances of violence and war, new taxes, and other hindrances to the old established commerce gravely affected the trading life of Europe.

This threatened throttling of the business of the European peoples came at just the period when, after ten centuries of readjustments, they were beginning to feel a great rebound of energies within the new forms of institutional and intellectual life which they had slowly evolved. Moreover, due to the steady northwestward thrust of the Turks, this superabundant energy, greater even than that of the Roman Empire, was compressed within a comparatively small area. To the south, the Sahara Desert and the hordes of Islam set an impassable barrier. To the west and north were unknown or frozen seas, mysterious and terrifying. European energy was rapidly rising but walls seemed to be closing in on it. It was as though a liquid were being brought to the boiling point in a container which was contracting. Vent or explosion was inevitable. Thanks to ocean exploration a vent was found, and within four centuries European civilization was to spread over the whole globe.

In the fifteenth century, sensitive to the increasing difficulties of the Oriental trade by the old routes, and ignorant of the great downward protuberance of the African continent, Portuguese explorers sought to find a way to the Orient by sailing eastward south of the Sahara. If successful they hoped to tap the trade at its source and to eliminate the land routes and the Turks. Finally after two generations of advance, Bartholomew Diaz rounded the Cape of Good Hope. He had proceeded far enough, before being forced to turn back by a mutinous crew, to make him sure that the goal lay just beyond. In 1498 Vasco da Gama, following the track of Diaz, reached India and saw the welcome domes of Calicut. After a voyage of 18,000 miles he returned to

Portugal with a rich cargo and yet more precious knowledge. Even his predecessor, Diaz, had discovered, however, a dozen years before, that this route to the Indies
would be portentously long.

Certain that the East could be reached by sea, and believing in the theory, thought by many to be incredible,
that the world was round, Columbus had conceived the
idea of reaching the Indies by sailing West. He hoped
thus to save the long and useless journey around Africa,
and had the globe been as small as he thought and had
the then unknown American continents not blocked the
way, he would have outflanked the Portuguese, as they
had outflanked the Turk. At last, helped by the Spanish
monarchs, Ferdinand and Isabella, he set sail from Palos
August 3, 1492, with his crew of eighty-nine in three
tiny vessels, of which only one had a deck.

COLUMBUS DISCOVERS AMERICA

With the days passing into weeks, and the weeks into
months, he and his companions voyaged westward until
on the evening of October 11 a flaring light was seen as
though on a shore. The next morning the explorers
landed on the beach of some small island in the Baha-
mas which we cannot accurately identify. The story has
been told so often that in the efforts to make a "fresh
presentation" of American history a number of recent
historians have gone so far as not to mention Columbus

at all! He belongs forever, nevertheless, with the small and select band of men who by novel vision and indomitable will have influenced the entire subsequent course of history. Even to his death, after subsequent voyages, Columbus continued to believe that he had attained Cathay or "The Indies" as the Orient was called, which error accounts for the name Indians given to the inhabitants of the lands which he explored. In reality he had found a New World in which Europeans could live and which would absorb their surplus energies for centuries.

Once it was demonstrated that land could be reached by sailing west and, quite as important, that a return was possible, the original discoverer had many successors. In 1497 John Cabot, an Italian like Columbus, sailed from Bristol in the employ of the English King Henry VII, and landed either on the Newfoundland, Canadian, or Labrador coasts. In 1524 Verrazano, under the flag of France, explored our shore possibly from Carolina to Newfoundland. The Spaniard Gomez was somewhere within the same limits the year following, and the maps of the time show the rapidly increasing geographical knowledge gained.

It is not necessary to chronicle the many explorations, along the coasts or in the interior, which were made in the ensuing century, for, with Verrazano, the chief three contestants to claims on America had appeared,—Spanish, English, and French. Nor is it necessary to relate the diplomatic struggles of the claimants or the first abortive attempts at settlement by the English under such dreamers of empire as Sir Humphrey Gilbert or Sir Walter Raleigh. We may pass on to the opening of the seventeeth century by which time the claims to what was at last realized to be a new continent and not the Indies had taken somewhat definite shape.

With the exception of Portuguese Brazil, Spain, with a well-established empire in Peru and Mexico, claimed— and in part possessed by colonization—all of South and Central America, our present Gulf coast, our Southwest, and the land between the Rockies and the Pacific. France claimed all of Canada and the Mississippi Valley, while England considered as hers the whole of the North American continent from Florida to Canada and from the Atlantic to the Pacific. The conflicting character of these claims is evident, and was more than once to plunge the world into war.

The new land which had been found by Columbus and his followers was no gorgeous East with silk-clad princes, teeming millions, spices, and precious jewels. For the most part it was a forbidding wilderness inhabited by naked savages. Only where the Spaniards, encountering the barbaric cultures of the Aztecs and the Incas, had discovered treasure of silver and gold, mines, and an ample labor supply, was there easy wealth to be reaped. Quickly a transplanted Spanish culture was established based on the riches and populousness of the

9

older barbaric kingdoms. The 160,000 Spaniards who it has been estimated were in New Spain by 1574 had libraries, printing presses, scholars, and universities long before a single Englishman had been able to establish a foothold in the North.

The French, after trying colonization in Florida, whence they were driven out by the Spaniards, established a fortified post at Quebec under the indomitable Champlain, who had explored and mapped our New England coast. From that year, 1608, they continued to hold Canada until 1763, although always with a sparse population. The French empire in America was to be ever far-flung, a sort of combined trading post and missionary enterprise gilded by imperial dreams. Since Canada apparently lacked mineral or agricultural wealth, the Indian fur trade became the dominant interest, and French traders and explorers roamed west to the Great Lakes and down the valley of the Mississippi, establishing forts and trading centres in the vast hinterland behind the Appalachians.

The influence of the French on the destinies of the continent, however, was to prove out of all proportion to the numbers and strength of the colonies. Had France not established New France and had she not been despoiled of it by the English in 1763, she would probably have had no motive to abet the English colonies in their revolt of 1776, and that revolt instead of being successful would have been merely one more of the innumerable suppressed rebellions in the history of the British Empire.

The year before Champlain built his fort at Quebec and faced the first terrible winter from which only eight of the twenty-eight settlers were to emerge alive, a handful of Englishmen had planted the first successful English colony far south in Virginia. To them the future belonged, but before picking up the thread of our own history, which will thenceforth be continuous, we must turn to observe the England of the seventeenth century, which with a population half that of London today was to send out the swarms which were destined to found a new English nation overseas.

In some respects that little, bustling, fast-changing England of 1600 was in the lead of the European nations. France was dissipating her energy in continental wars and entanglements. Spain, which in spite of the huge annual supply of gold derived from her American possessions had been steadily sinking in power and prestige, had received a staggering blow when the English defeated her Armada in 1588. Even before that the English sea-dogs—Drake, Hawkins, and the rest—had been yelping on her trail like wolves, and bringing down galleon after galleon laden with treasure. When the entire "invincible" Armada had been sunk or scattered to the winds, the daring and pretensions of English seamen rose to new heights. Spain was no longer a deterrent to any New World venture.

England was also the first of the great nations to pass from the stage of feudalism to more modern conditions, and, though both government and society were aristocratic, her plain citizens were the freest in the world. Under the Tudors, who were English to the core in all their aspirations, there had been a great outburst of conscious nationalism and patriotism. Henry the Eighth had declared the English Church independent of the Pope, and to the hatred of the French and Spanish as competitors and foreigners had been added that of Protestant for Catholic in an age when religion was a passion. Robust individualism was rampant and took many forms, whether in men of action like Drake, Raleigh, Frobisher, and others, or in the brilliant band of men of letters, with Shakespeare at the head, who are still the glory of English literature. This individualism extended to more ordinary folk, business men intent on extending trade, or independent-thinking citizens deciding for themselves the problems of their spiritual life.

Puritanism was one of the forces of the period. The word has been used in many meanings but we may here consider it as applied to the movement against what were considered errors, abuses, or evils in the ecclesiastical or moral life of the time. Protestantism, when it had denied the authority of the single Catholic Church, had opened the way to an anarchic individualism in the interpretation of the Bible as the Word of God; and in an era of increasing intellectual energy and personal liberty it was impossible that any organization should say to all individuals "thus far and no farther" in schism.

THE PURITANS

The Puritans were made up of all sorts of minds, from those of great noblemen, like the Earl of Warwick, or thinkers, like Milton, to illiterate cobblers or farmhands. Their protests against tenets or ceremonies of the English Church and against the manners and morals of non-Puritans were of all degrees of intensity. Some wished to reform Church or society from within, others, the Separatists, felt they must withdraw entirely. In those days, religious heresy aroused passions similar to those aroused today by economic heresies, and too radical religious beliefs were held to be as inimical to the safety of the State as are Socialism or Communism in the America of our own century. The extremer Puritans therefore suffered some persecution and feared worse. Moreover, among Protestants themselves, the demand to the right of individual interpretation of the Bible did not lead, as might have been expected, to tolerance. The individual, having found for himself what he believed to be the Truth, and convinced of its universal validity and importance, all too often felt compelled to force it on other men, and to found sects or societies in which it alone should be recognized.

About the beginning of the seventeenth century profound economic changes were also in progress. Among other things, the steady and vast flow of gold from New Spain had thrown the old price structure of goods and labor into confusion. Some classes were rising and others were falling in the economic scale. This, added to the changes from feudalism to capitalism and from agriculture to an incipient industrialism, was rapidly upsetting long-established conditions in the nation. There was much unrest and unemployment among the laboring and lower middle-classes. In the upper middle-class of "gentlemen" those who could not adjust themselves to the new order were slipping down, while others, making use of the rather abundant capital due to the great increase in Europe's gold supply, were making ventures in new trades overseas and growing rich.

Many "companies" were being formed to permit groups of these men to join in trading to Muscovy, the Levant, India, Guinea, and elsewhere, such companies being typical of a new form of economic adventure not only in England but in France, Holland, and other countries. In some cases they were formed to buy land and to colonize it, as in Ireland. In others they were primarily trading companies, but on account of the conditions of commerce this meant also control of the depot or trading station and its inhabitants established at the end of a trade route in a foreign and frequently uncivilized land.

Thus, at the time we have reached, all the conditions

were ripe for England to begin the attempted exploitation of some part of the New World. Briefly, there was an enormous reservoir of energy seeking an outlet. There were many people, only a part of whom were being drained off by the colonizing projects in Ireland, who were discontented with the religious, social, or economic situation in which they found themselves at home. Much unemployment on the one hand was offset by accumulations of new capital on the other in possession of energetic and adventurous merchants seeking profitable investment and accustomed to take large risks for corresponding gains.

Spanish profits from America had been colossal but that nation was no longer powerful enough to act as the growling dog in the manger of such parts of the New World as she did not actually occupy. France, although she had explored our Atlantic seaboard, had chosen to concern herself with Canada and the fur trade of the interior. The Portuguese had been excluded from North America by the Papal Bull of 1493, and the enterprising Dutch had as yet shown no interest in Western schemes or exploration. With the formation of the East India Company in 1600 the great English chartered companies had covered practically all quarters of the globe open to exploitation by English capitalists except the New World. Consequently the next step in commercial expansion inevitably pointed to North America.

THE VIRGINIA CHARTERS

On April 10, 1606, King James I granted a charter to two groups of capitalists, one group being mostly resident in London and the other in and around Plymouth.

VIRGINIA CHARTERS.

NUMBER I.

King JAMES I.'s LETTERS PATENT to Sir Thomas Gates, Sir George Somers, and others, for two several Colonies and Plantations, to be made in VIRGINIA, and other Parts and Territories of AMERICA. Dated April 10, 1606.

I. JAMES, by the grace of God, King of England, Scotland, France, and Ireland, Defender of the Faith, &c. Whereas our loving and well disposed subjects, Sir Thomas Gates, and Sir George Somers, Knights, Richard Hackluit, Clerk, Prebendary of Westminster, and Edward-Maria Wingfield, Thomas Hanham, and Ralegh Gilbert, Esqrs. William Parker and George Popham, Gentlemen, and divers others of our loving subjects, have been humble suitors unto us, that We would vouchsafe unto them and may in time bring the infidels and savages, living in those parts, to human civility, and to a settled and quiet government; Do, by these our letters patents, graciously accept of, and agree to, their humble and well intended desires.

IV. And do therefore, for Us, our heirs and successors, Grant and agree, that the said Sir Thomas Gates, Sir George Somers, Richard Hackluit, and Edward-Maria Wingfield, adventurers of and for our city of London, and all such others, as are, or

KING JAMES CHARTER

As the opening of it appears in *The Charters—A Narrative of the Proceedings of the North American Colonies in Consequence of the Late Stamp Act.* Printed in London in 1766.

From the Bancroft Collection, New York Public Library.

In this document, usually called the first Virginia Charter, England definitely claimed the right to that part of North America between the 34th and 45th parallels of latitude, or from about Cape Fear River to Passamaquoddy Bay. Each chartered group, or "company," was given the right to a hundred miles of coast, stretching a hundred miles inland, for colonization, the London Company having the exclusive right to plant south of latitude 38 and the Plymouth Company north of 41. The intervening strip was open to either of them, but neither was allowed to plant within a hundred miles of the other.

In spite of an ineffective protest from Spain, the London Company, under the chief patronage of Sir Robert Cecil, at once proceeded to make use of its privileges. The main hopes for profit lay in the possible discovery of precious metals and of a water passage through what was thought to be a narrow continental barrier to the markets of the East. A colony, however, was desirable for several reasons, and in December, 1606, 120 persons were sent out in three ships which did not reach the shore of Chesapeake Bay until the 6th of the following May.

About thirty years earlier Raleigh had made two unsuccessful attempts to plant a settlement in Virginia, one of them being notable for the birth of the first English child in America, a little girl who was christened Virginia Dare, and whose fate is shrouded in the mystery which surrounds the entire colony of 1587, no trace of which could be discovered when help was sent out to it four years later. They may have perished of starvation or been massacred by the Indians. When the attempt was again made to plant a colony in 1607, it is possible that the savages recalled the previous intrusion. In any case they at once attacked the first landing party of new settlers. The site chosen for what was to prove the cradle of the American people was at Jamestown, then called James Fort, and was marshy and malarial. What with sickness, the savages, an ill-devised form of government, and inexperience with pioneering needs, the first few years were stark with tragedy.

The tragedy is certain though the details are largely shrouded in mystery. One of the chief actors, the famous Captain John Smith, has left us an account of them but in the long and crowded career of that adventurous person it is difficult to pick out truth from fiction as told with great gusto by himself. We know, at any rate, that when the supply ships sailed for England the second time in April, 1608, 144 out of a total of 197 immigrants had died.

Renewed efforts were made by the London promoters, who grossly misrepresented conditions to intending emigrants, and in June, 1609, nine more vessels were despatched with about 500 persons of both sexes and all ages. One vessel sank. One ran ashore on Bermuda. Plague and fever stalked the decks, and when the survivors reached Jamestown they found there only a hundred whites, some encamped about twenty miles away and some living with the savages. There was no food on shore and hardly any on the ships. Disease and hunger worked on the immigrants like scythes on wheat. In their madness for food, men dug up dead and putrid

Indians, and sat by their dying comrades waiting to seize on their flesh.

It was more than humanity could stand and the decision was made to abandon the colony. There was in store, however, a sudden and dramatic turn in events. At the very moment when the 150 survivors of the 900 adventurers were sailing for home down the James, a ship was sighted bringing Lord de la Warr with food and help. All decided to make one more effort, and the frightful "starving time" of 1609-10 was a turning point in the settlement of the United States. A severe military government was instituted and order came to the colony. With the expiration of the seven years during which property was to be held in common stock, private ownership was instituted and did much to stimulate hope and ambition. Peace was bought with the Indians. Sir Thomas Gates, Sir Thomas Dale, and George Yeardley, all soldiers of a "hard-boiled" type, succeeded as governors in bringing the colony through its trials. Dreams of gold and silver or the Northwest Passage evaporated and the colony settled down to the cultivation of tobacco as its staple.

It has been estimated that by 1625, when at last the colony had become firmly established, 1095 persons were living in Virginia, but to secure this result and to establish what was to be the American nation, over 4500 had perished from starvation, massacre or disease. The 5649 immigrants who may be called the first Virginians, were of all types,—a few gentlemen with servants, a few genuine criminals, some soldiers and professional men, more or less riff-raff, and much excellent material in the way of artisans, mechanics, and so on. When stability and private ownership came after the first few horrible years, the types of newcomers most in evidence were men with capital to build plantations and those known as indentured servants. The latter, who were of considerable importance in our history, were of all grades. Some came from jails but that means little as in that day men were imprisoned in England for very minor offences and even trifling debts. Under an indenture, men, women, and children were sold or sold themselves into service in the colony for a term of years,—two or three up to seven or more,—to pay for their passage. Their term of service completed, they could claim land and start life afresh in the New World. Under the strain of the maladjustments in the economic condition of England, many of good standing at home took advantage of this way of making a new beginning, and the word servant, which covered schoolmasters, younger sons of good families, and others, is misleading. It meant merely in many cases those who sold themselves into service in exchange for the costly voyage to America which they could not otherwise pay for. As the trade became organized, wicked ships' captains began to kidnap boys and girls on the streets and sell their time in America.

The original charter granted by King James in 1606 was followed by others in 1609 and 1612, the last being revoked completely in 1624, when Virginia became a Royal Colony. There ensued, however, no disturbance to property rights or popular liberties. The first charter, happily, in words which the Americans were always to cherish and remember, had provided that the colonists and their descendants "shall have and enjoy all liberties, franchises, and immunities within any of our other dominions, to all intents and purposes as if they had been abiding and born within this our Realm of England or any other of our said dominions." That promise of liberty had been the original basis on which Englishmen had first been induced to settle in America.

For the first decade, however, the colonists had had little or no voice in managing their own political affairs. In April, 1619, Sir George Yeardley arrived from London with new instructions as governor, the most important of which was that thereafter the people were to have a share in their own government and that twenty-two burgesses were to be elected from nine "plantations" and three "cities" to form the lower house of the new legislature. Actually at first, there were eleven little local organizations, variously called "city," "borough," "hundred," or "plantation," each represented by two burgesses in the lower legislative house. This with the council of six as an upper house, and the governor, brought the governmental machinery to a type that was to be familiar in its broad outlines, though with local variations, throughout colonial America.

On July 30, 1619, the legislature met and political self-government was formally inaugurated on the American continent. The following year it was likewise instituted in the colony of Bermuda. A significant but less happy event in the same year that the burgesses thus started at Jamestown on their colonial Parliamentary career was the arrival of a Dutch ship whose captain sold twenty negro slaves to the planters.

Although the stability and prosperity of Virginia were now in striking contrast to the early years, disease continued to take an appalling toll, and in 1622 there was an unexpected attack by the savages, the result of both these factors being that after the massacre there were fewer than 900 settlers left in the colony. Nevertheless, emigrants continued to pour out from England, but the mismanagement and scandals connected with the London Company finally brought about the voiding of its charter, as we have stated, in 1624. However, in spite of all vicissitudes the colony grew, as did its confidence in governing itself, so that in 1635 the House of Burgesses dared even to depose a royal governor. The English character as well as race had indeed established itself in the New World.

Meanwhile efforts by the Plymouth Company to found a colony in New England had not succeeded, one experiment of wintering in Maine with inadequate resources having signally failed. Every year, however, French, Spanish, Dutch, or English ships were to be found along our shores for fishing, fur trading or exploring, and the New England coast had become well known. In 1609, Henry Hudson, often miscalled "Hendrik," an Englishman in Dutch employ, had discovered the river that bears his name; and in 1614 Captain John Smith was exploring and mapping the Massachusetts coast and acquiring unlimited faith in the possibilities of the region. Virginia, however, was thirteen years old before the first band of settlers were to effect a permanent lodgment in the North, and then by accident.

In 1606, the year when the first emigrants embarked on their ships for Chesapeake Bay, another small group made up of the Separatists we have mentioned above, fearful of being able to continue peaceably their religious life in England, had emigrated to Holland, settling in Leyden. Being English, they were not happy living among foreigners; they feared demoralization for their children; and found it hard to make comfortable livings. For these and other reasons, they determined, as an endless stream of emigrants of all races has since, to try their fortune in the New World.

The Virginia colony having proved successful, they decided to settle near that. Having secured the needed financial backing of capitalists in London, 102 passengers crowded into the *Mayflower* and set sail from Southampton in the summer of 1620. Only a third of these, under the lead of William Brewster, were "Pilgrims" from Leyden, the rest being a nondescript lot of

> 54.
>
> sett by them done (this their condition considered) might be as firme as any patent; and in some respects more sure. The forme was as followeth.
>
> In y name of god Amen. We whose names are underwriten, the loyall subiects of our dread soueraigne Lord King Iames by y grace of god, of great Britaine, franc, & Ireland king, defender of y faith, &
> Haueing vndertaken, for y glorie of god, and aduancements of y christian faith and honour of our king & countrie, a voyage to plant y first colonie in y Northerne parts of Virginia. Doe by these presents solemnly & mutualy in y presence of god, and one of another, couenant, & combine our selues togeather into a Ciuill body politick, for our better ordering, & preseruation & furtherance of y ends aforesaid; and by vertue hereof to enacte, constitute, and frame such just & equall lawes, ordinances, Acts, constitutions, & offices, from time to time, as shall be thought most meete & conuenient for y generall good of y Colonie: vnto which we promise all due submission and obedience. In witnes wherof we haue here vnder subscribed our names at Cap=Codd y .11. of Nouember, in y year of y raigne of our soueraigne Lord king Iames of England, franc, & Ireland y eighteen and of Scotland y fiftie fourth. An: Dom. 1620.]

THE *MAYFLOWER* COMPACT

The first part, from the original Bradford manuscript.

In the Massachusetts State Library.

settlers picked up in London or elsewhere and shipped by the capitalists. It may be pointed out that a "*Mayflower* descendant" may thus have had a far from desirable ancestor!

THE PILGRIMS LAND AND FOUND PLYMOUTH

It was November before they sighted Cape Cod and, after running into dangerous shoals in an effort to make southward for Virginia, they decided to disembark at some favorable spot near at hand. It was thus by chance that the famous landing at Plymouth was made. Finding themselves outside the limits of the Virginia Government, with no charter of their own, and with a very mixed lot of persons to control, the more substantial passengers decided before landing to draw up a covenant to be signed by all the men providing for a simple form of self-government under which officers were to be elected and laws enacted.

During the first few years of this second American settlement many of the troubles which the Virginians had encountered were met again,—heavy sickness, occasional attacks from the savages, and economic difficulties until private ownership replaced the partly communal form of economic life forced on them by their capitalist backers. Neither the disorders nor the trials were so severe, however, as they had been in the Southern adventure, and the little democracy governed itself with notable success.

Chief among the leaders which it developed was William Bradford, a Puritan at once determined and lovable, a man of strong will, high courage, sound sense, and, although a farmer's son, of scholarly tastes. His *History of Plymouth Plantation* is the earliest contribution of importance to American historical writing, and still has a charm that few other American books could claim until nearly two centuries later. The peppery tempered but loyal little soldier, Captain Myles Standish, was the sword of the colony.

Meanwhile other English settlers, some worthy and others distinctly not so, began to settle singly or in small groups along the New England coast. Colonies of English were also going out to the West India islands,—St. Kitts in 1623, Barbadoes and St. Croix in 1625, Nevis and Barbuda in 1628. These and other islands were to become of great value to the Empire later, and we cannot understand some points in our own subsequent relations to England if we do not bear that fact in mind. It is also important at this stage of our story to think of the movement of colonization, now setting out from England in every direction, as a whole.

By 1640 probably over 65,000 English people had left their homes for the New World, without counting the large numbers who went to Ireland. Many different motives animated them, these often being combined in the same individual. Religion was only one of the moving impulses, but it was to be especially notable in the next, and by far the largest, colony yet to be planted in America, just as it had been the chief motive with the minority Pilgrim band on the *Mayflower*.

In the eastern section of England Puritanism was particularly strong among a group of influential families and clergy, and in that same section economic distress among the lower middle and laboring class was unusually acute. In 1628 a group of men of that district, some of

FACSIMILE OF PART OF THE FIRST PAGE OF THE MANUSCRIPT OF BRADFORD'S *HISTORY OF PLYMOUTH PLANTATION*
From the original in the Massachusetts State Library.

whom had already been interested in a fishing company at Cape Ann, secured a patent for land running from 3 miles north of the Merrimac River to 3 miles south of the Charles, a strip about 60 miles wide and 3000 long, as it ran to the Pacific Ocean!

They at once despatched John Endicott with about 60 persons to take possession and prepare for a colony. There was already a little settlement at Salem and there

Endicott wintered. The next year 400 people were sent out, and a Royal charter was secured for a Massachusetts Bay Company, much on the lines of the other company charters. This provided, in part, that the members of the company, known as "freemen," should constitute the "General Court" which was to meet quarterly and once a year elect a governor, deputy-governor, and board of assistants. The "Court" was also given power to make such rules, or laws and ordinances, as should not be repugnant to the laws of England.

Events in that country were moving rapidly, and the future was becoming dark. The King dissolved Parliament in anger and was to rule for the next eleven years without one. Nine of the popular leaders had been imprisoned in the Tower. Important Puritan, and what we might call today "Liberal," families were deeply anxious, and were considering the New World as a possible asylum.

Probably on account of this situation, the influential men in control of the Massachusetts Bay Company decided upon taking an unprecedented and what was to be a unique step in the history of English company colonization. They determined to send the actual charter to the colony itself. By doing so they, in practice, transformed what was intended to be a mere trading company charter into what they came, without legal justification, to consider the constitution for an almost self-governing State. The step was to prove of great importance in the subsequent relations of Massachusetts to the British Government, and to the development of colonial political thought.

JOHN WINTHROP IS ELECTED FIRST GOVERNOR

The first governor elected, in England, was John Winthrop, a gentleman of good family and position who, like so many others, had found himself unable to keep up his accustomed scale of living under the altered economic conditions of the time. He had been used to living well, with seven or eight servants, and the future for himself and his children had already seemed black to him when a final blow fell with the loss of a government office which he held. He was also a Puritan, and the outlook seemed as unpromising from the standpoint of enjoying his religious beliefs as it did from that of maintaining his inherited social position in his county. In his case, as in most, various motives thus reinforced one another in urging him to the experiment of going out to the American wilderness. The letters of himself, his wife, and children reveal a singularly affectionate and cultured family life, and it must have been with heavy hearts that they left their old Suffolk home.

However, in 1630, Winthrop sailed for Massachusetts with a band of nearly a thousand colonists, who settled what later became the towns of Charlestown, Boston, Medford, Watertown, Roxbury, Lynn, and Dorchester.

By 1634 he estimated the total population at four thousand, and Massachusetts had become the most powerful settlement on the entire North American coast.

The new colony was as strong in convictions as in numbers. There was a marked Puritan tinge in all the colonies, as in England itself, and the laws passed by the settlers in Virginia with regard to manners, morals, dress, and church-going differed but little from those to be passed in Massachusetts, though Virginia established the Church of England and New England became Nonconformist. The Massachusetts leaders, however, both lay and clerical, were of the strictest sect of the Puritans and gave the tone to the whole community. They attempted to make their State a theocracy with themselves as the sole interpreters of the Word of God in civil and ecclesiastical affairs, which they considered practically as one, and in 1631 the General Court declared that only church members could be admitted as freemen, that is have a vote in the government. It was hoped by the leaders that by this device they could maintain strict political as well as religious control. They had come to the New World to worship as they chose and had no intention of being interfered with by those of different belief whether in England or within their own newly established settlements. John Endicott exemplified best the dogmatic, harsh, unyielding, and intolerant type which the movement evolved, but even gentler and sweeter characters, like those of Winthrop or the Reverend John Cotton, grew less broadly humane under the conditions of life in the Theocracy.

The hard years of first settlement, the sectarian's belief in his own monopoly of Truth, the subtle infection of suddenly acquired power both as civil rulers and religious prophets, all tended to emphasize what we have come to regard as Puritanism in its most exaggerated and least charitable form. The leaders disliked and distrusted democracy or even permitting the ordinary citizen a voice in government, and did their best to stave off civil as well as religious dissent. But if too often they seemed intent on making the wilderness blossom like the thistle instead of like the rose, they developed around the core of "the New England conscience" a character which, with all its ugly excrescences, was to form an invaluable strain in the nation of the future. It is only just to point out, however, that this same strain accounts for much of the fanaticism and intolerance which have too often marked our national life and opinion.

Colonizing had by this time passed beyond the stage of doubtful success, and in 1632 the foundations for yet another colony were laid next to Virginia. Lord Baltimore, a Catholic peer, received a charter from King Charles which permitted him to found a settlement where Catholics would be tolerated, named in honor of the Queen, Mary-land. Although this charter was not that of a trading company like the others, but created a Palatinate like the Bishopric of Durham, it was notable

that, whereas in England the Bishop had practically un-
controlled power of legislation, Baltimore could make
laws only "with the advice, assent, and approbation of
the freemen or the greater part of them or their representatives." Unlike the French and Spanish colonies, the
seed of liberty and self-government was thus dropped
into the ground of every English town, plantation, and
colony at its very beginning. From their inception, the
English colonies throughout the New World were the
freest communities then in the world, a fact which, combined with other conditions, immensely favored their
progress on democratic lines.

Our main concern has been thus far with the genesis
of the United States, but we must recall that during all
the period we have covered there was amazing activity
all over the globe,—England, France, and Holland, for
example, contending with one another for commerce
and empire out in India and the Islands of the Far East.
The dispelling of the mystery and terror of the earth's
open seas had afforded the needed vent to Europe, and
the danger of explosion had been replaced by a furious
burst of energy as the possibilities of world exploitation
dawned on the European mind. The rise of the United
States is but one, though for us the most important, of
the results of Europe having found a way to break
through the fifteenth-century encirclement of barbarous
races, forbidding deserts, and innavigable waters.

CHAPTER II

THE COLONIAL SYSTEM TAKES FORM

THE period covered by this chapter, roughly from 1634 to 1690, was notable for the gradual evolution of a colonial system out of the scattered beginnings made at haphazard by the commercial ambitions of a few groups of capitalists or needy courtiers, partly assisted in the process of colonization by the religious hopes or fears of particular groups. The evolution proceeded in two directions—first, the actual peopling of the American coast and the Caribbean islands in a vast semicircle extending from Maine to Barbadoes, and, secondly, in the attempt to develop in England a theory of imperial needs, obligations, and government. We shall speak of the second point later, and with regard to the first our attention must be almost wholly directed to the continental half of the semicircle. We may note, however,—to get the proper perspective from the imperial point of view,—that in addition to the greater importance of her natural products, the island of Barbadoes alone in 1642 had a larger English population than all the New England colonies combined.

The New England population, however, had in-

33

creased rapidly from the Puritan settlement until about 1640, when the prospects for Puritans in England altered completely, and for the better, with the Puritan revolution there. After that, the stream of emigration to New England dried up almost entirely for well on to two centuries. Within eight years after the arrival of Winthrop the number of settlers in the section had increased to perhaps seventeen thousand, and besides the colonies of Plymouth and Massachusetts four new ones had been founded—Rhode Island and Connecticut in 1636, New Haven in 1638, while there had been settlements in New Hampshire since 1622, and a number in Maine. The date of "founding" of many of the colonies is somewhat vague, for in many of them there were occasional stray single settlers or even small groups who had squatted on lands or more lawfully preceded larger bodies sent out after legal possession had been secured by charter or otherwise. There is no advantage in waxing too hot over what is often a verbal quibble. The settlement of a solitary, like the interesting Blackstone, for example, removing to live in Rhode Island, can scarcely be called the founding of a new colony, the term being better applied to the establishment of a permanent and fairly strong body of citizens with established forms of local government.

We may note that the establishment of New Hampshire, Rhode Island, and Connecticut was owing in each case to the opposition aroused in the minds of many by the narrow and tyrannical ruling Puritan oligarchy in control of Massachusetts. Just as the leaders of that colony had fled or been forced from England, so now many were fleeing or being forced from their colony in the New World to seek for greater liberty, as well as for new and well-located lands. As we have pointed out, resistance to intellectual or religious authority and insistence upon private judgment do not, unfortunately, necessarily result in tolerance. Indeed, the exaggerated importance given to his own views by the protesting individual seems rather to be likely to result in an aggressive *in*tolerance.

Moreover, there is no intolerance more overbearing than that springing from the belief by persons of rather narrow experience in their own superior morality or brand of religious truth. The local Massachusetts leaders had been people of no importance whatever in England when they suddenly found themselves ruling a commonwealth. They had also taken heavy risks to find a place where they not only could worship as they chose but could raise themselves in the social and economic scales. Having found it, they had no intention of allowing affairs to slip from their grasp. This was all quite human but militated strongly in some ways against the best interests of Massachusetts.

For many generations there were to be two strands in the history of that commonwealth,—resistance by the colony as a whole to any encroachments by England, and resistance by the more liberal elements among the colonists themselves to the ruling oligarchy, who believed not that the people should rule but that they should *be* ruled by the specially elect of God.

For a while, the leaders refused to allow the people even to see the charter, and carried matters with a high hand. In 1631 the men of Watertown protested against paying a tax levied on them, rightly claiming that only the freemen could tax themselves. It was in that year the oligarchy ruled that only church members could be freemen. In 1634 two representatives elected from each town were finally granted a sight of the charter, when they found that they had been deprived of their rights under it. It was then decided, after a mild uprising against Winthrop and the other leaders, that the General Court, made up of delegates from the towns, should meet four times a year, and that it alone should have power to pass laws, elect and remove officials, lay taxes, and grant lands.

Almost from the beginning, the Congregational form of church had been adopted in Massachusetts. By this system each church was independent of all others, chose its own pastor, and was composed only of such persons as could satisfy the rest of the congregation of their regenerate state. They were bound together by a covenant, and this church group and the political organization of the town became the two cells from which the New England social organism was built up. Adding the village

THE OLD SHIP CHURCH, HINGHAM, MASSACHUSETTS, BEGUN IN 1681

An example of the earliest type of town meeting-house which was a rectangular building
with hipped roof surmounted by a belfry containing a bell.

From a later print, courtesy of the State Street Trust Company, Boston.

OLD MEETING–HOUSE, SANDOWN, NEW HAMPSHIRE, BUILT IN 1774

Prior to the Revolution, the smaller meeting-houses outside of the towns were usually
without a steeple.

By courtesy of the Society for the Preservation of New England Antiquities.

AN OLD PRINT OF THE COLLEGE OF WILLIAM AND MARY IN VIRGINIA
SHOWING IT AS IT WAS ABOUT 1732

This print was taken from the so-called "Copper Plate" recently found in the Bodleian Library at Oxford by research workers on the staff of the Williamsburg Holding Corporation which is engaged in restoring a part of Williamsburg to its eighteenth-century appearance. The building in the centre is the Wren Building.

THE WREN BUILDING AS IT IS TODAY

or town school, soon introduced, the three ideas are to be found throughout our history wherever New England influence has penetrated. The tendency of all three was profoundly democratic, but this in no way altered the attempt of the leaders, such as even Winthrop and Cotton, who were opposed to democracy, to prevent its application to civil government.

Many complaints had been made in London about affairs in the colony when its peace in America was disturbed in 1635 by the ideas of Roger Williams. Williams had a gentle and winning personality, and soon fell foul of the bigotry of the Massachusetts lay and clerical leaders. Unfortunately, besides preaching religious toleration he added certain dangerous doctrines, claiming, for example, that title to American soil was vested in the Indians and not in the King. After a trial, in which both religious and political motives bore their part, he was sentenced by the Massachusetts authorities to be banished the following spring. Escaping from home in midwinter, after having heard he was to be shipped to England, he made his way through the snows and bitter cold of a New England January to Narragansett Bay where he founded the new colony of Rhode Island, for which he obtained a charter in 1644.

Meanwhile others wished, voluntarily, to emigrate from Massachusetts, and the beautiful valley of the Connecticut attracted some of these. In 1635 a law was enacted that no one could leave Massachusetts without consent of the authorities, but it was finally decreed that the Reverend Thomas Hooker and a band of settlers might go. By the end of the following year there were probably 800 people at Hartford and neighboring places, and thus our endless western migration from the "settled East" had begun.

The government of Massachusetts, as we have said, as much as the rich Connecticut meadows, was probably the cause of the exodus. When the form of government of the new settlements was under consideration in 1638, the settlers having no charter, Hooker preached his famous sermon, arguing for fixed laws and popular control of the government and magistrates. Those who have the power to elect, he claimed, have the power to control, and "the foundation of authority is laid, firstly, in the free consent of the people." When the "Fundamental Orders" were accepted as the basis of government, they contained no reference to the King, and, probably as a reaction against conditions in Massachusetts, provided that the governor should not be eligible for re-election and that there should be no religious qualification for the franchise.

In the same year, 1638, in which Hooker was preaching his liberalism at Hartford, New Hampshire received its most important early accession to population in a group of refugees from Massachusetts. This emigration was consequent upon the trial of Ann Hutchinson, followed by her banishment, and the fining or disfranchisement of many of her followers. Just when this affair was at its

Christenings

make not

CHRISTIANS,

OR

A Briefe Difcourfe concerning that
name *Heathen*, commonly given to
the INDIANS.

As alfo concerning that great point of their
CONVERSION.

Publifhed according to Order.

London, Printed by *Iane Coe*, for I. H. 1645.

A FACSIMILE OF A REPRINT OF THE ORIGINAL TRACT WRITTEN BY
ROGER WILLIAMS IN 1643
Contained in "Rhode Island Historical Tracts," 1st Series, No. 14.

39

height an important body of intending settlers arrived in Boston from England headed by the Reverend John Davenport and several wealthy laymen. Resisting entreaties to remain in Massachusetts, they decided on New Haven as the site for their rather rigid theocracy, and settled there in 1638. Like Hooker and his followers they had no charter, but unlike them they entered into a reactionary covenant, making church membership essential for freemen and entrusting all government to an elected body and governor who for many years were restricted in authority only by the laws of Moses. For various reasons the colony, although it grew, never prospered, and in 1661 was absorbed by Connecticut.

NEW ENGLAND MAKES PROGRESS

New England was thus rapidly expanding, and it was able to do so in comparative safety as a result of the terrible Pequot War in 1637. It was the story of white aggression and racial hatred which was unhappily to be repeated on almost all of our frontiers for two and a half centuries. The chief incident of this first New England war was the surprise by the Puritans, under the lead of Captain John Mason, of the main village of the savages. In the dark, with a strong wind blowing, the two entrances to the stockade were guarded to prevent any escape, and then a torch was applied. Five hundred Indian men, women, and children were burned to death, the Puritan leader merely remarking that by the Providence of God

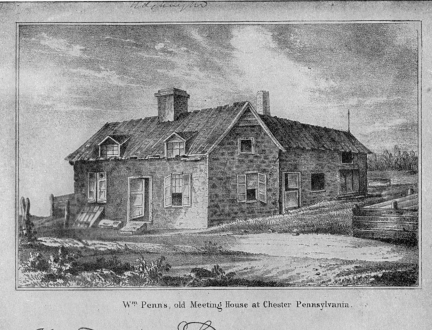

Wm. Penn's, old Meeting House at Chester Pennsylvania.

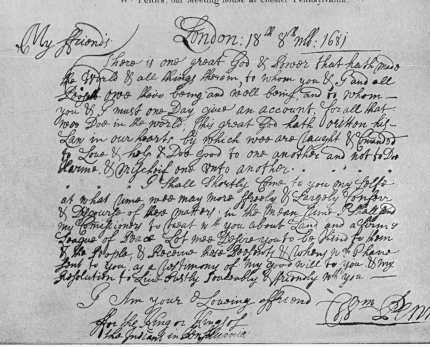

WILLIAM PENN'S MEETING–HOUSE AT CHESTER AND A LETTER FROM PENN TO THE INDIANS

This letter, reproduced in part, was addressed by Penn, and sent in care of three commissioners to the Indians living on the land for which Charles II had given him his grant. In it he expresses his hope for an amicable purchase of the land and a life of peace and accord for all.

From the Library of Congress.

HARVARD COLLEGE, CAMBRIDGE

From left to right the buildings are: Holden Chapel, 1737; Hollis Hall, 1762; Harvard Hall, built in 1766 upon the site of the original building which had been destroyed by fire; Stoughton Hall, the gift of William Stoughton, presiding judge at Salem witch trials, which was torn down and replaced in 1805; Massachusetts Hall, 1720.

From the engraving by Paul Revere, in the Essex Institute, Salem, Massachusetts.

BOWEN'S VIEW OF YALE COLLEGE, 1786

Left: the Athenæum erected in 1761.   Right: Connecticut Hall, 1750.

By courtesy of Yale University Library.

there were 150 more than usual at home that awful night.

The fear of a general Indian uprising in 1642 led to a league among the four colonies of Massachusetts, Plymouth, New Haven, and Connecticut. Under the name of the New England Confederation this league functioned rather feebly for forty years, and was of slight importance. Its chief significance is in showing how easily these colonies, which were beginning to plant themselves without charters or thought of King or Parliament, were slipping toward a belief in entire political independence in managing all their own affairs.

A step toward intellectual independence also was taken by Massachusetts in 1636 when Harvard College was established to train up a godly ministry. Much used to be made of this event, but when we contrast the courses of study and the scholarship produced in our first "college" with what the Spaniards had achieved long before at such universities as those in Mexico City or Lima, perhaps a more modest estimate of this event in our educational history may be preferable. It tended, moreover, to increase the provincialism of New England by encouraging it to keep students at home for an inferior training instead of sending them, as the other colonies later did, to enjoy the better opportunities in the universities of Europe.

By the mid-century, Massachusetts was hardening into the most cruel and narrow period of its long, and in many ways glorious, history. Winthrop died in 1649, and Cotton in 1652. Such mild restraining influences as there had been of gentleness, charity, and toleration appear for a while to have lost their power. Civil and ecclesiastical control passed to men of the type of Endicott. New England may well be proud of four such founders of her States as Bradford, Winthrop, Williams, and Hooker, but by 1657 only Williams remained, and his colony of Rhode Island was alone to play a noble part in refraining from the persecutions of the Quakers which blotted New England history between 1656 and 1663.

In the earlier of these years, a few weeks after the Massachusetts government had hung Ann Hibbens as a witch, two Quaker women, from England by way of Barbadoes, arrived in Boston. At once persecution began, and as others came it was increased in severity. The penalties, which included besides the selling of Quaker children into slavery in the West Indies, the imprisonment, beating, and torturing of their elders, culminated in the hanging of three men and one woman. At the request of Massachusetts all the other New England colonies, with the exception of Rhode Island, passed severe laws against the sect, though none tortured or killed them as did the leading Puritan State, then largely under the influence of Endicott and the Reverend John Norton.

Williams replied to the request of Massachusetts (though his colony was threatened with dangerous reprisals if it did not comply), that the Rhode Islanders had no laws against any one declaring by words only their religious beliefs, whatever they might be, and that although he conceived the doctrines of the Quakers tended to the subversion of civil government, nevertheless it would be found always that if Quakers were allowed to

The Wages of Sin;
OR,
Robbery juftly Rewarded:
A
POEM;
Occafioned by the untimely Death of

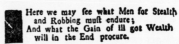
Richard Wilfon,

Who was Executed on Bofton Neck, for Burglary,
On Thurfday the 19th of October, 1732.

THis Day from Goal muft Wilfon be conveyed in a Cart, By Guards unto the Gallows-Tree, to die as his Defert.

Here we may fee what Men for Stealth and Robbing muft endure; And what the Gain of ill got Wealth will in the End procure.

NEW ENGLAND PUNISHMENT
A facsimile of a broadside in the Library of Congress.

preach in peace and were not persecuted, they would gain fewer adherents by their sayings than they would by suffering and martyrdom. The General Assembly of Rhode Island added that the colony prized freedom of conscience "as the greatest happiness that men can possess in this world."

In the forty years since the passengers on the *Mayflower* had unexpectedly been landed on the shores of

Massachusetts instead of Virginia, New England must have seemed to its old inhabitants to have made astounding progress. In spite of the terrible conflict with the savages yet in store,—King Philip's War of 1676,—the older settlements were now as safe as shire towns in England, though the frontier, that ever-present factor in American life, was open and liable to sudden attack and massacre. It would be a mistake to think even of Massachusetts as a land only of dour countenances, and hangings of witches or Quakers. Our first woman poet, Anne Bradstreet, had penned her love verses there, students ragged each other at Harvard, children played around school doors. Literature had begun in New England, and though much of it is musty theology that no one reads today, Bradford and Winthrop had written valuable histories, and Williams in Rhode Island and Hooker in Connecticut had wrought out the ideals of the rule of the people, and of intellectual toleration.

The ordinary citizen, living on his farm, owned in fee simple, untroubled by any relics of feudalism, untaxed save by himself, saying his say to all the world in town-meeting, had gained a new self-reliance. Wrestling with his soul and plough on week days, and the innumerable points of the minister's sermon on Sundays and Meeting days, he was coming to be a tough nut for any imperial system to crack. All were not farmers, though most were, and a merchant class of larger or smaller traders was springing up in the seaports and in villages along navi-

THE
TENTH MUSE

Lately fprung up in AMERICA.

OR

Severall Poems, compiled
with great variety of VVit
and Learning, full of delight.
Wherein efpecially is contained a com-
pleat difcourfe and defcription of '

The Four
{
Elements,
Conftitutions,
Ages of Man,
Seafons of the Year.
}

Together with an Exact Epitomie of
the Four Monarchies, *viz.*

The
{
Affyrian,
Perfian,
Grecian,
Roman.
}

Alfo a Dialogue between Old *England* and
New, concerning the late troubles.
With divers other pleafant and ferious Poems.

By a Gentlewoman in thofe parts.

Printed at London for *Stephen Bowtell* at the figne of the
Bible in Popes Head-Alley. 1650.

TITLE–PAGE OF THE FIRST EDITION OF
ANNE BRADSTREET'S POEMS
From the New York Public Library.

gable rivers, carrying on a commerce with the mother country, the Wine Islands, Africa for slaves, the West Indies, and their own fellow continental colonists to the south. For part of the century, however, between the English of New England and those of Maryland and Virginia lay colonies of Dutch and Swedes.

THE DUTCH AND THE QUAKERS

From 1610, the year following Hudson's discovery of the river named for him, Dutch traders had frequented its mouth to traffic with the Indians, and in 1614 had founded a fort and small trading post on the site of what is now Albany. In 1623 the Dutch West India Company, a trading company such as we have become familiar with, planted a small settlement on Manhattan Island, where a few huts had been built some years before. The Dutch claim to New Netherland, with its principal town of New Amsterdam, was more or less indeterminate but included New York and Long Island, New Jersey, and Delaware. Of course it was not recognized by the English.

The Dutch were in fact rather late claimants, though their brief history in America was picturesque enough, and many prominent New York families like to trace their ancestry back to them. Their stay was a troubled one for they were in almost constant dispute not only with the advancing New Englanders in Connecticut and eastern Long Island, and the Virginians in Delaware, but also with colonies of Swedes which had been planted at Wilmington and surrounding points. The latter were finally conquered by the Dutch in 1655, but nine years later an English fleet arrived at the mouth of the Hudson and forced the Dutch governor, the redoubtable Peter Stuyvesant, to surrender. In honor of the Duke of York, the King's brother, to whom the territory had been granted, the colony and town were renamed New York, and the Dutch sway within the present United States came to an end. The two favorites to whom the Duke of York granted the land between New York and Delaware Bay founded East and West, now New, Jersey, the two colonies soon coming largely under the control of the Quakers, Berkeley, who had received West Jersey, selling out his rights to them almost immediately.

The Dutch had not believed in self-government by their colonists, and the history of New Amsterdam had been turbulent. The small town early acquired its modern cosmopolitan aspect, and it is said that eighteen languages were spoken on its streets in the Dutch period. Except for a few words adopted into our language, some social customs locally, and many romantic legends, the Dutch influence, however, has been almost negligible in the development of our institutions and culture in spite of much written to the contrary.

Charles II, who had returned to the English throne in 1660, after the Cromwellian interregnum, was only too willing to use the vast lands of America as grants to noblemen for his own or their benefit, and just as he granted the Dutch territories to his brother, so he also granted to a group of eight nobles the lands south of Virginia which are now included in North and South Carolina. Colonization was rather slow, but Charleston was settled in 1670, and grew fairly rapidly, a large accession of French Huguenots arriving ten years later. Rice growing, which was introduced in 1693, resulted in a great increase in slavery, rapid fortunes, and a basis of wealth and leisure which was to make South Carolina, within a few generations, perhaps the leading American colony in æsthetic culture and social charm.

The last colony founded in the period of this chapter was Pennsylvania, a charter for which was granted to the Quaker William Penn in 1681. Planting his chief town of Philadelphia on the bank of the Delaware, he expressed the wish that each house should always be surrounded by a garden so that the city might remain "a green country town," and "always be wholesome," an ideal of city planning which, until too late, we have most unhappily forgotten. Notable also in Pennsylvania under the leadership of Penn, alone among all the colonies, was the benevolent and honorable attitude adopted and maintained toward the Indians. Treaties were not only made but kept, and the relation of Penn to the savages forms one of the few episodes in the long annals of our treatment of the native which honest Americans would not wish to have blotted out.

Lake HURON

Lake ONTARIO

Lake ERIE

Montreal
(French)

Lake
Champlain

MAINE
part of Mass.

N. H.

Dover
Portsmouth
Salem
Boston
Plymouth

Ft. Orange
(Albany)

MASSACHUSETTS

Hartford
CONN.

R.I.

Providence

NEW YORK

New Haven

Great
Plains

PENNSYLVANIA

Schu...

New Amsterdam
(New York)

Ohio River

N.J.

Philadelphia

Wilmington

Baltimore

APPALACHIAN MOUNTAINS

MARYLAND

Potomac River

St Mary's

DEL.

Chesapeake Bay

James R.

Jamestown

Point Comfort

VIRGINIA

NORTH
CAROLINA

Roanoke Island

SOUTH
CAROLINA

ATLANTIC OCEAN

GEORGIA

Savannah R.

Charleston

Savannah

EARLY SETTLE-
MENTS IN THE
ENGLISH COLONIES

FLORIDA
Spanish

49

Although, as we shall see in the next chapter, there was soon to be a large influx of Germans into Pennsylvania, the colony had been founded mainly as a retreat for Quakers, and thus one more sect found refuge among us, adding to the fast growing complexity of our life even in this early period. In the neighboring colony of Maryland, in order to protect the Catholics, a law had been passed in 1649 by the colonial assembly (in which Catholics were in the majority at the time), providing that no person professing to believe in Jesus Christ should in any way be troubled or molested. Maryland and Rhode Island thus led the way toward complete toleration, at least for professing Christians.

Before proceeding to consider the second point of which we spoke at the beginning of this chapter as characterizing the period,—that is, the development in England of a colonial theory and practice,—we may note briefly one or two aspects of American development thus far.

First of all, in the colonies, as contrasted with England itself or with the French and Spanish empires in America, there was the great diversity in both race and religion. Within two generations from the gaining of a permanent foothold by the dominant English, we have already found large groups of Dutch, Germans, Swedes, and Huguenot French coming to make homes here for the purpose either of bettering themselves socially and economically, or to escape from persecution.

THE NEW COUNTRY BECOMES THE HOPE OF MANY RACES

This diversity was greatly to increase in the future, but at its very inception the United States became both a hope and a refuge for those of many races, and not merely of a single one. There was also the marked variety in religion. Although all the colonies were under English rule, Catholics, Congregationalists, Lutherans, Church of England adherents, Quakers, and others could all find rapidly growing and prosperous communities in which they could make their homes, and be unmolested. The intolerance of individual colonies, notably the Puritan ones, should not obscure the remarkable religious freedom that had come to exist within a group of colonies of a single European power. It could have been found at that time under neither French nor Spanish rule, but only under English.

Owing chiefly to soil, topography, and climate, there had also come about a rapid but clearly marked differentiation in the social and economic life of the various colonies. In New England all the physical factors in agriculture tended toward small farms which could most profitably be tilled by the head of a family with little help other than that of sons or a hired man. The system of small holdings tended to emphasize that compact type of settlement which naturally developed from the New England form of migration, which was that of a group closely knit together by being members of the church which was their chief concern. The small holding, the church, and the town meeting in New England all militated in that section against a loosely scattered mode of settlement.

New York had been started purely as a trading post. For more than a century, the policy of huge land grants adopted by both Dutch and English rulers; the importance of the fur trade for the only colony which (by the Hudson-Mohawk Valley route) had easy access to the interior of the continent; and the magnificent harbor the colony possessed, were all to determine its character as mainly commercial in a group of colonies that were otherwise dominated by agriculture.

Passing southward to Maryland, Virginia, and the Carolinas, we find agriculture again holding sway. In them the staple and exhausting crop of tobacco (except for rice to the far South) demanded larger landholdings than in New England, and brought about a more scattered way of living, as well, eventually, as a seemingly imperative demand for that black slave labor which was economically unprofitable on the much broken and stony surface of the Puritan colonies. These effects were not all felt in the South during its earlier and economically struggling period, but were to be of great importance after 1700.

Another characteristic of the English colonies as contrasted with those of any other nation at that time was the extraordinary amount of liberty granted to the individual colonist. Looking back from the vantage ground of a different era, we are too apt to think that the colonists were naturally entitled to this, and that in their constant struggles for ever greater liberty they were fighting against a tyrannical government. This was far from the case. As well as we can, we have to judge each age by the ideas dominant in it and not in our own. Neither France, Spain, nor even liberty-loving little Holland dreamed of giving their colonists when they left the mother country anything like the freedom which England granted to hers.

Charles II was assuredly no lover of democracy or the liberty of the common man, yet although the charters which he granted for the colonies of New York, the Jerseys, Pennsylvania, and Carolina were of the type known as proprietary, and were based on the model of the Bishopric of Durham, they all contained, like that granted by the first Charles on the same model for Maryland, the clause we have noted, that the proprietor, unlike the Bishop, could make laws only "by and with the consent of the freemen."

All Americans under the proprietary charters were thus given much more liberty in self-government than was enjoyed by their fellows in England in the Durham Bishopric. The circumstances of distance and the inability to be properly represented in Parliament were to raise special and difficult problems for our ancestors in America, as well as for the government in England. Nevertheless, in studying the story of our incessant struggle against the English government it is only fair to bear in mind that ours were the freest colonies in the world during all of our colonial period.

Charles II, as we have said, was no lover of a too-great liberty of the subject, and the restoration of the Stuarts in his person in 1660 brought troublous times for the Americans in many colonies. According to the generally accepted theory of that day, which seemed not at all tyrannical but only natural to all statesmen in Europe, colonies existed chiefly for the benefit of the mother country. Following the breakdown of the unified world of the Roman Empire and the long incubation period of the Middle Ages, the modern theory and emotions of nationality were fast emerging.

Politics, religion, and commerce, which had been decentralized, were beginning to be considered as essentially clustering around each national State for its own inhabitants. According to the economic theory of the time, real wealth was believed to consist in a store of the precious metals. That State was thought to be best off which accumulated the largest store, either by mining or favorable trade balances. Thus developed the "Mercantile Theory,"—by no means dead today,—which demanded that a country should always have a balance in its favor to be settled by imports of gold.

When Europe broke its barriers and the period of overseas empires was inaugurated, the theory of empire was naturally based on this theory of wealth. In order that an empire should owe others as little as possible, each sought to be as nearly self-contained as might be, in both the supplies of its needed raw materials and the markets for its finished products, so as to absorb as much as might be of the profits throughout all the economic scale and be as independent as possible of others. Speaking generally, the colonies, plantations, and trading posts of the British Empire were supposed to supply the raw materials for British manufactures and such other materials, for food or other needs, as could not be produced in the British Isles. Thus, for example, England had its fisheries on the Newfoundland coast, the tobacco and rice colonies of our South, the sugar islands of the West Indies (to which the valuable island of Jamaica had been added in 1655), its fort in Guinea protecting its slave trade, and its settlements in India, Sumatra, Java, and the Celebes for the products of the Far East.

On the other hand, the colonists were supposed to increase the market for British manufactured goods, and to buy these with the money which they received from the sale of their raw materials. The increase of colonial population, beyond what was necessary merely for producing and shipping home the lumber, sugar, tobacco, and other raw materials, was considered of value solely from the standpoint of increasing the number of consumers of British goods.

According to this elaborate scheme, England was to remain the centre of manufactures, banking, and military resources, while the colonies were to confine themselves to the rôles of producers of raw materials and consumers of English manufactures. In a world of empires competing for over-sea territories, the duty of protecting colonies against, so to say, being kidnapped by another empire, and also to guard the trade routes, fell to the navies of the home countries in Europe. When in 1650 and 1651, under Cromwell, and in 1660 and 1663, under the returned Stuarts, England passed Navigation Acts placing certain restrictions on the freedom of colonial trade with the outside world, this was not deemed tyranny but only reasonable regulation in exchange for protection and the smooth working of the imperial trade machinery. This theory of empire was not simply English. It was universal at the time, and on the whole England applied it with a far more enlightened and generous spirit than did either France, Spain, or Holland.

This far-flung empire, which had come into existence almost haphazard, and in scarcely more than fifty years when Charles II came to the throne, had no co-ordinated system of government. Especially during the troubled years of the Cromwellian Commonwealth, the American colonies in particular had been left much to themselves, and had got in the habit, even more than usual, of going their own way with little or no thought of the governing power at the centre of empire. Massachusetts had even dropped the King's name from its legal writs. The years between the restoration of the Stuarts in 1660 and their fall in 1688 were marked in America by constant efforts to reassert royal authority and increase royal control over the colonists.

Some of the efforts were logical and reasonable in theory but all proved irritating in practice. Many of the royal governors were incompetent or venal, and in 1676 the people of Virginia finally broke into revolt against Governor Berkeley under a leader named Nathaniel Bacon. Tobacco was not only the staple crop of Maryland and Virginia but also served as currency in the absence of coin, and frequent trouble arose from fluctuations in value. Before 1675 there had been for some time much distress in the colony owing to the low prices of what was at once crop and currency. This was due in part to over-production and in part to the fact that the navigation laws cut the settlers off from all markets save that of England, and it was said that the planters were merely the slaves of the English merchants.

In all times of economic maladjustment the poor and weak are the worst sufferers, so there was a good deal of grumbling against the bad government of the colony and the richer classes allied to the governor's set.

Matters finally came to a head when the governor and the tidewater gentry declined to make any move to protect the frontier settlements against serious attacks by the Indians, and the poor people found a leader for armed revolt in Bacon. Although the rebellion collapsed in a few months with Bacon's death from fever, it was not unsuccessful. The King recalled Berkeley in disgrace, appointed one of the "rebels" governor, and remedied some of the grievances. The uprising has a special interest as indicative of the many minor cleavages beginning to appear between rich and poor, old settlement and frontier, in the several colonies.

New England never fitted into the scheme of empire based on the Mercantile theory. With the exception of some timber she produced no raw material needed by England. Her fishing fleets competed with those of the home country. Having no staple crop and always driven to find means of paying for her imports from the mother country, she tended to encroach on English manufacturing to supply her own needs, and to trade not only with the West Indies within the empire but illegally with islands and countries outside it. Many complaints reached the King that the New Englanders were disobeying the laws of trade, that they were persecuting the Quakers and others, and that they were beginning to consider themselves as practically independent. These charges were mainly true.

At first it had seemed as though Charles II might prove liberal. In 1660 he had despatched a special messenger to Massachusetts to restrain that colony from further persecution, and the next year he granted charters to both Rhode Island and Connecticut which were so satisfactory to the people that they continued to be used as State constitutions until well into the nineteenth century. In 1676, however, he sent as Collector of Customs at the port of Boston and special investigator to Massachusetts a certain Edward Randolph to report on conditions. From the standpoint of efficient imperial administration, these were bad enough but Randolph was also almost insanely prejudiced against the colonies, particularly the Puritan ones, and his reports for many years painted the colonists in the blackest colors to the home authorities. By 1684 he had succeeded in having the Massachusetts charter forfeited in England and the commonwealth transformed into a royal colony. Writs were also issued against the charters of Connecticut, Rhode Island, the Jerseys, and Delaware. Pennsylvania narrowly escaped, but although Stuart rule was nearing its end and these cases were never determined against the colonies, another scheme was put into execution.

ADMINISTRATION IN NEW ENGLAND

From the standpoint of administration there was much to be said in favor of uniting at least certain groups of colonies into larger units. Local character, pride, and jealousies were already so strong however that the thought sprang from bureaucracy rather than from practical statesmanship. As intercolonial jealousies and the impossibility of getting united colonial action on any common Indian or fiscal policy were among the causes which were to precipitate the Revolution in 1776, it is interesting to speculate on what might have happened, had the colonies,

almost a century earlier, been united. It is futile, nevertheless, to do so, for they would not have consented to become
so. Charles tried the plan in part, and in 1686 Sir Edmund
Andros arrived in Boston with a commission to rule over
all of New England, New York being added two years
later to the consolidated province, as were also the two
Jerseys.

The new Administrator was honest but without tact,
and in any case occupied an impossible position. He
greatly increased his difficulties by unnecessary stirring up
of trouble over such matters as censorship of the press,
Episcopal rights, land titles, registry fees, and the en-
closure of the common lands, but he was no tyrant though
his term is usually spoken of as the "tyranny of Andros."
The powers granted him in his commission were so broad
that he might have been a veritable tyrant had he so
desired. In truth he had no such wish and in his term as
governor of New York previously he had shown popular
tendencies by supporting the colonists' demand for the
re-establishment of an Assembly.

Under the plan for a "Dominion of New England,"
however, all popular assemblies had been done away with
and the governor was to rule and tax only with the advice
and consent of the council. After the colonists' long experience in self-government any such effort to rule them
from above was insane folly, but the end was near.

In March, 1689, young John Winslow arrived in Massachusetts from Nevis with authentic news that the Stuarts

had been overthrown in England and that William of Orange and his wife Mary had been proclaimed Sov-

AT THE TOWN-HOUSE in

BOSTON:

April 18th. 1689.

Sir,

OUr Selves as well as many others the Inhabitants of this Town and Place adjacent, being surprized with the Peoples sudden taking to Arms in the first motion whereof we were wholly ignorant, are driven by the present Exigence and Necessity to acquaint your *Excellency*, that for the Quieting and Securing of the People Inhabiting this Countrey from the imminent Dangers they many wayes lie open, and are exposed unto, and for Your own safety; We judge it necessary that You forthwith Surrender, and Deliver up the Government and Fortifications to be preserved, to be Disposed according to Order and Direction from the Crown of *England*, which is suddenly expected may Arrive, promising all Security from Violence to Your Self, or any other of Your Gentlemen and Souldiers in Person or Estate or else we are assured they will endeavour the taking of the Fortifications by Storm, if any opposition be made.

To Sr. Edmond Androſs Knight.

Wait Winthrop	*Elisha Cook.*
Simon Bradstreet.	*Isaac Addington.*
William Stoughton	*John Nelson.*
Samuel Shrimpton	*Adam Winthrop.*
Barthol. Gidney	*Peter Sergeant.*
William Brown	*John Foster.*
Thomas Danforth	*David Waterhouse*
John Richards.	

Boston Printed by *S Green.* 1689.

FACSIMILE OF A BROADSIDE OF 1689 CALLING UPON ANDROS TO SURRENDER HIS POWERS AND PERSON
From the original in the Library of Congress.

ereigns of Great Britain. The information also reached the other colonies and was received with popular rejoicing.

In Boston, Andros, Randolph, and other royal officials
were thrown into jail to await the new King's command.
In New York, Francis Nicholson, who had been serving

A

LETTER

From A

Gentleman

OF THE

City of New - York

To Another,

Concerning the Troubles which happen'd
in That Province in the Time of the late Happy
REVOLUTION.

Printed and Sold by *William Bradford* at the Sign of the ,
Bible in *New - York,* 1698.

FACSIMILE OF THE TITLE-PAGE OF A LETTER DENOUNCING
LEISLER AND HIS FOLLOWERS

From the original printed by Bradford in the New York Public Library.

as Andros's deputy, fled to England and the populace rose
under an impetuous German leader, Jacob Leisler, who
continued to rule that province almost as a dictator for

two tumultuous years. In Maryland also there was an armed revolution, colored by the religious animosity between Catholics and Protestants. Apart, however, from these three ripples that lapped our shores from the great storm overseas, the colonists waited in peace to learn what the sudden change in English rule might hold in store for them.

CHAPTER III

THE DUEL WITH FRANCE

WHEN James II dropped the Great Seal of England into the Thames as he fled to France the Stuart dynasty and tyranny were ended. The new monarchs, William and Mary, were not absolute, and from the nature of the Revolution which had brought them to the throne the influence of Parliament and of the merchant class in England were both increased. The colonies gained much by the change but not as much as they had expected.

The Stuarts had contemplated a colonial system in which the supreme power would reside in themselves and which would be administered locally in the provinces by governors and councils appointed by them with no bothersome popular assemblies. That dream was dropped in the Thames with the Great Seal, but on the other hand the eighteenth century was dawning, the age of reason, of logic and legality.

The colonial charters which had been threatened by James were safe under William, but the new one granted to Massachusetts in 1691 indicated a new trend. Under it the province became a royal colony, with a governor

OF THE

OATHS

That are appointed by Act of Parliament, made in the
First Year of Their present Majesties Reign; to be
Taken instead of the Oaths of Supremacy and Allegiance, and the Declaration appointed to be made,
Repeated and Subscribed

I A. B. do sincerely Promise and Swear, That I will be Faithful, and bear true
Allegiance to Their Majesties, King *WILLIAM* and Queen *MARY.*
So help me God, &c.

I A. B. do Swear, That I do from my Heart Abhor, Detest, and Abjure, as Impious and Heretical, that Damnable Doctrine and Position, *That Princes Excommunicated or Deprived by the Pope, or any Authority of the See of Rome, may be Deposed or Murthered by their Subjects, or any other whatsoever.*
And I do Declare, That no Foreign Prince, Person, Prelate, State, or Potentate, hath, or ought to have any Jurisdiction, Power, Superiority, Preeminence, or Authority Ecclesiastical or Spiritual within this Realm.

So help me God, &c.

I A. B. *do solemnly and sincerely in the presence of God, profess, testifie and declare, that I do believe that in the Sacrament of the Lords Supper, there is not any Transubstantiation of the Elements of Bread and Wine into the Body and Blood of Christ, at or after the Consecration thereof, by any person whatsoever, and that the Invocation or adoration of the Virgin Mary or any other Saint, and the sacrifice of the Mass as they are now used in the Church of Rome, are Superstitious and Idolatrous. And I do solemnly in the presence of God, profess, testifie and declare, that I do make this Declaration and every part thereof in the plain and ordinary sence of the words read unto me, as they are commonly understood by English Protestants, without any Evasion, Equivocation or mental Reservation whatsoever, and without any Dispensation already granted me for this purpose by the Pope, or any Authority or Person whatsoever, or without any hope of any such Dispensation from any Person or Authority whatsoever, or without thinking that I am or can be acquitted, before God or Man, or absolved of this Declaration or any part thereof, although the Pope or any other Person or Persons or Power whatsoever should dispence with, or annul the same or declare that it was null and void from the beginning.*

FACSIMILE OF THE OATH OF ALLEGIANCE TO KING WILLIAM
AND QUEEN MARY

From the Library of Congress.

appointed by the King, an assembly elected by property owners, and a council elected by the assembly with the governor holding a veto power over nominations and legislation. Freedom of conscience, however, was provided for all Protestants, and the old Puritan theocracy was denied further control, a property and not a religious qualification being provided for the franchise.

The eighteenth-century policy of colonial administration was to be marked by the desire to reduce all the colonial governments to a more or less uniform status of royal provinces; the royal officials, from governor down, were to be expected to maintain the prerogative; and Parliament was to take a more active part in passing laws designed to regulate trade and other imperial concerns within colonial borders.

THE THREE MAIN CURRENTS OF EVENTS

The period from 1690 to 1763 was to be notable for three main currents of events. First, in America itself, there was to be a shift from the mere planting of new colonies to the consolidation and expansion of those already planted, with much increase of population and new racial admixtures. Secondly, in England, there was to be a logical and understandable, if unwise, effort to consolidate the colonial administration and to bring a uniformity consonant with the eighteenth-century mind out of the extreme variety left by the less logical and legalistic seventeenth. Thirdly, on both sides of the water, there was to be the long duel with France, which was to result, in 1763, in the ejection of that nation from Canada and the West.

During her history America has enjoyed exactly one century, from 1814 to 1914, of more or less isolation from the struggles which have almost incessantly torn Europe. Both before and after that century we have always perforce taken an active part in international affairs. Until the peace of 1814 we were caught in almost every eddy of European policy, and although the hundred years of isolation was in many ways of inestimable advantage to us in our formative period, that has now passed forever, whether we would wish it so or not. Even in that period of comparative isolation, however, there was constant interchange of cultural and other influences between Europe and ourselves, and to understand both our past and the problems of our future it is better to think in terms of that constant inter-relationship rather than of our merely partial and temporary isolation.

The fall of the Stuarts in England at once precipitated war between England and France, which automatically involved the colonies of both empires in America. To the south of the English colonies, there was Florida,—then a province much more widely extended geographically than the modern State,—where were the hostile Spaniards. North of Maine, and everywhere to the west of the Allegheny Mountain chain, were the French. English America occupied merely a narrow strip of coast, a thousand miles long and only two or three hundred miles wide,—much in shape like Chili today. To the east was the sea, and to the west the wooded heights of the mountain frontier. Between these two, in the narrow thousand-mile strip, were our towns or scattered farms and plantations.

In 1690 there were about 215,000 English as against possibly only about 12,000 French. The French, however, were a unit and could carry out a single, highly centralized policy. The English were under twelve different local governments, of varying efficiency, developing different policies, and all so extremely jealous of one another as to make united action practically impossible. In addition, there was the Indian.

Racial pride or prejudice had prevented any fraternization between the English settlers and the savages. Moreover, in most of the colonies the fur trade was of very minor importance. The English were fundamentally farmers and home-builders. With the exception of the Iroquois in central New York, the native for the English was neither a business partner nor a military ally. He was, for the most part, a dangerous animal, like the panthers, wolves, and wild-cats, or a nuisance like the stones and tree stumps, to be cleared away before advancing settlements.

The French, on the other hand, had no racial antipathy. They became brothers of the savages, lived with them, and took Indian mistresses or wives. They were traders, adventurers, explorers, not settlers, and roamed thousands of miles in the interior of the continent, making friends of

FRENCH
SETTLEMENTS
in North America

@ French Forts

all the Indian tribes, and erecting forts and trading posts. By about 1700 they had established these as far west as Minnesota, and up and down the Mississippi River and its tributaries, although New Orleans was not founded until 1718. If the French had no objections to taking squaws for wives, neither had they any scruples about using the savage braves as allies in war and turning them loose to scalp, torture, and murder our ancestors along our whole frontier. This was what made the mere 12,000 French so formidable to the English.

The war begun in Europe in 1689 between two civilized nations was almost immediately echoed back from the American forests by the warwhoop of the savages. With much cruelty, parties of French and Indians fell on our settlements at such far separated points as Portland, then called Falmouth, Salmon Falls, and Schenectady. The New England colonies and New York, burning with desire for revenge, called a joint meeting to plan a common campaign against the enemy, but, as was almost always to prove the case, they were unable to co-operate efficiently. An expedition sent out by Massachusetts under Governor Phips got as far as attacking Quebec unsuccessfully, but the French and Indians continued to harry the New England frontier unmercifully, and when peace was declared in Europe in 1697, "King William's War," as it was called in America, had been entirely indecisive on our side of the water.

Peace was of short duration, and in 1701 began the struggle which European historians call "the War of the Spanish Succession" and which we call "Queen Anne's War." Lasting until the Peace of Utrecht in 1713 it was of much the same character as the preceding one, save

for the not unimportant fact that England tried to assist
the colonists by sending out naval expeditions to work
in concert with them for the conquest of Canada. The
Spanish, being allied with the French, also raided our
Carolina settlements from Florida. New England suffered most, however, and the attack on Deerfield in 1704,
when fifty French, with a couple of hundred Indians,
killed fifty-three of its inhabitants and carried off more
than a hundred captive, was merely one of the best-
known of many episodes in our border wars.

Unfortunately the attempted co-operation between the
British fleet and the New Englanders in several successive
years brought only losses and irritation to the colonists,
owing mainly to the incapacity of the British com-
manders. Nevertheless, when peace was signed England
had made several notable gains in America. Besides the
Hudson Bay region, Acadia, which became the province
of Nova Scotia (New Scotland), and Newfoundland
were ceded to her by France, with a beneficial effect on
the American fisheries. Spain granted her special privileges in the slave trade, which greatly increased that
traffic and was not unimportant as a factor in fastening
slavery on our later South.

The eighteenth century was one of favoritism, patronage, and venality in politics. England was no worse, and
rather better, in the tone of her public life than most
countries, but the evil system made for confusion, lack
of efficiency, careless and incompetent statesmanship. In

spite of constant squabbling between the popularly elected American assemblies and the royally appointed governors, America was a loyal part of the empire.

Unhappily, whenever the Americans and English tried to work together, as in the several abortive Canadian expeditions in Queen Anne's War, the only result had been mutual exasperation. Thus in the war with Spain which began in 1739 under the odd name of "the war of Jenkins's ear," the colonists made a notable display of loyalty. American volunteers were asked for by the British for a joint expedition against the Spanish West Indies. Over 3700 Americans, mostly from New England, volunteered and went, of whom over two thirds died, chiefly as a result of the total inefficiency of the British naval and military officers. The disgraceful conditions in the British Navy at that time, the darkest period in its glorious history, were, perhaps, no worse than those in our own army department at the time of the Spanish War, but whereas in the latter case we were all Americans in the mess together, in the first case the colonials naturally contrasted their own willingness to help with the incapacity of the government overseas.

Co-operation was much more successful in the War of the Austrian Succession, 1744-1748, when in 1745 a joint attack was made on the strong fortress of Louisbourg by the British fleet under Commodore Warren and an American force, largely made up of men from Maine, under command of William Pepperell of Kittery. The colonials and English, as well as both branches of the service, worked together in harmony for once and captured the French stronghold. Unfortunately the favorable effect of this on American sentiment was largely destroyed by the fact that in the treaty of peace England returned to the enemy the fortress stronghold, so important to America and in the capture of which all the colonies had taken great pride. Under the conditions of the moment, England, which was always thinking of the empire as a whole, and herself as centre, could do nothing else. The Americans, however, naturally felt that their efforts had been thrown away and their interests sacrificed, although England made a heavy payment in cash to Massachusetts to reimburse her for a large part of the cost of the expedition.

A much more important struggle was now imminent. The various treaties between England and France had never settled the questions between them. The desires of the two empires were clashing in many parts of the world, but our own story is confined to America. There also the two contestants were closing in on each other.

WAR BETWEEN FRANCE AND ENGLAND IN AMERICA

The English government was beginning to look westward across the mountains to the fertile lands beyond, where also a group of Virginians, including two brothers of George Washington, had obtained a grant to 200,000 acres of land south of the Ohio River, and another large land company, likewise west of the mountains, had been organized. On the other hand, the French, whose posts and settlements extended up and down the whole Mississippi Valley from New Orleans to Lake Superior, had been working eastward. They also coveted the Ohio Valley and the country between the mountains and river.

In 1753 the two currents met. After some preliminary parleys, an expedition was sent out by Governor Dinwiddie of Virginia under command of George Washington, then a lad of twenty-one, as lieutenant-colonel. The French were too strong for him, and he had to surrender to the enemy at Fort Necessity on the 4th of July, 1754. The question was now clearly posed. Was the whole of the country west of the mountains to remain in the possession of the French with their savage allies, or was it to be open to settlement and development by the English colonists? That was the *American* problem.

The *imperial* one was far wider, and ranged from the Mississippi to the Ganges. England realized the desperate nature of the struggle upon which she was now to enter. The world was at stake,—not simply the American continental colonies but the rich West Indies, the balance of power in Europe, the African trade, India, the wealth of the Orient, the life of empires. Every resource would be needed and have to be strained. How far could the Americans handle alone their own end of the affair? United they had great potential strength, but could they, jealous as they were, unite?

74

England suggested that we call an intercolonial conference to consider the question from the standpoint of a joint Indian policy, for it was the Indian allies of the French rather than the French themselves that counted. Twenty-five delegates from seven colonies met in the old City Hall at Albany in 1754, the most distinguished gathering of native American ability that had yet been seen. Among others, there were Thomas Hutchinson of Massachusetts, later to be bitterly hated as a Tory but at this time regarded as one of the best and greatest of Americans; James De Lancey, like Hutchinson a man of great wealth and Lieutenant-Governor of New York; Benjamin Franklin from Pennsylvania; Stephen Hopkins of Rhode Island; and others, all notable in their colonies. The Indians were also there, "King Hendrick" of the Mohawks, representing the Six Nations. He complained bitterly that whereas the French were men and building forts everywhere, the English were "like women, bare and open, without fortifications anywhere."

A treaty was made with the savages, but the larger problem of a Plan of Union, advanced by Governor Shirley of Massachusetts, failed of success. A plan proposed by Franklin was, indeed, agreed upon by the convention but did not meet acceptance generally when referred back to the several colonies for approval. Jealousies and provincialism of outlook are characteristic of all colonies at a certain stage of their growth, as the later histories of Canada and Australia witness, but it is only fair to keep our failure of 1754 in mind when we shall come to consider the later policy of England.

The following year England sent over two regiments of regulars under command of General Braddock to strike at the French by capturing Fort Duquesne at the junction of the Allegheny and Monongahela Rivers. The story of his defeat and death in the wilderness and the saving of the remnant of his army by Washington is well known. Braddock was a brave officer but obstinate, lacking in tact, and, with his long experience in European warfare, disdainful of advice by the Americans. A regular army officer is rarely an easy person for civilians or militia to get along with, and there was much ill-feeling between the English regulars and our colonials who had had experience in Indian raids but did not suffer discipline gladly.

The English General Loudon, in New York and New England, also did nothing to raise the Americans' respect for British official efficiency or tact. Nevertheless, these facts should not make us forget that as the war went on it was waged more and more by the forces sent over by England and less by the militia of the colonies. The years 1756 and 1757 were full of disasters, but after the great William Pitt swept away the lesser politicians in England and became Prime Minister, the trend of events changed swiftly.

In 1758, 41 British warships and 11,000 troops, with only a few Americans, recaptured Louisbourg. Colonel

Bradstreet captured Fort Frontenac on Lake Ontario. General Forbes with 1200 Highlanders and four times that number of colonials marched against Fort Duquesne, to find it abandoned by the French, and the place was renamed Pittsburgh. In his attempt to attack Canada by the Lake Champlain route, General Abercrombie made a bad failure, but the following year, 1759, Fort Niagara, Ticonderoga, Crown Point, and Quebec were all taken from the enemy by British forces in which there was but a sprinkling of colonials, the capture of Quebec being effected under the immortal Wolfe. More than twice as many New Englanders took part in the attack on Havana in 1762 as were included in the capture of the French city. Although Spain had come to the aid of France, England was victorious in all quarters by 1763. France's naval power was temporarily destroyed; she had lost India; and in the Treaty of Paris she ceded all her possessions in North America east of the Mississippi to England except the small island at the mouth of that river. By a secret treaty she also ceded all of "Louisiana" west of the river to Spain. Her North American Empire had crumbled to dust.

It is well that it did so, for had England, fighting with Prussia against France, Spain, and Austria, lost instead of won, the effect on our history would have been almost incalculable. Even if a defeated England had not been forced to turn over her American colonies to the rule of France, those colonies at best would have been encircled for an indefinite period by the successful Catholic powers, without the English ideas of liberty, and in control of perhaps a hundred thousand savages to unleash on our borders. There could have been no expansion for us westward across the mountains. There would have been in the next generation no American Revolution and no United States. It was the strength of England and not that of the colonies which had achieved the world victory, a point on which we shall have to dwell later. Deferring the larger aspects of the end of the war, we must return to consider local American affairs.

Although the duel for empire, lasting for seventy years, had been fought in many quarters of the world as well as in America, it was naturally the part that the Americans had taken which interested them most and seemed to them all-important. We minimized our constant inability to unite, and on the other hand magnified all our own local successes and examples of bravery in border war. We had been in close co-operation with the British regulars on many occasions and almost without exception had gained a poor impression of them, both for inefficiency and bad manners.

Just as the city man is inclined to think himself superior to the country man, so the citizen of any home country is likely to adopt a somewhat superior attitude toward the colonial, always and everywhere. We could not have ousted the French without the power of England but the general picture remaining in our minds was

78

well exemplified in the popular contrast between the brave but overbearing and pig-headed Braddock and the quiet young Washington who knew so much better the needs of our frontier form of war. The sum total of irritation between British subjects on the two sides of the water had thus been notably increased by a couple of generations of joint undertakings.

In civil government there had also been a constant cause for irritation in all the colonies, except Connecticut and Rhode Island, neither of which had a royal governor. That official occupied everywhere a very difficult position. As the representative of the King and of the central authority in the empire, he was expected to maintain the royal prerogatives. On the other hand, he was dependent for his salary not on England but on the votes of the colonial assemblies. Every governor, as Benjamin Franklin said, "has two Masters; one who gives him his Commission, and one who gives him his Pay."

Owing to the excessive space usually given to New England in our earlier histories, the struggles in Massachusetts between the assemblies and such governors as Shute or Burnet have tended to make it appear that the fight for liberty was peculiarly a New England product. In fact, such contests were waged everywhere, in the Proprietary and Royal Colonies alike, nowhere more constantly and openly, for example, than in New Jersey and Pennsylvania. Some of the governors sent out were excellent men, such as Spotswood or Burnet, but England had not then developed that civil service for colonial administration which has become the finest in the world. Many colonial governors in the eighteenth century were mere needy adventurers, but, good or bad, they were bound to be storm centres of bitter political controversy.

Control of the purse has always been the strongest bulwark of freedom, and it was fortunate that England left this control to the colonists. They, on their side, naturally employed it to the fullest extent, and the whole history of this period is the story of constant use of financial pressure by the assemblies to secure the approval of the governors to popular measures and even to force them to disobey their instructions and the terms of their commissions. Under the circumstances of distance, lack of direct representation in Parliament, and other matters incidental to the colonial status, such contests between the popularly elected assemblies in America and the governors from overseas, generation after generation, came to appear like a contest not merely between the subject and the Crown as it would have in England, but as a struggle by the Americans for their rights as Americans against the power of the mother country.

Against local opposition of one sort or another it was almost impossible even for a good governor to adopt a wise policy. Governor Burnet's experience in New York before he was transferred to Massachusetts well illustrates the difficulties of the whole colonial situation. One of the greatest, if not the greatest danger, to the American colonies was the French; and the power of the

FACSIMILE OF A MAP IN COLDEN'S *HISTORY OF THE FIVE NATIONS*, PRINTED IN LONDON IN 1747

From the Lenox Collection, New York Public Library.

French was their control of the Indians by means of the fur trade. In 1726 Burnet, having consulted with the expert on Indian affairs, Cadwallader Colden, author of the *History of the Five Indian Nations,* sought to check the French influence by establishing an American trading post at Oswego and also by stopping the sale of Indian trading goods to the French at Montreal by the

Albany merchants. The English trading goods were better and cheaper than the French, but selling them to the
French to use with the Indians was almost like selling
firearms to an enemy.

New York, of all the colonies, was the best situated,

July 14th. 1703.
Prices of Goods

Supplyed to the

Eastern Indians,

By the several Truckmasters ; and of the Peltry received
by the Truckmasters of the said *Indians.*

One yard Broad Cloth,*three* Beaver skins,*in season.*
One yard & halfGingerline,*one* Beaver skin,*in season*
One yard Red or Blew Kerfey,*two* Beaver skins,*in season.*
One yard good Duffels, *one* Beaver skin, *in season.*
One yard& half broad fineCotton,*one*Beaver skin,*in season*
Two yards of Cotton, *one* Beaver skin. *in season.*

*What shall be accounted in Value equal
One Beaver* in season : *Viz.*

One Otter skin in season, is one Beaver
One Bear skin in season, is one Beaver,

INDIAN TRADE—A FACSIMILE OF A BROADSIDE
In the Library of Congress.

on account of its easy entry to the interior of the continent by the Hudson-Mohawk Valleys, to engage in the
fur trade on a large scale. By a shrewd use of its superior
goods and location, the colony could have done much to
alienate the Indians from the French in the very heart
of their central empire. This would have been of great
advantage not only to New York but to other colonies
whose frontiers were constantly ravaged. The New
Yorkers, however, cared nothing about the other colo-

nies, and the merchants of Manhattan and Albany, who were getting rich from selling goods to Montreal, thought little of the frontier. They took care therefore, after the manner of "big business" always, to block sound social policy for the sake of profits. They not only wrecked the governor's plan but his own career.

THE BEGINNINGS OF CONFLICT WITH ENGLAND

Throughout this period there was constant effort to resist imperial control and to demand larger rights; and almost invariably the colonists won. Sometimes this was accomplished peacefully, as in Pennsylvania, where the proprietor Penn agreed to a new Charter of Privileges in 1701, enlarging the rights of self-government; or was the result of tumultuous revolution as in North Carolina, where for seven years before "Cary's Rebellion" in 1711 the poorer people had been carrying on armed resistance against the authorities and wealthier elements.

England, as we have said, thought of the American colonies, when she thought of them in statesmanlike fashion at all, as merely one part of an interdependent and nicely balanced economic empire. Our ancestors naturally thought of them as their own, with which they could do as they liked and whose natural resources and trade opportunities were to be exploited to the limit, primarily for their own benefit. Just as capital and labor rarely look at economic problems from the same point of view, so the metropolis of any empire and one of its colonies often clash in their views without either of them suspecting that they may be narrow-minded or selfish. The point of view evolves unconsciously from all the surrounding conditions of each.

Such a clash of views and interests left a landmark in this period in the "Molasses Act" passed by Parliament in 1733. The colonies had always tacitly acknowledged the right of that body, becoming more active in imperial legislation as the century advanced, to pass laws designed to regulate the trade of the empire as a whole. It was part of the price paid for being a member of a strong empire instead of a waif outside in days when such a waif was sure to be pounced on by some imperialistically minded nation. The expanding commerce of the colonies, however, was beginning to be hampered by the restrictions of the Navigation Acts, and there was much smuggling and clandestine trading with countries outside the imperial system.

New England, as we have noted, had always fitted least easily into the mercantile scheme from the nature of her products. She had gradually built up a trade which rested to a considerable extent on rum. Selling horses, timber, and other products to the sugar planters in the West Indies, she got in exchange molasses from which she distilled rum which she used in the slave trade and for heavy domestic consumption, lay and clerical. By 1730 the British Sugar Islands were fast running down, and the French islands were far richer and more fertile.

As New England trade was being diverted to them, the British West Indian planters brought the matter up in Parliament and asked for a bill prohibiting the Americans from trading with the French.

Clearly the interests of two integral parts of the empire were in conflict. As a member of Parliament wrote, "our Northern Colonies tell us, 'If we pass the Bill, we destroy their Trade,' and our Southern Colonies say, 'If we do not pass the Bill, they are undone.' " There was also a larger question. The whole period was dominated by the contest between England and France. Was it wise for Parliament to allow the New Englanders to build up French commercial power in the West Indies at the expense of the British? It was decided to sacrifice New England's local interest to the larger ones of the empire as a whole, and a bill was passed laying a prohibitive duty on the import of rum or molasses from the French islands.

Had the law been obeyed by the New Englanders their trade would have been ruined and their whole economic structure, none too strong, would have toppled. They naturally felt that Parliament had completely sacrificed them. The tremendous danger of Parliamentary interference with American affairs had become evident. On the other hand, England made no serious effort to enforce the law, and the French trade went on as before, only thenceforward as illegal smuggling. The lessons, however, of the latent danger from the power overseas, and the ease with which it could apparently be flouted, were not lost on our ancestors. To the just wrath of Pitt they continued to do a highly lucrative business with the French islands even during the French and Indian War, when such trading was having a serious ill effect on their own struggle with the enemy.

The growing self-confidence and self-consciousness of Americans in this period was due not only to contacts with English officers, constant and successful struggles to control governors, and easy nullification of Royal orders and Acts of Parliament. Between 1690 and 1763 the population increased from 215,000 to about 1,800,-000. Only one new colony had been founded, that of Georgia in 1732, and most of the increase thus occurred in the older ones. The Georgia colony had been started by General James Oglethorpe, an English philanthropist, who secured a charter with the sole idea of making a retreat in the New World where poor people from the debtors' prisons might start life afresh. Being granted the land between South Carolina and the Spaniards in Florida, he set to work but the colony grew slowly. Comparatively few debtors emigrated, but on the other hand Scotch Highlanders and Germans both settled in considerable numbers.

What happened in Georgia was symptomatic of what was occurring in all of the colonies. There was little English immigration during the eighteenth century, the marvellous growth in population being mostly due to native births and to large influxes of Scotch, Irish, Germans, and to a lesser extent, Swiss. All these facts tended to make the American of 1760 feel himself more of an American and less of an Englishman than his ancestors had done some generations before.

In the early part of the century there was great distress both in Ireland and Germany. In the former, drought, sheep-rot and disease seemed destined to complete the ruin wrought by the political and economic policy of the British. Those who suffered most were the Scotch Presbyterians in the north of the island, whose standard of living had been higher than that of the Catholic Irish in the south. In the second decade of the century long term leases for farms fell in in great numbers and stony-hearted landlords demanded double and treble rents to renew them. A vast exodus of these people began to America, where they arrived chiefly in Philadelphia and from thence poured out into the frontier counties of Pennsylvania and down into the Shenandoah Valley.

Though they came to all of the colonies, notably the Carolinas, they always went out to the frontier, where land was cheap, and made the finest frontiersmen we have known. Of the social effects of this great movement of a people we shall speak in the next chapter, and are here concerned only with what we may call its imperial aspect. It is impossible to calculate accurately the number who came, but historians have estimated them as high as 500,000, and I think we may conservatively place it at 300,000 to 400,000, counting the immediate descendants of the immigrants. When it is recalled that great numbers of these came to us with hatred for England as one of their strongest passions, it becomes evident that something very momentous had happened in the re-

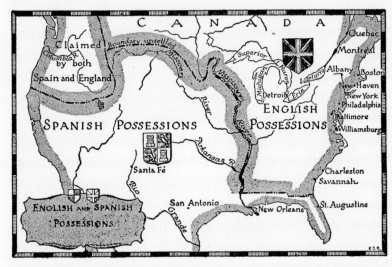

lations between the mother country and the American colonies.

Germany had not recovered from the terrific slaughter and devastation of the Thirty Years' War, and in the Palatinate and other provinces, as in the German cantons of Switzerland, there were intense poverty, suffering, and religious persecution in the early eighteenth century. From this mass of human misery came another great movement of population to our shores, the Germans settling largely in Pennsylvania, Maryland, and Virginia, the Swiss going mostly to Carolina. For these

Germans also there are no statistics in the modern sense, but I think it safe to say that by 1763 there were at least 100,000 of them in the colonies, and quite possibly many more. This stock had no hatred of England, but on the other hand, no knowledge of her or loyalty to her. They knew only their new homes in America and their struggles to win them.

By 1763 England had won her duel with France. She owned North America from the Atlantic to the Mississippi, and from the Gulf of Mexico to the Arctic Sea, although in 1784 she ceded back Florida to the Spaniards. But in this vast territory were the irreconciled French in Canada, possibly 300,000 savages who were hostile to English rule, several hundred thousand Scotch-Irish with a tradition of hatred for English oppression, 100,000 Germans who cared nothing about England, perhaps 400,-000 black slaves who knew nothing of her, and a sturdy population of possibly 600,000 of her own sons and their descendants who were loyal but who were chips of the old block in their love of liberty and who had been used to a greater degree of self-government in all their daily concerns than even Englishmen enjoyed at home. Here was a problem that would call for the wisest possible statesmanship. Before we consider it further, and the failure to solve it, we must pause to get a better idea of what sort of life our ancestors had built up by the time that they were forced into a bloody civil war with the nation from which a majority of them had sprung.

CHAPTER IV

AMERICAN LIFE IN 1763

ALTHOUGH by the period now reached by our story there was much diversity among all of the thirteen colonies, they also fall easily into three quite clearly differentiated groups,—the Southern, Middle, and New England. It was in the tidewater and older sections of these that the differences between colonies and groups were most noticeable. Back of all of them, from Maine to Georgia, ran the frontier where conditions were comparatively uniform, as were also the attitudes of the frontiersmen toward the wealthier residents of the old settlements. We shall come to this important point later in the chapter, and must consider here the broad differences between the groups named.

The Southern one, which included the oldest colony, Virginia, extended from Georgia to Maryland. It was not a region solely of big plantations. There were many small planters who tilled the land themselves without slaves or with only two or three. But as we shall see, life had been getting harder for these poorer people, many of whom had gone to the frontier; and the wealth which the rich had gained had come from securing in one way

and another large estates in land and ample slave power
with which to work them.

Slavery was recognized by law and practiced in every

March 10, 1752.

RAN away from the Subfcriber, living in *Prince George* County, about a Fortnight
ago, a lufty well-fet *Virginia*-born Negroe Man Slave, named *Vallen*; he is a
fmooth-tongued cunning Fellow, and it's probable will endeavour to impofe on People,
by pretending to be what he is not; and it's not unlikely will change his Name; he is
between 30 and 40 Years of Age, about 5 Feet 10 Inches high, and had on when he
went away, an Oznabrigs Shirt, a Cotton Waiftcoat and Breeches, dy'd Yellow, and
a Pair of Breeches not dy'd. Whoever will take up and fecure him, fo that I may have
him again, fhall have Two Piftoles if taken up on the South Side of *James* River, if in
Carolina, or the North Side of *James* River, Three Piftoles Reward, befides what the Law
allows, paid by

William Broadnax.

AN ADVERTISEMENT FOR A RUNAWAY SLAVE
The reward offered for capture varied according to the location.
From "The Virginia Gazette" of 1752.

one of the colonies, but it was economically profitable
on a large scale only in the South, with its milder climate
and its simple and undiversified agriculture. In Mary-

Cleared Outwards.

March 26. The Warren, of Whitehaven, Robert Letham, for Whitehaven, with 238
Hhds. of Tobacco.
April 4. Sloop Molly, of Virginia, Solomon Ewell, for Barbados, with 416 lbs. of
Tobacco, & 1950 Bufhch of Corn.

ADVERTISEMENT OF CARGOES IN VESSELS OUT OF VIRGINIA
From "The Virginia Gazette" of August 7, 1752.

land, great landowners like the Carrolls, who had one
grant of 60,000 acres, and the Dulanys, also with large
grants, had made fortunes by settling German immigrants on their properties as tenant farmers. But for the
most part through the South the important families,

socially and economically, were the owners of large plantations, for tobacco or rice, who lived on them in a sort of patriarchal life with their troops of blacks. The only town larger than a village was Charleston, which may have had a population of 9000, and the type of life of the Southern gentleman was much like that of well-to-do squires in the counties of old England, modified by climate and slavery. His ties with the old country were close. London merchants bought his staple crop once a year, looked after his money or debts, and shipped over on order his clothes, silver, books, and mahogany. His sons frequently went to England to study at the universities or master law in the Temple, and to get their social training in London or in Tunbridge Wells and other fashionable English spas, as depicted by Thackeray in *The Virginians*.

In the middle colonies of Pennsylvania, New Jersey, and New York, we find quite different ways and occupations. In the first, the mixed population of Quaker English, Germans, Welsh, and Scotch had modest farms or were acquiring wealth in manufacturing, such as breweries and iron works, or in trade. Philadelphia was the largest city on the continent and a bustling place of over 20,000 people of whom so many were Germans that the street signs were painted in the two languages. Money and social position there belonged rather to the city merchant or manufacturer than to the planter, as in the South.

THE GIBBS HOUSE, CHARLESTON, SOUTH CAROLINA. BUILT IN 1752

IN THE VIEUX CARRÉ, THE OLD FRENCH AND SPANISH PART OF
NEW ORLEANS

Photographs by Edward Larocque Tinker.

JOSEPH CABOT HOUSE, SALEM. BUILT IN 1748

VAN COURTLANDT MANSION, NEW YORK. BUILT IN 1748
From the Essex Institute, Salem.

New York was the second largest city, having just outdistanced Boston, and was a cosmopolitan town chiefly interested in commerce. Thanks largely to having had a succession of peculiarly unscrupulous governors early in the century, such as Fletcher and Cornbury, many New York families had acquired huge grants of land up the Hudson and elsewhere, and there was a social distinction in the possession of such spoils. They had developed, however, no such plantation life as in Virginia southward, and had been too grasping as landlords to succeed in planting tenant farmers as had, in such a business-like way, Carroll and Dulany in Maryland.

The great manorial families in New York, nevertheless, were extremely influential in the government and in controlling the distribution of offices. Seven townships belonged to the Livingstons; the Beekmans and Schuylers owned most of Dutchess County; the Phillipses and Heathcotes, six manors in Westchester; and the van Rensselaers nearly 700 square miles near Albany. Lord Cornbury, as governor, had made one single grant of 2,000,000 acres, and it was chiefly out of such favoritism or bribed gifts, that had come the old New York "aristocracy." Besides the landed proprietors, including the old Dutch "patroons" along the river, there was also growing up a class of rich merchants, whose power and influence increased with their wealth. These were especially numerous and rich, of course, in the city of New

York itself, whose commerce vied with that of its greater competitor, Philadelphia.

Crossing into the Puritan colonies we would at once have sensed a great difference, as all travellers of the day did. Boston was a town of 15,000 and Newport about half as large, but for the most part New England was a land of small farms closely grouped in villages about the church. There were a neatness and a thriftiness lacking farther south, and the village greens and the landscape with its elms and meadows and hedgerows could almost be mistaken for a bit of old England. As in the Middle Colonies, wealth came chiefly from manufacturing or shipping, but the sturdy farmer, of pure English descent, having his say in town meeting or as church member, counted for more in the scene than he did in plutocratic New York or in polyglot Pennsylvania. As each New England town had been settled, its inhabitants had been allotted lands in fee simple, and with no fresh immigration for many generations and no alien stocks, a native yeomanry had grown up with a remarkable degree of tenacity and independence.

In a hundred and forty years, the stony ground, a cruel climate, and a profound preoccupation with religious problems according to Calvin, had "set" the New England character. Since 1692, when a hundred and fifty persons were imprisoned for witchcraft in Massachusetts and twenty were killed, the devil had not been thus fought there with carnal weapons of the law, but there were still a certain strength of beliefs and a grim determination in New England that was not to be found in money-making New York, or among the Quakers or German Pietists of Pennsylvania, or the easy-going Southerners. New England was a land apart, and desired to remain so, its inhabitants having always been taught by their clergy to consider themselves as peculiarly the people of God in a wicked world. It was in a sense the Scotland of America.

The original immigrants who settled all the colonies were from much the same social grades in England whether they had settled North or South. Everywhere there had been a sprinkling of "gentlemen," as the term was then understood, among the great mass of farmers, artisans, and others, but practically without exception the whole of the colonial population had sprung from the laboring and the middle classes, upper and lower, scarcely a single titled aristocrat and only a comparatively few "younger sons" having made their homes over here. The origin, for example, of such Virginia families as the Beverleys, Byrds, and Carters had been merely good middle class in Europe, as had been that of the French families in South Carolina or Dutch in New York which were to become notable. Both virtues and vices vary in different classes, and those in America were almost wholly untinged by the aristocratic. This does not mean that there were not social distinctions, clearly made and sharply insisted upon, in colonial days. There most assuredly were. But America generally, then as always, was based on the middle-class outlook, using the phrase in no invidious sense, rather than upon the aristocratic.

OUR EARLY SOCIAL AND ECONOMIC LIFE

On the other hand, men are moulded by different forms of social and economic life, and as these came to vary in the different sections, the ideals of each became

---

To be SOLD, by the Subscriber, near the Capitol, *in* Williamsburg,

GENUINE *French* Claret, at 40 *s. per* Dozen, Samples whereof may be had at 4 *s.* a Bottle, net *Barbadoes* Rum at 5 *s. per* Gallon ; also fine *Madeira* Wine, *English* Beer, and *Hughes*'s Cyder, at the common Rates ; also a Cask of fine Hogs-Lard, of about 230 *lb.* Weight, with several Pots of Capers and Anchovies.

2   *Daniel Fisher.*

AN ADVERTISEMENT OF A SALE OF A SHIPMENT OF LIQUOR, CAPERS, AND ANCHOVIES

From "The Virginia Gazette" of 1752.

---

different from the others. The aristocrat has been the product of generations who have been in a position to rule others, and who have learned the habits and responsibilities of such rule; who from wealth and leisure have developed the art of manners and social life; and who from possessing an assured social position, buttressed by visible emblems, have acquired independence of public opinion. The man who has a notable estate on which his family has been living for generations, who devotes his time to hunting, social life, and governing, develops a different set of qualities and ideals from one who may be just as wealthy and educated, but who lives a town life and is constantly preoccupied with the making of money from trade in severe competition with others.

By the middle of the eighteenth century, the ideals of the South with its great plantation economy and of the North with its rising mercantile interests had begun to draw apart. The rich Southerner, like the second William Byrd of Westover, for example, with his 180,000 acres, living on his large and well-known estate, with a public recognition that came quite as much from his family and place as from his own efforts, having little to do with trade and not understanding it very well, responsible for ruling and looking after his numerous slaves, regarding himself from boyhood as belonging to a superior race, devoting himself to sport and cultivating a social life of great charm, often too heedless as to expenditure and his scale of easy living, began to develop the aristocratic qualities. The entailing of the larger estates upon the oldest son also helped to build up the types and ideals of an aristocratic life.

On the other hand, in New England, without such estates, without entail, and with fortunes made or lost in trade, there was little or no tendency to modify middle-class ideals of the best and also sometimes of the narrowest sort. Business dynasties are usually brief. The richest man in New England, for example, John Hancock, inherited a fortune made by his uncle and lost it himself. Both in the Northern and Middle Colonies, the period was notable for the constant rise of new men to financial eminence. The money of the upper social class of New England was based on trade, and as ever in history, there was a vast difference in outlook between the agrarian and commercial groups. The New Englander handled his business affairs shrewdly and well, far better

ADVERTISEMENT OF THE BRIGANTINE *JANE* CARRYING
PASSENGERS AND FREIGHT

From "The Pennsylvania Gazette," October 27, 1748.

than the Southerner. He took both his intellectual and religious life more seriously, and just as his class in England disliked the aristocracy there, so the New Englanders disliked the very mild aristocracy which had begun to develop in the South. On the other hand, the Southerner looked down upon and disliked the New Englander. He regarded him much as an old Tory, hunting county squire in the old country would have regarded a tradesman or a London merchant. The beginnings had already been made for one of the most disastrous sectional cleavages in our history, to be steadily widened for nearly a century following.

Although the first American guide book had been published in 1732, travel between the colonies was difficult, and this helped to maintain the differences between them and to foster local peculiarities. In 1754 a combined stage and boat line was advertised to run twice a week between Philadelphia and New York, and a few other lines were started in the next decade, but the roads were bad, as were most inns, and the traveller had to rely almost solely on his own private carriage or even more, on riding horseback. New England merchants carried on some commerce by boat with the Southern colonies, but there was extremely little social intercourse between the sections. A Carroll of Maryland might go to old England, but it was as unthinkable that he would go to New England for pleasure as it was that a John Adams should tour Virginia or the Carolinas. If each had done so, they would have discovered that as compared with their fathers' times, wealth had greatly increased as well as the scale of living.

OUR EARLY HOUSES AND THE ARTS

In all the colonies they would have found their richer friends living in beautifully designed houses of the Georgian type. The earlier architecture of the first few generations had derived rather from the mediæval in Europe, and there had been much variety in the styles introduced by English, Dutch, Swedes, Welsh, Germans, and others, but these pleasant differences tended to disappear after about 1720. Foreign strains in America have always been quickly absorbed into the prevailing English, and the new mansion of a rich German, Dutch, or Welshman came to be built uniformly in the Georgian which spread up and down the whole coast.

The change of style from the earlier period correctly interpreted a change in colonial conditions. The frontier had come to be far off from the older settlements. Life in the latter was as safe, stable, and almost as conventional as in any county of England. Wealth had accumulated and its possessors desired a dignified setting in which to display it and to conduct their social life. For this, both the architecture of the Georgian house and its furnishing were admirably adapted. They were at once dignified and homelike. The two interiors preserved in the Boston Museum of Fine Arts, one of 1690 and the other of 1750, mark vividly the change that two generations had brought. The beamed ceiling had given place to plaster (often in the larger houses of exquisite design in decoration); the rough boarding of the wall had become beautiful panelling, painted white or covered with paper imported from England; the bare floor had been covered with oriental rugs; the oak chairs with wooden or rush seats had been replaced by mahogany upholstered in satin or brocade. As we study the furniture or the rooms of this period, happily preserved in many places

Room from West Boxford, Massachusetts. *Circa* 1675–1704.

Room from the Jaffrey House, Portsmouth, New Hampshire. *Circa* 1750.

TWO INTERIORS PRESERVED IN THE BOSTON MUSEUM OF FINE ARTS

SANTA BARBARA MISSION, CALIFORNIA, 1787–1800

Left: ST. MICHAEL'S CHURCH, CHARLESTON, SOUTH CAROLINA, BUILT IN 1742

Right: SAN XAVIER DEL BAC, TUCSON, ARIZONA, BUILT BY THE FRANCISCANS ON THE SITE OF FATHER KINO'S MISSION, FOUNDED ABOUT 1700

beside the Boston and Metropolitan Museums, we are struck by their perfect taste, their dignity, and sense of peace.

In New England, although the mansions were often as spacious as in the South, there was a certain compactness about them which befitted the long hard winters, and the town dwelling. In the South they were often in three sections, a large central portion and two smaller ones on either side, sometimes connected with the main portion and sometimes not. None of them would have been "great houses" in the English sense, but all, North and South, were roomy, comfortable, and often of exquisite proportions and of daintier craftsmanship in their decorative carving than those contemporary with them in England.

One Marylander, Doctor Alexander Hamilton, who did venture North, found in Rhode Island "the largest and most magnificent dwelling house" he had seen in America, that of Captain Godfrey Malbone in Newport. Wealth in New England being concentrated in the towns, the finest domestic architecture of the period has to be looked for in such places as Boston, Marblehead, Salem, and Portsmouth. Mostly of wood in the North, the larger houses were of stone in the Middle Colonies and of brick in the South. Innumerable examples might be cited of these beautiful and dignified dwellings in every colony of the period, but we may suggest as examples the McPhaedris house in Portsmouth, the Vassall in Cambridge, the Jumel in New York, Cliveden in Germantown, Westover and Mount Airy on the James in Virginia. In South Carolina, plantation wealth was being expended also in town life, and such houses as that of Miles Brewton were being built to provide a luxurious setting for a social scene as brilliant as any on the continent.

For the rich who lived in these houses, English culture, so roughly transplanted more than a century before, had come to perfect flowering. The long narrow strip of the English colonies had been settled. The rough work of pioneering seemed about over. Life was much what it was in English provincial towns and counties, only a little freer, a little less hemmed in by old conventions, customs, and class restrictions. Within a few years the storm of war was to overwhelm this old English-American life, the West was to be opened, and for more than a century a wild scramble was to ensue for untold riches, while the frontier leaped from the Appalachians to the Mississippi, from the Mississippi to the Rockies, from the Rockies to the Pacific. In the vast turmoil of it all, modern America was to be born, and the life of these old Georgian house dwellers was to come to seem as remote and un-American as that of English squires. But just before all this was to burst upon us it seemed as though America had come of age and settled down to maturity as a fully developed English provincial civilization.

Life had been hard in the early days and in the work of pioneering there had been little chance to cultivate the arts. Something had perforce to be given up in the struggle to plant a civilization where there was nothing but wilderness and savage foe. The farmer or artisan who in the settled life of the Old World had satisfied his craving for self-expression by carving the beams of his house, making chests and other pieces of furniture,

WHEREAS fome ill-difpos'd Perfons have reported, that the Subfcriber hath not fufficient Entertainment : This is to give Notice, That all Gentlemen who will favour me with their Company, may depend on good Entertainment, at the *Crown* Tavern, oppofite to the *Printing-Office*, in *Williamfburg*, by
Their humble Servant,
William Dunn.

A RIVALRY BETWEEN TAVERN KEEPERS APPARENTLY INSPIRED
THIS ADVERTISEMENT
From "The Virginia Gazette," 1752.

carving or painting them in the winter evenings, found his time and strength occupied by sterner tasks. The man who in England might have sat by the fire and read his book, found his time and hands more than occupied in wresting a farm or plantation from forest or stony upland. Folk art and the cultivation of the mind tended to disappear, and products and activities to become wholly utilitarian. Perhaps 1700 marked the lowest artistic and mental period of the colonies. But with wealth accumulated and the wilderness conquered, an indigenous American culture, though on English models, sprang up, and while folk art did not return, there came to be a ready market for the professional artist or craftsman.

In the middle of the century, B. Roberts, Alexander Gordon, and Jeremiah Theuss were all painting portraits in South Carolina of the leading families there—the Ravenels, Porches, Manigaults, Izards, and others. In Virginia, Charles Bridges was painting the wealthy planters with their wives and daughters. Hesselius in Maryland, Robert Feke in Newport, and John Smibert in Boston were among the other portrait painters, of whom each colony had its favorite. Copley was perhaps the most fashionable, and Benjamin West, who was to become President of the Royal Academy in London, was beginning his career. Landscape painting was also becoming popular, and in 1757 there was an exhibition in New York of work which was entirely that of Americans.

Music was cultivated and in the larger towns there were frequent concerts of the best compositions of the time rendered by orchestras capable of playing operatic overtures and symphonies. In 1759 the first musical society, the "Orpheus Club," was organized in Philadelphia, and in 1762 was founded the well-known "Saint Cecelia Society" in Charleston after a less formal existence during the preceding quarter of a century. Both musicians and actors from Europe usually went first to the rich and luxury-loving West Indies, and thence to America by way of the South Carolina capital, where there were probably more and better drama and music to be heard than anywhere else in the colonies. New

ISAAC ROYALL, FOUNDER OF THE ROYALL PROFESSORSHIP IN THE
HARVARD LAW SCHOOL, AND HIS FAMILY

From the painting by Feke in Harvard University.

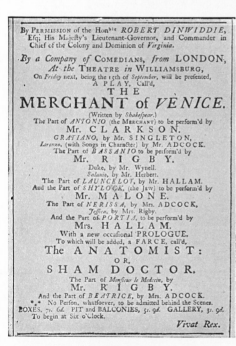

ANNOUNCEMENT OF THE FIRST AP-
PEARANCE OF THE HALLAMS IN
AMERICA

From "The Virginia Gazette" of August 28, 1752.

MRS. HALLAM AS "MARIANNE" IN
"THE DRAMATIST"

*From the Theatre Collection of the Harvard College
Library.*

NASSAU HALL AND THE PRESIDENT'S HOUSE, PRINCETON, 1764

From an engraving by Henry Dawkins, in the Princeton Library,
after the drawing by William Tennent.

GEORGE WHITEFIELD PREACHING

From the portrait by John Woollaston in the National Portrait Gallery.

England still forbade "stage plays" as being of the devil, but from New York south there was ample opportunity to hear the works of Shakespeare, Addison, Congreve, and others, among the best or most popular dramatists of the day. This was especially the fact after the arrival of the noted English actors, Mr. and Mrs. Lewis Hallam, who came in 1750 and found so much encouragement that they remained for twenty years, playing not only in

An Addreſs from the Society called *Quakers*, was preſented to the Houſe and read, ſetting forth, that they have, with real Concern, heard that a Company of Stage Players are preparing to erect a Theatre, and exhibit Plays to the Inhabitants of this City, which they conceive, if permitted, will be ſubverſive of the good Order and Morals, which they deſire may be preſerved in this Government, and therefore pray the Houſe to frame and preſent to the Governor, for his Aſſent, a Bill to prohibit ſuch enſnaring and irreligious Entertainments.   *Ordered to lie on the Table*

A PROTEST OF THE QUAKERS OF PHILADELPHIA AGAINST THE APPEARANCE OF DAVID DOUGLASS AND HIS PLAYERS IN 1759

From the original Journal of the General Assembly, in the Genealogical Society, Philadelphia.

the large cities but in such small towns as Port Tobacco, Petersburg, Fredericksburg, and others in the South. The minor arts, such as silver-smithing, glass blowing, furniture making, and others, were also developing craftsmen whose work is eagerly sought after by collectors of today.

EDUCATION AND RELIGION

By the end of this period, eight of the colonies had their own colleges, Harvard in Massachusetts (1636), William and Mary in Virginia (1693), Yale in Connecticut (1701), Princeton in New Jersey (1746), University of Pennsylvania (1751), Dartmouth in New Hampshire (1754), Columbia in New York (1754), and Brown in Rhode Island (1764). Some of these institutions were, it is true, but the germs of the later ones, of which even the names have been changed, but the beginnings are note-

THE EARLIEST BUILDING OF THE BOSTON LATIN SCHOOL, ABOUT 1645

For the first ten years of its existence, school was held in the house of the head master. In the picture is shown also the rear of King's Chapel.

worthy of what was to be a continuous growth. Probably New England led in the matter of education, although her excellent school laws were far from being generally observed. In that section as elsewhere the statute books give very unreliable evidence as to real conditions, and Massachusetts taxpayers were not seldom as averse as those elsewhere to spending money on schools. These were not compulsory and the so-called "free" village and town schools of New England were so only for those children whose parents could not afford to pay. The New England system theoretically, however, was the best of all colonial ones, and the Boston Latin School possibly the finest in the country, though there were excellent private schools elsewhere, notably in Philadelphia.

New York was strikingly backward in educational, and to a considerable extent in intellectual, interests. In

---

NOTICE is hereby given, That *Symes's* Free School, in *Elizabeth-City* County, will be vacant on the 25th of *March* Inst. a Tutor of a good Character, and properly qualified, may meet with good Encouragement, by applying to the Trustees of the said School.

N. B. The Land Rent of the said School is 31 *l. per Ann.* besides Perquisites.

AN OPENING FOR A "TUTOR OF GOOD CHARACTER" IN THE SYMES'S FREE SCHOOL IN ELIZABETH CITY COUNTY
From "The Virginia Gazette" of March 12, 1752.

the South it is rather difficult to judge of conditions, although clearly they were not as inferior to New England as used to be thought from a mere study of the laws. Southern children of the richer classes usually had tutors, and when this training was followed by a few years at an English university they got a better education than fell to the lot of the New Englanders of the same social grade. The scattered mode of settlement in the South made the problem of educating the poorer children more difficult than in the compact New England villages, but there were a good many schools in existence, and the Southern apprenticeship laws provided that the apprentice must be taught at least to read and write.

The original object aimed at in American education had been to make good Christians rather than good citizens. William and Mary College in Virginia, like Harvard and Yale in New England, had been founded to train up a godly ministry. The New Englanders had made their schools town schools at a time when the suffrage was limited to church members, but when that restriction was withdrawn in the new charter of 1691, they found that the school system had been secularized. Nowhere was there a realization of the value of education merely for citizenship. The general secularization of thought, however, proceeded apace in the colonies and in this, America as usual reflected the dominant current of thought in Europe.

By 1763 our religious life was very different from what it had been a couple of generations earlier. Even in New England the first fervor of the original refugees had been cooling and the theology petrifying. Everywhere in the colonies, the people were deprived of much that in the customs and surroundings of the Old World, rich in human experience and accomplishment, had afforded color and emotional outlets. The great mass of colonists had become emotionally starved in their narrow, dull and hardworking lives. Over these, whether in the Anglican South or Puritan New England, the extraordinary years of revivalist meetings known as "the Great Awakening" swept like a forest fire.

A number of preachers, such as Gilbert Tennent and

the great Jonathan Edwards, had been preaching in a way deeply to stir the religious emotions of their hearers, and there had been minor revivals in the colonies before George Whitefield came over from England in 1738. As he and lesser preachers toured the colonies, the repressed emotions of their hearers wrought congregations to frenzy. Under the lead of the evangelicals, churches were split into what were called "Old Lights" and "New Lights," and for the first time all of the colonies were caught up in the wave of a common movement. There was intense bitterness mixed with the emotions which broke congregations in twain, but when the excitement subsided about 1744, American religious life had undergone a profound change.

The complete domination of the ministers of the old sects of whatever sort had been broken, and the influence of the conservatives who had opposed the movement, much weakened. It was in a sense a popular uprising, and the new evangelicals of all denominations felt themselves bound closer to one another than to the conservatives of their own sect. Whitefield, like John Wesley who came over in 1735, was almost more interested in pure humanitarianism than in religion, and after the first reaction of indifference following the surges of emotion, the whole movement left Americans with a greater interest in education and humanitarian reforms, in what may be called the secular aspect of religion, and with greater independence toward the individual clergyman, against whom they had asserted their own views. This was notably true even throughout Puritan New England. In that section the old ideal of the theocratic State had passed, and everywhere the field of secular interests had widened as religion had become more personal.

This drift in the spiritual life of the colonies is exemplified both in the character of the literature produced in them as the century advanced and in the shift of the intellectual centre from New England to Pennsylvania and the South. In 1705 Robert Beverley in Virginia had published his *History and Present State of Virginia* and three years later an unknown author in Maryland produced a satiric poem of genuine interest and power called *The Sot-Weed Factor*. Although both of these are more living today than most of the printed matter turned out in Boston, that town unquestionably held the primacy in intellectual matters in the period.

For sheer bulk of writing probably no American author has ever equalled Cotton Mather, then the leading clergyman in the New England metropolis, who is credited with over four hundred titles. His *Diary* and his most celebrated work, the *Magnalia Christi Americana,* have much historical and antiquarian value but it is doubtful if any one outside of local New England enthusiasts ever reads him for pleasure today. This is not true of a much greater *Diary* of another Bostonian of the period, Judge Samuel Sewall, which is not only a mine of information for the life of the time but affords a very living picture of a man who is much nearer to us in character and outlook than the warped and self-tor-

PART II.

WHEREIN IT IS CONSIDERED, WHETHER THERE IS OR
CAN BE ANY SUCH SORT OF FREEDOM OF WILL AS
THAT WHEREIN ARMINIANS PLACE THE ESSENCE OF
THE LIBERTY OF ALL MORAL AGENTS; AND WHETHER
ANY SUCH THING EVER WAS OR CAN BE CONCEIVED OF.

SECTION I.

SHEWING THE MANIFEST INCONSISTENCE OF T HE ARMINIAN'NO-
TION OF LIBERTY OF WILL CONSISTING IN THE WILL'S SELF-
DETERMINING POWER.

HAVING taken notice of those things which may be necessary to be observed concerning the meaning of the
principal terms and phrases made use of in controversies
concerning human liberty, and particularly observed what
liberty is according to the common language and general
apprehension of mankind, and what it is as understood and
maintained by Arminians; I proceed to consider the Arminian notion of the *freedom of the will*, and the supposed necessity of it in order to moral agency, or in order to
any one's being capable of virtue or vice, and properly
the subject of command or counsel, praise or blame, prom-
ises or threatenings, rewards or punishments; or whether
that which has been described as the thing meant by liberty in common speech be not sufficient, and the only liberty which makes, or can make, any one a moral agent;
and so properly the subject of these things. In *this* Part

A PAGE FROM JONATHAN EDWARDS'S *FREEDOM OF THE WILL*
From a reprint in the New York Public Library.

turing Mather and was also, perhaps, more typical of
the upper-class Massachusetts of the day in which he
carried on his profession, wrestled with his daily problems, and carried on his amusing wooings.

Jonathan Edwards, pastor of the church at Northampton, and a far greater man than Mather, was to prove in the mid-century the greatest theologian New England or possibly America has produced, but it is noteworthy that unlike Mather he neither sought nor possessed any influence on political life. As a clergyman of such dominating power he could not have escaped, a century or half century earlier, being one of the chosen leaders of the theocratic State. No one has ever carried out with more impeccable logic the Calvinistic theology, and his great treatise on the *Freedom of the Will* is one of the books of world importance published in America. His theory, however, of the utter depravity of the human soul did not suit the growing optimism and comfort of the times. Dismissed by his congregation and made president of Princeton he well illustrates the passing of the old theology from popular to mere academic interest.

The man who both in his writings and his life best exemplifies the new preoccupations of the colonists was Benjamin Franklin, who abandoned Boston in his boyhood, was thereafter identified with Philadelphia. In the aphorisms that he scattered through his enormously popular *Poor Richard's Almanac,* such as "God helps them that help themselves," he struck a chord to which the people responded as they no longer would to the divines, and in his *Autobiography,* not published until after the Revolution, he not only gave for the first time the story of the rise from poverty to riches and power of a typical American career, but did so in words that went home to the simplest understanding. Not only was the most influential American writer no longer a New Englander, but more books of all sorts now came to be published outside that section than in it.

Just as the æsthetic life of the other colonies, notably in music and the drama, had become richer than that of New England, so also was the lead in scientific research passing to them. Franklin of course was to be our most noted scientific philosopher of his day, but even before the middle of the century Colden in New York, James Logan and John Bartram in Philadelphia, all had European reputations for their botanical studies. In Virginia, John Mitchell was writing the first American treatise on the principles of science, and throughout the South Mark Catesby had been carrying on his researches in natural history. In Charleston, Doctors John Lining and Lionel Chalmers were studying problems of weather and the only man in America, Doctor William Bull, who had a genuine degree as Doctor of Medicine (from Leyden), was established in that town.

The public library movement, which has been one of our notable contributions to civilization, got under way in this period, and of the seventeen subscription libraries started between 1745 and 1763 not only was the most important one that founded by Franklin, in Philadelphia, but one third of the whole number were in Pennsylvania. Massachusetts had led the way in journalism with the publication of our first newspaper, *The Boston*

News-Letter in 1704, but by 1763 the best papers were all published south of New York. The most influential was *The Pennsylvania Gazette,* but the literary interest of *The South Carolina Gazette,* which published the best original verse in America, and of the various *Virginia Gazettes,* whose prose articles, in the one published by William Hunter, were quoted all over the colonies, exceeded those of any of the other score or so of colonial journals. New York was notable not only for *The New York Gazette* published in that city by William Bradford, but also for the important struggle carried on there for the freedom of the press by Peter Zenger. It was a little early yet for magazines, but a dozen, all short-lived, had been started of which four had met their deaths in Boston and eight in the Middle Colonies.

By 1763 there was thus in the colonies a well-established cultural life conforming to the eighteenth-century English pattern. So shrewd a man as Franklin considered that the country was completely settled, and the richer classes had become conservative in their outlook on what they considered to be a properly organized and well stratified society. As we shall see, the "lower classes" gave them plenty of anxiety but the magnates hoped to keep these in hand. The task, however, was not to be easy, for especially in such centres as New York, Boston, and the other larger towns, the mechanic and artisan classes were advancing rapidly in both self-consciousness and demands for political power. Under astute leaders, notably Samuel Adams, they were a few years later to form one of the most important elements in bringing the legal disputes with England into the fires of social and class passion. Another group, of different sort, which quickly increased in prestige and influence from the mid-years of the century was that of the lawyers, often despised in some communities and even legislated against a generation or two earlier, but who, in their own way, were also, like the artisans and mechanics, to become of prime importance as the struggle with England grew more serious.

If society throughout the more settled portions of the colonies was English, it was, however, English with a difference,—a difference that may be noted in many ways. It was not merely that the "American language" was already beginning to diverge from English by the retention of many Elizabethan words which had become obsolete in the old country but also by the introduction of new ones. The American psychology itself was becoming subtly different. Owing to the influence of many conditions, the American had become more gentle in his instincts. In spite of cock-fights, eye-gouging, and more or less brutality, the more cruel sports of the days of colonization, such as bear baiting by dogs which delighted English audiences, had never been brought over here. On the whole, our legal punishments were much lighter than those in England, and, probably owing to better economic conditions, violent crimes, especially those involving property, were comparatively rare with us. Duelling never had as much vogue here as in Europe, and the American was already becoming something of a pacifist as regards war.

Humor is often a subtle key to the intricacies of national psychology, and it is notable that in Franklin's writings we already find American humor to have become the reverse of English, ours being founded in absurd exaggeration of statement whereas the English derives from under-statement. Class feeling had much shallower roots in our soil than in the old country; and the life and opportunities of the New World had tended to develop a greater sense of independence in the individual. There was, nevertheless, ample loyalty to King and empire, so long as claims to authority might not be pushed too far. All spoke of England as "home" and scarcely an American had any thought of fatal disputes with the mother country.

More than a century and a half had passed since Virginia had been first planted, and many of our institutions, such as churches and schools, were more than a century old, while many families traced their purely American ancestry for longer than that. A New Englander, New Yorker, Virginian or South Carolinian considered himself quite as good as any stay-at-home Englishman, was proud of his colony, and confident of the future. He thought only in terms of his own colony and England, and on the whole there was little love lost between the colonies themselves, the old jealousies still persisting. The last thing that almost any colonial politician would have thought of in 1763 would have been of the possibility of placing them all under one government.

There were, nevertheless, other forces at work in America. We have thus far spoken chiefly of the rich, but most colonists were not rich. America was far from being peopled only by those who lived in the big Georgian houses and dressed in brocades and satins and lace. We need not here speak of the several hundred thousand slaves, who were so submerged in the scale as not to require thinking about at that time except for the fear, constant in every plantation owner's heart, of a possible insurrection. But there were some hundreds of thousands of submerged Americans who were to be of immense importance in the next twenty-five years.

It is true that the general economic and social level of the entire white population was higher in the America of 1763 than anywhere else in the world, but the American of whatever nationality, whether he was recent immigrant or descendant of early settler, had become something different from the European he or his ancestor had been in the Old World. The first had come here fleeing from intolerable conditions at home, in England, Ireland, Germany or elsewhere, lured often by fantastic hopes. On the voyage over, the immigrant had usually suffered almost unspeakable hardships, sometimes two thirds of them in a vessel in the early eighteenth century dying on the way. Often cruelly fleeced by business sharks on arrival, the newcomer settled down or started for the frontier with anger and the grim determination to make his way. Descendants of the older English settlers could also hark back enviously to the earlier and simpler days when life was easier for the poor man.

Except for the scrabble for existence in the most primitive beginning of any settlement, there had always been distinction even in earliest America between the rich and poor, but that distinction had been steadily increasing. While the rich had progressed from the first rough shacks to the Georgian houses, there had been no such advance for the poor. In a new country where land was the prime source of capital even when not its final form, the rich and favored of the governor's set had been securing their huge holdings by means denied to the poor and socially lowly. There had been practically no improvement in agricultural implements, and the work of tilling an original grant of fifty acres or so had become no more remunerative and no less back-breaking in a century and a half. In New England the favorites of even the Puritan legislatures could manage to get grants of townships and farm lands by the ten thousand acres, and gradually become rich merchants in the seaboard towns or "Lords of the Valley" along the Connecticut. We have already noted the huge grants and landholdings of the favored in New York and the South.

With the increasing scale of business operations the small man found it more and more difficult to compete, whether in the size of boats for trading or the size of crops to be marketed. In the South the great increase in slavery in the century had brought its special problems. The planter who at the beginning could afford to buy slaves and breed them had a tremendous advantage in control of power to develop his land over those who could not; and as the numbers of black laborers rapidly increased after 1700 and racial pride came into play, the poor white farmer found himself not only poor but working on a level with the despised African.

In the early days, when land had been plenty, a man could find land for his sons not too far from his own home, but as population grew and land became scarce both from that reason and from the huge engrossing of tracts by the rich, the young generation found themselves more and more forced out to the frontier. In the beginning the frontier had been at every one's door and all had shared its hardships, but now with the settled life of the seaboard, the frontier was not only far off and open to dangers long past in the old settlements, but the frontiersman was beginning to be looked down upon as an ignorant, uncouth fellow. In New England when a man did go out to some new town which speculative grantees had opened for settlement, he often found that the favored owners had retained all political rights in their own hands, and that the settler had nothing to say about taxation, the building of roads or other matters in

TO BE SOLD on board the
Ship *Bance-Ifland*, on tuefday the 6th
of *May* next, at *Afhley-Ferry* ; a choice
cargo of about 250 fine healthy

NEGROES,
juft arrived from the
Windward & Rice Coaft.
—The utmoft care has
already been taken, and
fhall be continued, to keep them free from
the leaft danger of being infected with the
SMALL-POX, no boat having been on
board, and all other communication with
people from *Charles-Town* prevented.
Auftin, Laurens, & Appleby.

N. B. Full one Half of the above Negroes have had the
SMALL-POX in their own Country.

ADVERTISEMENT FOR SALE OF NEGROES ON BOARD THE
BANCE-ISLAND AT CHARLESTON
From a broadside in the Library of Congress.

the town which he was building himself for their benefit.
Although the suffrage was much more widely extended than in England, it was limited by qualifications which disfranchised many growing classes, such as servants, artisans, small shopkeepers, and others even in the old settlements. The frontier counties in practically every colony, however, had a special grievance in this

respect. For example in Pennsylvania, when Lancaster was erected as an outlying county in 1729 it was allowed only four votes in the Assembly instead of the eight which each of the older counties had. Although the population further out grew rapidly, no new counties were created for twenty years, and when they were they were given only two votes each. When, with the further spread of population, it was necessary to create two more counties, these were yet more discriminated against by receiving only one vote each.

By one such method or another, in all the colonies, the frontier was thus almost disfranchised, and the control of the politics of the colony was retained by the old settlements. In all the colonies a few families were usually in political control. John Adams said that six or a dozen at most ruled Connecticut in company with the clergy. In New York it was the Smiths, Duanes, Schuylers, de Peysters, and a few others. Family influence, the alliance of business with the legislatures, the growing power of the rising class of lawyers, favoritism of the governor,—all these and other forces seemed to be nullifying the power and opportunity of the common man. In 1763 there was special discontent as the dislocation of the economic life due to the recent war, with its high wages and prices and subsequent collapse, had created much debt and distress.

There were thus two marked cleavages beginning to show in the life of the period. There was a growing conflict between rich and poor, voters and non-voters in the older settlements; and also against those older settlements as a whole was ranged the entire frontier from Maine to Georgia, becoming angrily resentful over the denial of its rights. From time to time there were armed clashes here or there, and both aggrieved classes, in old and new counties everywhere, were beginning to find leaders from among themselves to voice their anger and their hopes. The dwellers in the Georgian houses, solidly conservative, were doing no little worrying, all along the coast, as to how these radical ideas among "the people" could be curbed.

CHAPTER V

THE INSOLUBLE PROBLEM OF THE
NEW EMPIRE

THE British Government in England had colonial problems of a different sort to solve. Even if the statesmen across the water had not handled them very badly, as all English historians of today agree was the case, it is only fair to admit that the difficulties were practically insoluble at that stage of the world's political experience.

When the Peace Treaty of 1763 was being negotiated it was bitterly debated in England whether France should be made to cede Canada or the immensely rich sugar island of Guadaloupe. This conflict of views was of great significance for it indicated that a change was in progress in the theory of empire. According to the old Mercantile theory there was no question that Guadaloupe, supplying a valuable raw material,—sugar,— should have been taken rather than what were considered the vast and barren wastes of Canada and the savage infested Mississippi Valley. The old theory, as we have explained, envisaged only the building up of a self-sufficing *commercial empire* made up of the mother country and a group of colonies which would all contribute their particular share to the economic life of an empire which should thus be as independent as possible of all others. Such colonies were immediate and valuable assets to England, and involved no expense except that of naval protection, which England had always borne.

The change from that theory to the new one of *territorial empire,* in which huge tracts in foreign lands should be secured with an eye to the distant future and their potential value as affording, when populated, markets for British goods or homes for British subjects, was a momentous one. When the die was cast, and England chose the almost illimitable continental empire of the American North and West instead of the immediately valuable and easily governed island of Guadaloupe, it became evident that she would have to face a wholly new set of problems in imperial government and organization.

These fell chiefly into two sets: first, how should the new domain be organized and governed, and, second, as it was evident that the expense would be heavy, who should meet it and how?

Gradually during the eighteenth century a sort of standard type of colony organization had evolved. In most of the thirty or so colonies, island or continental, there were a royal governor and council, some royal customs and other officials, and an assembly elected by the colonists. Except for the regulation of trade by Parliament, the colonies had been left to a great extent to themselves, had raised their own taxes, and defended themselves on land with the occasional co-operation of the British fleet. This had been the case until the French and Indian War which ended in 1763.

Obviously such a scheme could not be put into operation in the Canada-Mississippi Valley territory, filled only with a few thousand recalcitrant French and several hundred thousand hostile Indians over whom French influence was still supreme. There was no use thinking of royal governors and popular assemblies there. What, for the most part, was called for were military posts and garrisons, and a unified control over the vast native population. The Indian policies of the thirteen colonies, with the partial exception of Pennsylvania, had always been both bad and conflicting. The Indians had continually been enraged by land-hungry settlers and by the English-American fur-traders who for the most part were a low and cheating crew. In 1754, when the magnitude of the impending struggle had become apparent in Europe, England had asked the colonies to devise some sound Indian policy in which they would unite, but, as we have seen, they had been unable to do so at Albany.

In addition to this first problem there was also that of expense. The colonists had not only been unable to agree on a common treatment of the important native question but the old theory that England should be responsible for naval defence had broken down. Although Massachusetts had been public-spirited, each colony had shown itself uninterested outside its own borders, and not always self-reliant even within them. More than half the total number of troops engaged on land, and a considerable part of the expense of even the colonial troops, had had to be provided by England. The debt of that country had risen to the then huge figure of about $650,-000,000, and the annual cost of its army and navy from $350,000 pre-war to $1,750,000 post-war.

THE INDIAN PROBLEM

Many in England felt that the Americans had not done their fair share in ridding their continent of the French, with whom, in the West Indies, they had even been carrying on a lucrative trade during the struggle. They felt, moreover, that the haphazard formation of western land companies, the pushing out of settlement, and the despoiling of the Indian hunting grounds, would keep the newly acquired territory, which had to be governed by England, in constant turmoil.

In the new British Government which came into office in 1763, Lord Shelburne at once set to work to decide how the Indian problem could be handled, whether an army would be necessary, and whether the colonies should be asked to defray part of its expense. Shelburne, who was young but had marked ability and was perhaps the best disciple of William Pitt, headed a group in Parliament which was thoroughly friendly and sympathetic toward America, and the method by which he hoped to solve the difficult problem was not intended in any way to be hostile to the interests of the colonists.

The plan evolved called for an administration of all the Trans-Allegheny Indian lands which would assure the savages that they would not be interfered with until honest purchases had been made. A line was to be run between the English and Indians, which would be slowly advanced westward as settlements proceeded based on treaties. Ten thousand troops were to be sent to maintain order, the cost to be borne at first by England and later shared by the colonists in some way which might be agreed upon as least objectionable and burdensome. Unfortunately these plans were interfered with by events on the American frontier and in the English Cabinet.

In spite of the Treaty of Peace, the French had been stirring the savages to revolt against the English, suggesting that France was sending an army to help them and pointing out how their hunting fields were never interfered with by French traders, whereas the English settlers cleared them of game as they moved steadily westward. The incitements of the French fell upon ready ears, for the colonists, as always, had been encroaching rapidly on Indian lands, and in doing so and in their fur trading subjected the Indians to abuses, thinking only of immediate and personal profit and without consideration of either justice or sound policy. In May, 1763, the savages rose under an able native leader named Pontiac and in a few weeks captured all the posts in the North-west, from Pennsylvania to Lake Superior, except Detroit and Fort Pitt, the latter being saved by Colonel Bouquet with 500 Highlanders.

That same summer, owing to political changes in Eng-land, the Grenville-Bedford party came into power, and Shelburne was replaced by the Earl of Hillsborough, of whom even George III was to say some years later that he had never known a man "of less judgment." On that, at least, the King was right, and that such a politician should have been placed in charge of American affairs at such a critical juncture was the first of the colossal blunders which the British Government was successively to make in the next decade.

Frightened into quick action, without ability and with inadequate knowledge of America, Hillsborough within six days prepared the Proclamation of 1763, as it is called, which established a dividing line between the colonists and the Indian territory. (See map on page 159.) The line so hastily adopted, running, roughly, along the Appalachian watershed, took no acount of settlements already long made. Nor did it of territory granted to cer-tain colonies in their charters, and within which grants had been made to land companies. Moreover, future sale by the Indians, except to the Crown, was prohibited by the Proclamation, settlers who had already entered the now forbidden territory being required to withdraw. Outside of the Indian preserve, the Proclamation also set up on the continent three new royal provinces,—Quebec and East and West Florida. The Americans were naturally deeply resentful toward what they considered an unjustified attempt to keep them from developing the western country, which they had, in part at least, helped to win for the empire.

The British Government had been right in its basic assumption that the vast hinterland could not be left to be exploited, governed and defended by thirteen wrangling colonies which had never been able to agree on anything. The ministers had been extraordinarily careless and clumsy, however, in taking the initial step to govern it themselves. That step taken, the second problem of cost at once came up. Meanwhile, George Grenville, who was hostile to America, had little knowledge concerning it, and possessed the mind of a bureaucrat, had become Prime Minister. Dangerously for a statesman, he began with statistics, and found that owing to colonial smuggling connived at by royal officials, it cost England $35,000 a year to maintain American custom houses that produced only $10,000 revenue.

THE STORM BREAKS

As we have seen, molasses was the base on which New England commerce, at least, rested, and had the old

Molasses Act of 1733 with its prohibitive duty been observed by the colonists they would have had no money to buy goods in England. All of the colonies, without exception, were always hard put to it to find enough exchange to pay their English debts. Grenville, with the intention of reducing the duties on molasses to a point at which they might be paid and collected, secured the passage, in 1764, of the so-called "Sugar Act," lowering the duties from 6d. to 3d., and also imposing duties upon other imports into America, such as wine from the Azores and Madeira, coffee and the products of the East and the foreign West Indies. Moreover he showed that he intended to see that the new laws should be obeyed. Warships were sent to the American coast, naval officers given power to collect duties, and prosecutions for smuggling were taken from the colonial courts and put under the jurisdiction of Admiralty courts.

An Act was also passed declaring any future issue of colonial paper money not to be legal tender, thus extending to all America the prohibition which had been enacted against New England only in 1751. This greatly frightened the colonists, who, from the constant scarcity of coin, had had frequent recourse to issuing paper. What perhaps frightened them most of all was the provision that customs duties were to be paid into "His Majesty's Exchequer," which they mistakenly assumed meant that the gold or silver paid for all duties and fines would be shipped to England and leave them with nothing with which to pay their foreign trade balances. It was really intended, although not worded clearly by the government, that this money should remain in America and there be used to pay one third of the cost of maintaining the ten thousand troops, whom Parliament undertook to station there, England expecting to pay the other two thirds herself.

The fear of a gold drain affected all the colonies but the class most alarmed by the new customs duties in the "Sugar Act," and even more by the prospect of duties really being collected, were the merchants of New England. Uneasiness had already been caused in that Puritan section by a rumor that an Anglican bishop was to be appointed with all North America as his see, which made the still influential body of congregational clergy hostile to the thought of any encroachments by England on complete local liberty of action.

In addition, there was in Boston one of the most remarkable Americans of the period. Samuel Adams was the son of a well-to-do brewer and had been educated at Harvard. He had no capacity for business and managed to lose the comfortable estate which he inherited. In 1764 he was in debt and his family were partly dependent upon charity. In later life, after the Revolution, he was to show no more capacity for constructive statesmanship than he had for business. He was narrow and provincial, but in the single groove in which his mind ran it operated so powerfully and cut so deep that he may be counted as one of the men who have profoundly influenced the course of history in their day.

That one groove, into which flowed the whole of his intellectual and emotional nature, was bitter hostility to England, and insistence upon the complete freedom of the citizens of Massachusetts. For him, that colony was all that existed in the political world, and almost alone among Americans of this period he seems early to have conceived the thought of achieving independence of the empire. He was extremely provincial and, not unlike some other Bostonians, felt that his town was the hub of the universe, and that salt had no savor outside of New England.

In December, 1765, his fellow radical at the other end of the colonies, Christopher Gadsden, had written from South Carolina that "there ought to be no New England men, no New Yorker, etc., known on the Continent, but all of us Americans." Such broader vision was beyond Adams, who even in later years only hesitatingly yielded to the necessities of nationalism. He had, however, consummate ability as a revolutionary agitator in manipulating the opinions and emotions of the ordinary people, and for the next ten years he was to devote himself to inflaming the public mind on every possible occasion.

When Grenville's plans for the new duties became known, a town meeting in Boston appointed a committee to draw up resolutions for their representatives in the General Court, which Adams drafted. Committees of merchants in the leading seaports of several colonies had sent over protests to England, pointing out the disastrous effect on trade of the new laws, but Adams went far beyond this. "If our trade may be taxed, why not our lands? Why not the produce of our lands, and in short everything we possess?" If taxes are laid upon the colonists without "legal representation where they are laid," he added, "are we not reduced from the character of subjects to the miserable state of tributary slaves?"

This was a wholly new doctrine, advocated also by James Otis in his pamphlet entitled the *Rights of the British Colonies Asserted and Proved,* in which he suggested that the colonies be given representatives in Parliament. Hitherto the colonists had always accepted the doctrine that Parliament could pass Acts regulating imperial trade and laying duties. They had merely nullified the Acts by smuggling or pointed out their inexpediency without ever claiming that they were unconstitutional or tyrannical. The British Government could scarcely have been expected to acquiesce supinely in the new constitutional theories put forward by Adams and Otis but the vigor of the radical group combined with the remonstrances of the conservative merchants should have warned them to walk warily. Instead they made a fatal blunder.

Even although England expected to pay a large share of the future imperial expenses in America, it was considered that the Americans' own share would not be covered by the new duties, and Grenville had been looking about for additional taxation. One of the simplest forms is that of a stamp tax on legal or business papers, and this, already in use in England, had been discussed for some years as possibly applicable to the colonies. Grenville, in fact, had asked the opinions of the Colonial Assemblies about it and requested alternative suggestions as to forms that might be preferable to them, without getting any helpful advice.

It is clear now looking back that such a tax, being internal instead of external, might raise a storm of protest, but, little of a statesman as Grenville was, he cannot perhaps be blamed too heavily for not foreseeing the full effect of what he was doing. Even Benjamin Franklin, who was then in England, although he opposed the passage of the Act, did not think the colonists would object, and advised two of his friends at home to take office as stamp distributors, and Richard Henry Lee, the future patriot, also applied for the position in Virginia. In view of such opinions Parliament passed the Act without the slightest thought that there would be any serious objection to it, in spite of some speeches against it, notably by Colonel Isaac Barré. The Act, which received royal assent March 22, 1765, levied taxes of varying amounts on newspapers and almost all legal documents, the stamps having to be paid for in coin.

The news was received quietly for the most part in

America as Franklin had anticipated. Then suddenly the storm broke. Two years before, out in the western mountain region of Virginia, a young man named Patrick Henry had won a case for the people against the payment to the local Anglican clergyman of his salary according to the terms of what was called the "Two Penny Act." Henry's case was weak and the verdict unjust but his success won him rousing popularity in the frontier section, and before news of the Stamp Act came he had been sent to the legislature as a member of the House of Burgesses, where he was regarded with fear and dislike by conservative Virginians.

On May 29, 1765, when the House was considering what action to take on the Stamp Act, Henry leaped to his feet and proposed a series of resolutions in a speech which, although often quoted, has not come down to us in authentic form. It called forth a rebuke from the Speaker, who avowed that Henry had uttered treason. Passage of the resolutions was bitterly opposed by such men as Peyton Randolph, Edmund Pendleton, Richard Bland, and George Wythe, who were all to become prominent on the American side, and it is impossible to tell just how many of the proffered resolutions were actually passed by the House. However, six were published in the newspapers, and, as "the Virginia Resolves," they ran like a flaming torch up and down the entire coast. It was claimed in them that the local legislature was the only body which had any legal right to tax the Virginians.

135

Economic conditions were bad in America and had been made worse by the Acts of the preceding year. At first the merchants had suffered most from them but the Stamp Act brought the newspaper editors and lawyers into sharp opposition to Britain, and the whole population feared stagnation of business both from the new taxes (which in reality were light), and from the mode of their collection. Massachusetts called for a meeting of representatives from all the colonies to be held in New York in October. Before that, some action had to be taken. America was almost a unit against the imposition of the new Stamp tax. The only question was how to avoid it. In many colonies the merchants agreed not to import English goods until the law was repealed, and that summer American orders in England declined £600,000.

Organizations called "Sons of Liberty" were formed almost everywhere, mostly from the extreme radical groups. Stamp distributors were threatened, and personal violence used against them. Mobs broke windows, burned houses, and intimidated people from using the stamps had any one been so inclined. In Boston the costly home of the Chief Justice, Thomas Hutchinson, was sacked. All his furniture and the priceless documents which he had collected for writing his *History of Massachusetts,* were thrown into the street and burned. America was in turmoil from one end to the other, the mobs often getting out of hand. In some colonies business was suspended and in others carried on without use of the legal stamps.

One strange feature was the slight interest taken in the meeting of the Stamp Act Congress in October. Only nine colonies were represented, and its proceedings passed almost without notice in the newspapers of the day. In spite of the difficulty of reconciling the views of the twenty-seven delegates, resolutions were passed claiming, as Virginia already had done, that the colonies could not be taxed save by their own assemblies where alone they were represented. It was found difficult to claim rights common to all if based on varying charters, and the broader ground of "natural rights" was therefore entered upon from this time.

THE DIFFERENCE IN POLITICAL IDEAS

The people at large, however, were not interested in fine-spun political or constitutional theories. With them it was rather a surge of emotion at interference with their accustomed freedom and fear of what might come, instilled into them by such men as Christopher Gadsden in South Carolina, Henry in Virginia, and Adams in Massachusetts, with others of like sort elsewhere. "No taxation without representation," "the rights of man," and "tributary slaves" were words which burned deep into the minds of the crowds, and the search for a legal basis for constitutional relations was left to the intellectuals.

When in March, 1765, chiefly as a result of pressure brought to bear on Parliament by the English merchants, the Stamp Act was repealed, the news was received almost as emotionally as had been that of its passage. America went wild with rejoicing, and no attention was paid to the Declaratory Act passed simultaneously asserting the right of Parliament to bind the colonies in all cases whatsoever and denying their claim to taxation solely by their own legislatures. Even Pitt, who with other statesmen had demanded the repeal in Parliament and had declared that he rejoiced that America had resisted, stated that he believed in the full parliamentary control over the colonies except to take "money out of their pockets without their consent."

The fact is that unconsciously the two parts of the English race had drifted far asunder in fundamental political ideas. The change had come about so gradually that neither had realized it. The idea of representation is a case in point. In England, Parliament was considered to be representative not of individuals but of classes. If some members of the landed interest and of the commercial and professional classes could elect representatives, then those classes and interests were considered to be represented. Representation, until long afterward, was not thought to have anything to do with territory or numbers. There were great centres of population in England which had no direct representatives at all. Yet these considered themselves represented because all classes in them were represented by men elected from members of their particular class elsewhere.

The Englishman thus found it hard to understand why the American landowner or merchant claimed that he was unrepresented merely because he did not himself vote for a member of Parliament. On the other hand, from historical reasons a new system had grown up with us and seemed almost the order of nature. In spite of our limited franchise and many abuses, the general theory had early developed that as new towns or counties were formed they should be given representation, and thus the idea of representation came with us to be connected with numbers and locality. So much so that by this time the practice was almost universal of electing a representative from the district in which he lived. "No taxation without representation" thus meant something quite different on the two sides of the ocean, as did Pitt's taking of money without "consent."

Again, in England, Parliament, as the great body representative of the whole nation, had come to be supreme. There was nothing it could not do in legislation. With us there had developed an idea of a fundamental law, derived from our constant reference to the charters in squabbles with governors or the home government. From this we slipped easily into the eighteenth-century doctrine of "natural rights," rights inherent in every individual simply as a human being. This was as little likely to be taken seriously by the British statesmen when demanded only by Americans as it would have been by us in 1765 if demanded by our 400,000 black slaves.

Finally, we had come to look upon our local legislatures as practically co-ordinate with Parliament, glimpsing a sort of commonwealth of nations such as the British Empire is now becoming. Such a theory offers many difficulties in practice even today, and in 1765 it was quite outside the realm of political realities.

The ideas of English and Americans were largely the product of their environment in each case. It seemed natural to the Englishman at home to accept a system into which he had been born, just as it seemed natural to the American to adapt that system to the new conditions of colonial life. A small farmer in Yorkshire who never had voted for a member of Parliament did not trouble his head about it, but a small farmer in a Massachusetts town or Pennsylvania county who had been accustomed to personal representation in the legislature and moved out on the frontier to settle a new town or county, did not see why he should be disfranchised for doing so.

In a new country not only does the new environment operate on old ideas and ways of doing things, but the absence of any accumulated stock of traditions, institutions, and vested interests allows of the rapid growth of new ideas. In my boyhood, for example, I remember that the then small town of Cheyenne, Wyoming, had electric lights when New York had only gas in its streets, and was running electric trams when New York had horse cars. It was not due to any superior virtue in Wyoming but to the fact that it was perfectly free to install the new without considering the old, whereas in New York the new came into conflict with all sorts of established interests connected with the old.

How fast new America had moved as compared with old England is shown by the fact that it was the conservatives in America who were closest in thought to the most advanced liberals in England. Had each of these classes been in control in the respective countries, an adjustment of the quarrel would have been likely. In the mother country, however, the most die-hard of the politicians held the power at critical stages, and in America the extreme colonial radicals kept stirring trouble.

It has been said that America was like a boy who had grown up and could no longer be kept in subjection. There is truth in the simile and at the same time danger for clear thinking. A father who does not let his boy go his own way after a certain age and become independent is naturally considered stupid or tyrannical, but there is no similar code of conduct for nations or empires when a part wishes to secede from the whole. The British statesmen of this period assuredly could not have justified themselves if, without a struggle, they had simply allowed the Americans to disclaim every shred of authority over them by Parliament, any more than a century later we ourselves allowed the Southern States to secede peaceably because they desired to do so. Nor would we allow any part of our nation or empire to do so today solely of its own volition. The British statesmen were stupid, but they were also confronted with a problem which was practically insoluble.

Briefly, our political philosophy had become different from the British. Our interests seemed to us the most important in the empire, as England's did to her. They conflicted at several points. We quickly realized, once the quarrelling started, that even if we could send some representatives to Parliament we would merely confer supreme power on that body with only a trifling minority of members from America. "No taxation without representation" could only mean that we must forever deny to Parliament any power of the purse over us. The difference which had been tacitly accepted in the past between internal and external taxation came to seem no difference at all when analyzed. English logic had to insist on the power of Parliament to legislate for the empire or there was no empire. American logic led to an almost total denial of such power.

With the good feeling, and the innate loyalty to the empire existing in the minds of most Americans, affairs might have slipped along with little friction had English statesmen let sleeping dogs lie or had there been no extremists in the colonies like Adams and Henry and Gadsden. This was true in spite of bickerings with the governor of Massachusetts over demands for damages on account of the Stamp Act riots or with General Gage in New York over the operation of the Act (1765) quartering troops.

In 1766, in a new Cabinet in England, Charles Townshend became head of the exchequer. Undeterred by the views of Pitt, who as Earl of Chatham was nominal head of the Cabinet, but ill, Townshend at once set himself to get money out of America. Few statesmen can ever have handled delicate situations worse. In 1767 he secured the passage through Parliament of a number of Acts, all calculated to arouse the resentment of the colonies. In one of these a duty was laid upon tea, red and white lead, glass and painters' colors, designed to produce a revenue of about £40,000 a year.

In part this was to be applied to the support of the army in America and in part to paying the salaries of the colonial governors and judges, thus removing them entirely from control by the assemblies. It also provided for a new administration of the customs service and made it clear that every Navigation Act of the old commercial system from 1660 on, most of which had been dead letters, were to be enforced. Writs of Assistance were also legalized, although it had been James Otis's fiery denunciation of these which had first made him a popular leader in 1761. Another bill suspended the New York Assembly on account of its refusal to furnish supplies for the troops, and another created a board of commissioners to supervise the collection of duties in America. Having sown this field of dragon's teeth, Townshend let himself out by dying, and was succeeded by Lord North as Secretary of the Exchequer, Hillsborough occupying the new office of Secretary of State for the Colonies.

Protests were sent to England and to a great extent the non-importation agreements were put into force again. In Philadelphia John Dickinson, a Pennsylvania lawyer who had received his legal training in the English Inns of Court, began publishing his famous *Letters of a Farmer* which, reprinted everywhere, were perhaps more widely read than any of the rest of the rapidly increasing literature of controversy. He declared that laying duties to raise a revenue instead of to regulate trade was an innovation, and that although there was a certain power in Parliament (which like all Americans he found more and more difficult of definition), "we are only as much dependent on Great Britain as one perfectly free people can be on another." He suggested that three successive lines of action might be taken against England,— first, remonstrance and petition, second, refusal to buy British goods, third, as a last resort only, forcible resistance to the Acts of Parliament. For the first time he suggested, not independence, but the thought that the colonies were beginning to form a nation. They are separated, he wrote, "from the rest of the world, and firmly bound together by the same rights, interests, and dangers." It was indeed danger, forced upon them by the mistakes of English statesmen, which was beginning to make them feel, in Dickinson's words, that "they form one political body of which each colony is a member." The new board of customs commissioners made their

(6)

caufe, for *three shillings* and *four-pence*, was tried, all the people of *England*, with anxious expectation, interested themfelves in the important decifion ; and when the flighteft point, touching the freedom of *one* colony, is agitated, I earneftly wifh, that *all* the *reft* may, with equal ardour, fupport their fifter. Very much may be faid on this fubject ; but, I hope, more at prefent is unneceffary.

With concern I have obferved, that *two* affemblies of this province have fat and adjourned, without taking any notice of this act. It may perhaps be afked, what would have been proper for them to do ? I am by no means fond of inflammatory meafures ; I deteft them. I fhould. be forry that any thing fhould be done, which might juftly difpleafe our fovereign, or our mother country : but a firm, modeft exertion of a free fpirit, fhould never be wanting on public occafions. It appears to me, that it would have been fufficient for the affembly, to have ordered our agents to reprefent to the king's minifters, their fenfe of the fufpending act, and to pray for its repeal. Thus we fhould have borne our teftimony againft it ; and might therefore receive reafonably expect that, on a like occafion, we might receive the fame affiftance from the other colonies.

* *Nov.* 5. A F A R M E R.

Concordia res parvæ crefcunt.
Small things grow great by concord

The bey of King W i l l i a m *the Third's landing.*

(7)

<hr>

L E T T E R II.

Beloved Countrymen,

T H I R E is another late act of parliament, which appears to me to be unconftitutional, and as deftructive to the liberty of thefe colonies, as that mentioned in my laft letter ; that is, the act for granting the duties on paper, glafs, &c.

The parliament unqueftionably poffeffes a legal authority to *regulate* the trade of *Great-Britain*, and all her colonies. Such an authority is effential to the relation between a mother country and her colonies ; and neceffary for the common good of all. He, who confiders-thefe provinces as ftates diftinct from the *British* empire, has very flender notions of *juftice*, or of their *interefts*. We are but parts of a *whole* ; and therefore there muft exift a power fomewhere, to prefide, and preferve the connection in due order. This power is lodged in the parliament ; and we are as much dependant on *Great-Britain*, as a perfectly free people can be on another.

I have looked over every *ftatute* relating to thefe colonies, from their firft fettlement to this time ;
B 4 and

THE BEGINNING AND ENDING OF TWO LETTERS FROM *DICKINSON'S
LETTERS OF A FARMER,* PUBLISHED IN LONDON IN 1768
From the Ford Collection in the New York Public Library.

headquarters in Boston, and from the imperial standpoint the improvement in the service was notable, the American duties collected rising from £2000 a year to £30,000. Owing mainly to the unenforcement of the early Navigation Acts and of the impossible Molasses Act, smuggling had ceased to be looked upon in America as reprehensible. Every one, even leading merchants like John Hancock, smuggled regularly. Hancock was the richest man in New England, and because of his wealth was later to be chosen President of the Continental Congress. Owing to the lightness of his character, his excessive vanity, and love of popularity, unballasted by either moral depth or intellectual ability, his motives for joining the patriot party are difficult to appraise correctly or even, perhaps, fairly, but there was no question of patriotism in much of his smuggling. That was for profit.

The new customs commissioners had several times asked for a ship of war to patrol the coast and had been growing more and more angry over the smuggling they could not prevent when a particularly outrageous case occurred. There was a duty of £7 per tun on Madeira wine, and merchants did their best to make an additional profit by avoiding this. In the spring of 1768 the man-of-war *Romney* had finally been stationed in Boston Harbor, and, not long after, Hancock's sloop *Liberty* arrived from Madeira. The customs inspector who went on board was confined in the cabin and the cargo hurriedly unloaded at night. The commissioners on hearing of this ordered the sloop seized and had her towed out and anchored off the *Romney*. At once the mob, now ready to rise on every occasion, attacked the houses of the commissioners, who took refuge in Castle William. There had been similar outbreaks elsewhere, and in

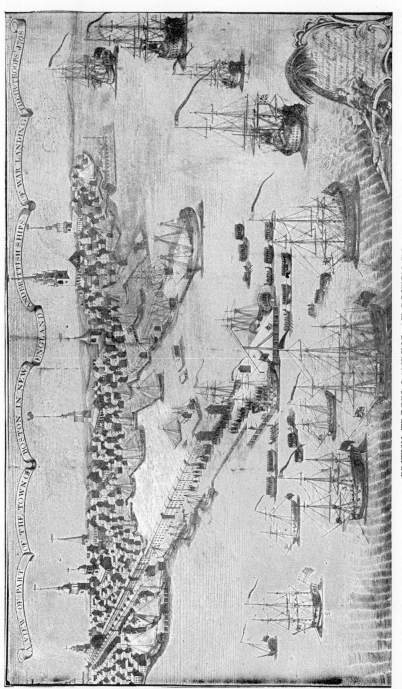

BRITISH TROOPS LANDING AT BOSTON IN 1768

The description reads that after landing at Long Wharf "they marched with insolent parade, drums beating, fifes playing and colors flying, up King Street, each soldier having received 16 rounds of powder and ball."

From the engraving by Paul Revere in the Stokes Collection, New York Public Library.

THE ABLE DOCTOR OR AMERICA SWALLOWING THE BITTER DRAUGHT

From an engraving by Paul Revere after a caricature in "London Magazine," April, 1774. In the Spencer Collection, New York Public Library.

October the British Government stationed two regiments in Boston to maintain order. Events were marching.

Early in the year the Massachusetts House of Representatives had sent a circular letter to the other colonies suggesting that they all unite both in discussing the situation and in petitioning the British Government with regard to the Townshend Acts. The royal governor in Massachusetts, Francis Bernard, was peculiarly lacking in tact, knowledge, and judgment, and unhappily it was this incapable official, always at loggerheads with his somewhat troublesome Bostonians, who formed the official opinions of his equally incapable superior, Hillsborough. The earl instructed Bernard to demand that the House of Representatives rescind the Resolutions in connection with the circular letter, and to dissolve that legislative body if it declined. He also sent instructions to the governors of all the other colonies to dissolve their assemblies if they should act favorably on the request of Massachusetts. The House of Commons backed Hillsborough and were for even more extreme measures.

Massachusetts voted in the House, 92 to 17, not to rescind, and the legislature was promptly dissolved. An extra-legal convention of delegates from all the towns then met in Boston, and adopted resolutions similar to those which under the leadership of Samuel Adams had been drawn up on many occasions. Parliament, which with utter lack of statesmanship had brought on this new crisis, now lost its head yet more and sent an address to the King asking that the inciters of "rebellion" be brought to England for trial for treason under an old and inapplicable statute.

All the colonies were deeply stirred and in the Virginia House of Burgesses, George Washington introduced a set of Resolutions, known to history as the "Virginia Resolves of 1769," which had been drawn up by George Mason. They marked a distinct advance in clarity of thinking over the earlier ones and proclaimed that the Colonial Assembly, with the approval of King or royal governor, was the only body which could tax the colonists. They also stated that the colonists had the right to petition the King for redress of grievances, and that to transport any person overseas to stand trial for "any crime whatsoever" was "highly derogatory" of his rights as a British citizen.

It was not only in the legislatures that the growing confusion was evident. The attempt to renew the non-importation policy led to much bitter feeling and actual violence among the colonists themselves. The chief financial loss of such a policy fell on the merchants who instead of entering upon the policy willingly were to a large extent coerced. In South Carolina, for instance, they were forced to suspend imports only by threats of personal violence from the Sons of Liberty led by the radical Gadsden. In Boston, Adams had his mob ready, and intimidation, destruction of property, and tarring and feathering were freely used to bring the merchants into line with the radicals' political plans, as in New York and elsewhere.

Meanwhile, following the death of Townshend, there had been another change in Cabinet posts in England, and Lord North, who now became Prime Minister, decided that the government was stirring up resistance in America for little actual gain. He therefore secured the passage of a bill in Parliament voiding all the new duties of the Townshend Acts, except that on tea which was kept as a symbol of the right of Parliament to levy duties. The administrative machinery erected for the American customs was also retained as were the older established duties.

FERMENT IN NEW ENGLAND

It is a mistake to think of the colonists as all burning with "patriotism" and hatred of England. We must recall that although events were fast bringing about unprecedented unity of sentiment and action among the several colonies, they were still very distinct from one another. A Virginia planter, for instance, would have felt much more at home with an English squire than with a Boston merchant. Speaking broadly, however, there were three groups which severally developed the same attitude toward England in all the colonies. Two of these were comparatively small, the ultra-Loyalists at the top, who defended all that England did, and the extreme Radicals at the bottom. In between was the vast mass of Americans who wanted above all else to be allowed to live their lives and earn their bread in peace, unmolested by new and annoying British laws or the violence of American radical mobs. They were willing to stand up for their rights, and were made both angry and anxious at the trouble that the injustice and stupidity of the politicians in Parliament were making, but hoped for a change. They also, however, feared the growing violence and breakdown of order in America.

As we have seen, there were many grievances felt here by different classes and sections,—artisans in the towns, men of the frontier, and others. America was full of combustible material, and with the growing unrest of the times it was easy to kindle this with a spark. Within a few years popular leaders had sprung up whose power and local importance came from stirring up all the discontented elements. They played with mobs, and not always with the singleness of purpose and hatred of a Sam Adams against English policy. All sorts of local aims were also being served. As in all such cases, the influence of these popular leaders depended upon the stirring up of emotion and the creating of a seeming constant need of their leadership.

In Massachusetts, Adams had proved a master at keeping the public mind in ferment. Opinions will always differ widely about him but I think he was consistently honest in his purpose. His narrow mind, however, was always as firmly convinced that he was indubitably right as was ever that of old John Endicott himself. On the other hand, we are all human, and he could hardly escape, unconsciously, the effect of finding himself, after a life of somewhat humiliating failure, in a position of tremendous influence over the populace, with his real talents for drawing up remonstrances and inciting to revolt in constant demand. His whole importance, unlike that of John Adams, Washington, and other greater men, was dependent upon keeping alive the passions of the mob. This he did constantly, in public meetings, in the legislature, in newspapers, and more mysterious ways, "cooking up articles, paragraphs, occurrences" as John Adams said of him.

Steadily throughout the two years the British soldiers had been in Boston, Adams had seen to it that their presence should create as much friction and be as thoroughly resented as possible, although the soldiers had maintained perfect discipline. Finally, on the very day that Lord North moved the bill doing away with the Townshend duties, March 5, 1770, the long-expected clash occurred between citizens and soldiers in Boston.

A sentry at the Custom House was pelted with snowballs by some young roughs and called out the guard. A crowd gathered, and one soldier was knocked down and another beaten with a club. Mistaking a shout for an order to fire, the soldiers did so, killing four of the crowd. The officer in command at once surrendered to the civil authorities, and at the trial, in which the soldiers were defended by John Adams and Josiah Quincy, Jr., all were exonerated except two of the privates, who were convicted of manslaughter and burned in the hand as punishment. Immediately after the affray the two regiments had been removed to Castle William by Lieutenant-Governor Hutchinson. This "Boston Massacre," brought on by the constant incitement of Adams and others, was long used by them to stir up feeling against the British, and passionate orations were delivered for some years on each anniversary.

The news of the repeal of the Townshend duties was received by the merchant class everywhere with feeling of deep relief, and they and other conservative elements decided to stop further bickering with England. The quality of British political life was at perhaps the lowest point it ever reached, but there were constant changes and as long as a working compromise seemed to have been brought about and England had made a partial retreat it was thought that the more or less theoretical disputes could be shelved.

Moreover, the merchants had not liked at all the coercion practised on them by the radicals to force them not to import, and the conservatives had all become alarmed by the disorders brought on by the Sons of Liberty and the dangerous turmoil of mob-rule. If they did not wish their profits interfered with or their liberties infringed by England, neither did they want to find themselves controlled in America by the lower classes, as they con-

New-York May 30th 1770.

The FEMALE PATRIOT, No. I.

ADDRESSED TO THE

TEA-DRINKING LADIES of NEW-YORK.

WHEN ADAM first fell into SATAN's Snare,
    And forfeited his Blifs to pleafe the Fair;
GOD from his Garden drove the finful Man,
And thus the Source of human Woes began.
'Twas weak in ADAM, for to pleafe his Wife,
To lofe his accefs to the Tree of Life:
His d ar bought Knowledge all his Sons deplore,
DEATH thir Inheritance, and SIN their Store.
But why blame ADAM, fince his Brainlefs Race
'Will 'ofe their ALL to obtain a beautious FACE;
And will their Honour, Pride, and Wealth lay down,
Rather then fee a lovely Woman frown.
The Ladies are not quite, fo complifant,
If they want TEA, they'll ftorm and rave and rant,
And call their Lordly Hufbands Afs and CLOWN,
The jeft of Fools and Sport of all the Town.
A pleafent Story lately I heard told
Of MADAM HORNBLOOM, a noted Scold,
Laft Day her Hufband faid, " My deareft Life,
My Kind, my Fair, my Angel of a Wife ;
Juft now, from LONDON, there's a Ship come in
Brings noble News will raife us Merchants Fame,
The Fruits of our non-importation Scheme.
The Parliament, dear Saint, may they be bleft
Have great part of our Grievances redreft:"
" Have they indeed," replies the frowning Dame,
" Say, is there not fome Tea and China come."
" Why, no! We can't import that Indian Weed,
That Duty's ftill a Rod above our Head."
" Curfe on your Heads, you nafty fumbling Crew,
Then round his Shoulders the hard Broom-Stick flew,
Go, dirty CLOD-POLE! get me fome Shufhong,
This Evening I've invited MADAM STRONG.
--- Silence --- you BLOCKHEAD --- hear, the Lady
    knocks!

A BROADSIDE CONDEMNING TEA-DRINKING LADIES
From the original in the New York Public Library.

sidered them, of town or frontier, in whose ability to govern they had no confidence whatever. The complete breaking off by John Hancock of relations with Sam Adams was symptomatic of what was going on elsewhere. The merchants soon began importing freely again, and business began to boom at last after the hard years.

To be sure, the British Government was still intent on collecting what duties remained, and smuggling continued. It was merely for profit's sake, however, and was on a huge scale. Occasionally there were physical clashes with customs officers, and in June, 1772, the revenue schooner *Gaspée* was seized and burned in Rhode Island waters. It was the third vessel so destroyed in that nest of smugglers and the royal commission could get no witnesses who would testify against their friends and neighbors.

In the autumn a rumor came over that England was contemplating paying judges' salaries out of the customs revenue, and Sam Adams, who had been doing his best throughout the past two years of prosperity and calm to keep the political pot of protest boiling, seized on this as a new and intolerable grievance. In a town meeting he secured, not without much opposition, the appointment of twenty-one men as a "committee of correspondence," which was to state the rights of the colonists "as Men, as Christians, and as Subjects," and to correspond on the subject with committees from other towns.

Gradually radicals in other colonies formed similar committees, and thus a revolutionary organization was built up throughout America, and did its best to stir the people, as Sam Adams said, from "stupor and inaction."

It was not so much stupor as it was the Anglo-Saxon's mental habit of not bothering about fine-spun theories, and of letting matters drift and adjust themselves so long as there is no crisis to get excited about. The country generally was prosperous. The merchants, who could afford to lose one complete cargo of tea in three and yet make large profits, were contented. In spite of all the agitators from Adams in Massachusetts to Gadsden in Carolina, the substantial classes everywhere refused to consider their liberties in danger. The country had settled down to calm after the storm, and was glad to do so. Then suddenly the English Government made what was to prove an irretrievable blunder.

Until 1773 the East India Company, and not the British Government, was the ruler of India. It had been in frequent trouble with native princes, and several times in financial difficulties. The interests were vast and in 1773 an Act was passed which gave Parliament a voice in administration. The company was in trouble and had 17,000,000 pounds of tea stored in London. North decided, solely with thought of the extrication of the company and with none at all of American colonial policy, to allow the company to sell this tea in the colonies, paying the regular American three-penny duty but none of the charges and duties imposed in England. The idea was that this would clear off the company's surplus and at the same time allow the colonists to buy their tea cheaper than ever, even when smuggled.

The effect, however, was to give the company, temporarily at least, exclusive rights in America, where the radicals at once raised the cry of "monopoly." For three years they had been trying to find an issue without success, and they probably would have failed again on tea had all American merchants who had been tea importers been made the agents for the sale of the government-company tea. Instead of this, certain agents only were appointed, most of whom were unpopular from having taken sides against the great bulk of American merchants in previous troubles. What Sam Adams had been unable to accomplish was now achieved by Lord North, who threw the powerful American merchant class over to the side of the radicals again, just when they themselves were least inclined for such an unnatural union.

When the first tea ships arrived under the new plan, they were nowhere allowed to discharge their cargo except at Charleston. From some ports they were forced to return to England, but Boston staged its famous "tea party." Governor Hutchinson, who had become extremely unpopular, refused to sign clearance papers permitting the ships to leave until their cargoes had been discharged. A number of public meetings had been held, and feeling ran high. It is hard to say which was the more stubborn, the royal governor or the radicals. The latter might have allowed the tea to be landed as in Charleston and stored in warehouses without its being permitted to be sold; or Hutchinson might, like other governors, have allowed the ships to sail. As it was he played straight into the hands of Sam Adams.

According to a preconcerted plan, when the governor's final decision was made known to a great public gathering in the old South Meeting House, a band of men disguised as Indians boarded the vessels and threw all the tea into the harbor. Opinion in America was divided on the action. Even some New England town meetings condemned it, speaking of "liberty degenerating into anarchy," and although John Adams applauded it such patriots as John Dickinson and Benjamin Franklin heartily disapproved. One of America's best friends in England, William Pitt, then Earl of Chatham, denounced it as "criminal."

The work of the mobs in Boston, New York, and elsewhere was once more beginning to make the owners of property fearful and to cause them to withdraw their new support temporarily given to the radicals on account of the Tea Act when yet another blunder by the British Government, which seemed determined to force conservatives and radicals together in America on every opportunity, caused a vast wave of united sentiment, hostile to England, to flow over the whole of the colonies.

If American conservative opinion was opposed to the

destruction of private property in Boston, English governmental opinion was furious about it. In March, 1774, at Lord North's request, Parliament passed a bill, since known as the Boston Port Act, removing the Custom House from that town and closing its harbor to all inward and outward commerce until restitution should have been made to the East India Company for the destroyed tea, which was estimated to have been worth £15,000 Sterling. The Act went into operation June 1, and on that day Governor Hutchinson sailed for England and turned the province over to the commander-in-chief of the British forces in America, General Gage. The news of the terrifically severe punishment which had been meted out to the third largest port in America roused all the colonies. Resolutions of sympathy and cargoes of food poured from the whole continent into the closed town.

Three other Parliamentary Acts relating to Massachusetts were also soon passed. The first of these altered the charter of that colony and provided that the members of the council should thereafter be appointed by the Crown, that minor officers were also to be appointed instead of being elected, and that no more town meetings could be held without the consent of the governor. Another provided that officials charged with capital crimes might be sent to England for trial, together with all the witnesses, and a final Act renewed in somewhat harsher terms the earlier one as to quartering of troops.

Inset map labels: Quebec; to Quebec; QUEBEC ACT LINE 1774; PROCLAMATION LINE 1763; THE THIRTEEN COLONIES; LOUISIANA (to Spain 1763); FLORIDA (Br. 1763-83)

Main map labels: Montreal; Champlain; Crown Point; Ticonderoga; NEW HAMPSHIRE; Connecticut R.; L. Ontario; Saratoga; Mohawk R.; Fort Niagara; Bennington; Concord; Boston; Albany; Cape Cod; MASS.; Hartford; CONN.; R.I.; Newport; NEW YORK; West Point; NORTHWEST TERRITORY; Lake Erie; Delaware R.; Morristown; New York; LONG I.; Brooklyn; PENNSYLVANIA; Valley Forge; Princeton; Trenton; Philadelphia; N.J.; Ohio River; Baltimore; Washington; Mt.Vernon; MD.; DEL.; Delaware Bay; Boonesboro; Potomac R.; Chesapeake; VIRGINIA; Richmond; James R.; Williamsburg; Yorktown; ATLANTIC OCEAN; Dan R.; Roanoke R.; Guilford Court House; Raleigh; NORTH CAROLINA; King's Mountain; Cowpens; Camden; Wilmington; SOUTH CAROLINA; Savannah R.; Augusta; Charleston; GEORGIA; Savannah; FLORIDA (to Spain); St.Augustine

GENERAL BATTLEGROUND OF THE REVOLUTION AND (INSET) THE
LINE ESTABLISHED BY THE QUEBEC ACT, 1774

159

General Gage was made governor. There were voices raised in Parliament against the severity of all these Acts. Notably Chatham pointed out that the day was coming when the colonies would vie with the mother country in arms and arts, and that the colonists should be treated as children worthy of their sire. But the members generally were overwhelmingly on the side of coercion.

In the same session of Parliament another Act, the Quebec Act, was passed without thought of our thirteen colonies, but was considered by them as aimed at themselves. The problem of the government of Canada had never been satisfactorily solved, and this Act was directed to that end. The French were guaranteed freedom of religion, and certain administrative arrangements were made. In addition, the province was extended southward to the Ohio, which conflicted with the claims westward to lands which Massachusetts, Connecticut, and Virginia all believed were theirs under their charters. This was a mere blunder on the part of the English statesmen, but such careless blunders are costly, and this Act, which with the other four came to be known as the "Intolerable Acts," did much to unite the sentiment of the colonies against England.

THE FIRST CONTINENTAL CONGRESS AND THE FIRST CONFLICT AT LEXINGTON

Meetings now followed one another in quick succession in America, from those of towns and counties to

State conventions. Then, at the suggestion of Virginia, heartily welcomed by the other colonies, the first Con-

ADVERTISEMENT.

THE Committee of Correspondence in New-York, having on Monday Night laſt proceeded to the Nomination of five Perſons to go as Delegates for the ſaid City and County, on the propoſed General Congreſs at Philadelphia, on the 1ſt of September next; the five following Perſons were nominated for that Purpoſe,

Philip Livingſton,
James Duane,
John Alſop,
John Jay,
Iſaac Low.

The Inhabitants, therefore, of this City and County, are requeſted to meet at the City-Hall, on THURSDAY next, at 12 o'Clock, in order to approve of the ſaid five Perſons as Delegates, *or to chooſe ſuch other in their Stead, as to their Wiſdom ſhall ſeem meet.*
By Order of the Committee,

ISAAC LOW, CHAIRMAN.

TUESDAY, 5th
July, 1774.

THE SELECTION OF DELEGATES FROM NEW YORK TO THE FIRST
CONTINENTAL CONGRESS

From a broadside in the New York Historical Society.

tinental Congress met at Philadelphia, September 5, 1774, delegates being present from all the colonies except Georgia. Among others were John and Samuel Adams from Massachusetts; Roger Sherman from Connecticut; Stephen Hopkins from Rhode Island; John Jay and Philip Livingston from New York; John Dickinson, Joseph Galloway, and Thomas Mifflin from Pennsylvania; Cæsar Rodney, Thomas McKean, and George Read from Delaware; George Washington, Patrick Henry, Peyton Randolph (who was chosen President), and Richard Henry Lee from Virginia; Richard Caswell from North Carolina; and from South were Edward and John Rutledge and Christopher Gadsden.

Opinion ran from ultra-conservative to extreme radical, and the action of the Congress was a compromise. The Declaration of Rights drawn up to be sent to England was moderate and dignified. The rights of the colonists were based upon nature, the British constitution, and the charters. As the colonies could not properly be represented in Parliament, the Declaration asserted, their local assemblies should have exclusive power of legislating, but, it was added, for the best interests of the whole empire, the colonists would submit themselves to Parliamentary Acts designed solely for the regulation of trade. It was also stated that the colonists could not submit to an enumerated list of Acts which had been passed since 1764.

An association was entered into by which the colonies bound themselves not to import or export goods to or from English ports, nor consume English goods, until redress of grievances was obtained. Committees were to be appointed in every town and county who were to report the names of such as refused to sign the association agreement or who violated it. This was the most important part of the work of the Congress, and these local

By *the* LION *&* UNICORN, Dieu & mon droit, *their Lieutenant-Generals, Governours, Vice Admirals, &c. &c. &c. &c.*

A HUE *&* CRY.

WHEREAS I have been informed, from undoubted authority, that a certain PATRICK HENRY, of the county of Hanover, and a number of *deluded followers,* have taken up arms, chosen their officers, and, styling themselves an *independent company*, have marched out of their county, encamped, and put themselves in a posture of war; and have written and despatched letters to divers parts of the country, exciting the people to join in these *outrageous* and *rebellious* practices, to the *great terrour* of all his Majesty's *faithful* subjects, and in *open defiance* of *law* and *government ;* and have *committed other acts of violence,* particularly in *extorting* from his *Majesty's Receiver-General* the sum of 330l. under *pretence* of *replacing the powder* I *thought proper* to order from the magazine; whence it undeniably appears, there is *no longer* the least security for the *life* or *property* of any man: Wherefore, I have *thought proper, with the advice of his Majesty's Council,* and *in his Majesty's name,* to issue this *my* proclamation, strictly charging *all persons,* upon their *allegiance,* not to *aid, abet,* or *give countenance* to the said PATRICK HENRY, or *any other persons* concerned in *such unwarrantable combinations ;* but, on the contrary, to oppose *them,* and *their designs,* by *every means,* which designs must otherwise inevitably involve the *whole country* in the *most direful calamity,* as they will call for the *vengeance* of *offended Majesty,* and the *insulted laws,* to be *exerted here,* to vindicate the *constitutional* authority of government.

Given, *&c. this 6th day of* May, 1775.

D * * * *;

G * * d * * * the P * * * *.

A BROADSIDE OF 1775 DENOUNCING PATRICK HENRY
AND HIS FOLLOWERS
From the original in the Library of Congress.

committees became of extreme importance as the struggle advanced into its later stages. Before adjournment provision was made for a new Congress to meet May 10,

163

WILLIAMSBURG, Saturday, *April* 29, 1775.

LATE last night an express arrived from Philadelphia, with the following melancholy advices from the province of Connecticut, forwarded to the committee of correspondence in this city.

The blow (so much dreaded by our noble friend LORD CHATHAM*) is now struck, a great deal of blood spilt, and much more, it is likely, than the present advices communicate. That great man, in his speech upon the necessity of withdrawing the troops from Boston (delivered in the House of Lords the 20th of January last) says:* " *Perhaps, even whilst I am now* " *speaking, the decisive blow is struck, which may involve millions in the* " *consequences; and, believe me, the very first drop of blood that is spilled* " *will not be a wound easily skinned over; it will be* irritabile vulnus, *a* " *wound of that rancorous and festering kind, that, in all probability, will* " *mortify the whole body.*"

PHILADELPHIA, *April* 24, 1775.
An express arrived at five o'clock this evening, by which we have the following advices, viz.

WATERTOWN, *Wednesday morning, near* 10 *o'clock.*

To all FRIENDS *of* AMERICAN LIBERTY.

BE it known, that this morning, before break of day, a brigade, consisting of about 1000 or 1200 men, landed at Phipps farm, at Cambridge, and marched to Lexington, where they found a company of our colony militia in arms, upon whom they fired, without any provocation, and killed six men, and wounded four others. By an express from Boston, we find another brigade is now on its march from Boston, supposed to consist of 1000 men. The bearer, Trial Brisset, is charged to alarm the country, quite to Connecticut; and all persons are desired to furnish him with fresh horses, as they may be needed. I have spoken with several, who have seen the dead and wounded. Pray let the Delegates from this colony to Connecticut see this; they know Col. Foster, one of the Delegates.

J. PALMER, one of the committee.

A true copy from the original, by order of the committee of correspondent of Worcester, April 1775.

Attested and forwarded by the committes of Brookline, Norwich, New London, Lyme, Saybrook, Killingsworth, E. Guilford, Guilford, Brandford, Newhaven.

HOW THE NEWS OF LEXINGTON AND CONCORD WAS RECEIVED
BY THE OTHER COLONIES

(*Above*) Williamsburg and Philadelphia dispatches and (*opposite*) Fairfield.

From a broadside in the Library of Congress.

FAIRFIELD, SATURDAY, *April* 22, 8 *o'clock.*
Since the above written, we have received the following, by a
second express.

THURSDAY, 3 *o'clock after noon.*

SIR.

I AM this moment informed, by an express from Woodstock, taken
from the mouth of the express at two of the clock after noon, that
the contest between the first brigade that marched to Concord was still
continuing this morning at the town of Lexington, to which said
brigade had retreated; that another brigade, said to be the second
mentioned in the letter of this morning, had landed with a quantity of
artillery at the place where the first did. The Provincials were
determined to prevent the two brigades from joining their strength,
if possible; and remain in great need of succour.

1775, unless grievances had been redressed before that
date.

Meanwhile, Gage was in Boston with 5000 troops, and
warships lay in the otherwise empty harbor. He had been
ordered to seize Sam Adams and John Hancock and
ship them to England for trial, but had failed to catch
them. Regardless of the royal governor, Massachusetts
was governing herself by a Provincial Congress. The
winter of 1774-75 passed peacefully for Gage in Boston
but he knew the country everywhere outside was buzz-
ing as with angry hornets. In September he had made
a foray a few miles beyond the town limits and seized
some powder, but almost before he was back, the country
"minute men," estimated at 40,000, had swarmed after
him.

As spring came on he decided to make an effort to
capture stores which he understood had been gathered
at Concord. On the famous 19th of April, 1775, a detach-

ment of British regulars marched through the streets of Boston on what was to become one of the most cele-brated military expeditions in history despite its appar-ent unimportance at the time. Few, if any, undertaken lightly for a minor objective have had such resounding consequences.

Although the troops started before daybreak, the alarm was at once given and Paul Revere and two others rode through the country to rouse it, so that by the time the thousand advancing British soldiers reached Lexing-ton they found about fifty men blocking the way. Eight of these were killed, and the column proceeded. Most of the stores at Concord had been removed, but the British destroyed what little remained, and then started on the return march to Boston. By that time the whole country-side was alive with minute men, who shot at the moving British column from behind trees, stone fences, rocks, and any shelter. The retreat became a rout, and even when reinforced by 1500 troops under young Earl Percy who had hurriedly been sent to their aid, the exhausted British reached Boston and safety only with difficulty. More than 270 were killed, wounded, or missing, and the successful Americans settled down to besiege the town, closed this time by Massachusetts and not by Lord North. On that 19th of April, the shot had been fired that was "heard round the world." The great empire so hardly won in 1763 had begun to dissolve in blood.

CHAPTER VI

THE REVOLUTION

THE news that the long years of bickerings, arguments, appeals and legal reprisals had at last ended with open warfare between colonies and British troops was carried rapidly down the whole coast by messengers on horse-back. The fact that, although the galloping horsemen travelled with great speed for those days, they took five days to reach Philadelphia and six to give their tidings in Virginia, which were not heard at Edenton, North Carolina, for two weeks, helps us to understand some of the difficulties which both Congress and the army would have to face. Everywhere the startling news of fighting called forth resolutions of protest against England, and stirred the war spirit.

On May 10 the Second Continental Congress met in Philadelphia as agreed the previous year, and that same day Ethan Allen with a force of Vermonters surprised the British commander of Fort Ticonderoga. According to Allen's story in later years, he demanded the surrender "in the name of the Great Jehovah and the Continental Congress." However, one of the witnesses of Allen's triumph, giving a different version, reported that what Allen really said to the British officer was "You d—d old rat, come out!" which sounds more authentic. At any rate, a most welcome addition to the scant stores of colonial powder was secured and two days later Crown Point was also captured.

In Boston, the 6000 or more British regulars were besieged by a motley crowd of possibly 20,000 New England militiamen, whose only "training" (a rather bibulous and festive one) had been from two to four days a year. The town was at that time connected with the mainland by only a narrow neck, and was dominated by two eminences, Breed's Hill and Bunker Hill, the peninsula from which they rose being likewise connected with the mainland by another—Charlestown-neck.

THE FIRST BATTLES OF THE REVOLUTION

On the morning of June 17, the British were unpleasantly surprised to discover that Breed's Hill had been fortified in the night. Colonel William Prescott and his regiment, who had done the work, were entrenched there, with none too much ammunition. Had the British seized the Charlestown "neck" they would have trapped the Americans, but with a folly equal to Prescott's rashness, a council of war determined upon a frontal attack up the hillside by troops ferried across from Boston. General William Howe, in command, was a brave officer

THE FIGHT ON LEXINGTON COMMON

From a painting by Howard Pyle.

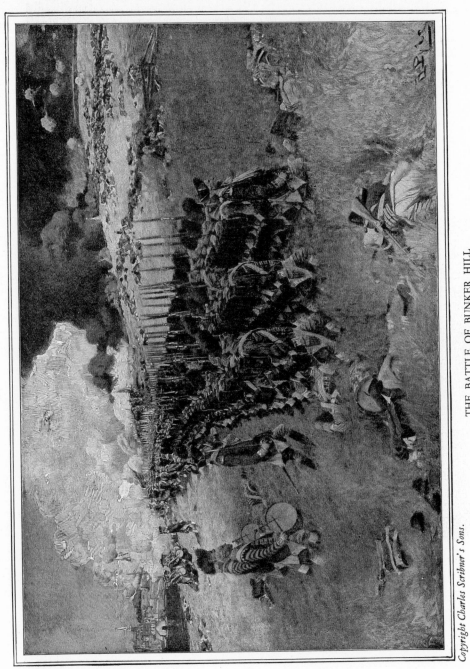

THE BATTLE OF BUNKER HILL

From a painting by Howard Pyle.

with a high reputation, and in the face of galling fire he led his lines up the steep incline again and again. The carnage was terrific, from one third to a half of the British being killed by the New Englanders who held their deadly fire against the enemy each time until they could aim "at the whites of their eyes."

Suddenly the firing stopped. The American ammunition was exhausted. Without disorder the Americans retreated to the mainland, and the British occupied the peninsula. In spite of the retreat, the "battle of Bunker Hill," as it came to be called, was an overwhelming victory for American morale. The British had obviously had to show the greater courage, but the fact remained that raw New England militia had faced British regulars and inflicted heavier casualties than any other enemy had done in the whole Seven Years' War. The English had met English.

Lexington, Concord, Ticonderoga, Crown Point, Bunker Hill settled the matter. With these attacks on British troops and with a Congress of all the colonies sitting in Philadelphia, there could be no turning back for America, nor could any English statesman of the eighteenth century have considered anything except the putting down of what was open rebellion. On June 15 Congress appointed George Washington Commander-in-chief of the American forces.

This action, the wisest and most pregnant with good of any that the Continental Congresses took, was due chiefly to the conflicting ambitions and jealousies of the various sections. New England disliked the thought of a commander from outside her borders, but the rest of America feared even more a New England army commanded by a New Englander. Much to the chagrin and mortified pride of Hancock, who had hoped for the post, John Adams, seconded by Sam, engineered the compromise, although after the matter was settled the formal nomination was left to a Marylander. Although Washington had a high reputation throughout the colonies, one of the main reasons for picking him at this stage was that he was one of the richest and most prominent men in Virginia, which was a much more populous and important colony than Massachusetts. Moreover, he was one of the few colonials who was well known for his military experience, and for all these reasons, his choice to head the rebel army would carry unusual weight both in England and the colonies. The choice would help to show positively that New England did not stand alone in her resistance and that a Southerner of wealth and influence, with everything to lose, was willing to stand in the very forefront of the rebellion.

WASHINGTON TAKES COMMAND

On July 3 Washington reached Cambridge and inspected his army. Numbering 20,242 officers and men, of whom 17,215 were present for duty, it was such only in name, and we may here glance at some of the difficulties which were to beset Washington throughout the entire war. He never in truth had more than the nucleus of an army. It is a mistake to think of our America of the Revolution as a nation of patriots all rising to their own defence. When Independence came, John Adams thought that one third of the people were in favor of it, one third opposed, and one third neutral. The New England historian Channing suggested forty per cent of the population as a fair percentage to be considered "militant revolutionists."

This estimate should give us, from a population of 2,200,000 whites, about 250,000 revolutionists of military age. In the Boer War in 1900, a population of 300,000 Boers put over 40,000 men into the field, and if we had done as well in our own self-defence from 1776 to 1783 we might have had 280,000 combatants. Yet Washington never had over 18,000 in any one engagement or over 22,000 at one time in his army, and during much of the war only a fraction of such a force. Of course, owing to short terms of enlistment and constant changes in personnel, many times those numbers served during the course of the struggle for a few days, weeks or months. On the other hand, however, Van Tyne, the leading authority on the subject, estimates that 50,000 of the Americans who remained loyal to England served with the British forces.

When Washington had had time to look over the situation at Boston he was nearly in despair. He found many of the officers, who were elected by their men and stooped to curry favor with them instead of enforcing orders, thoroughly incompetent. He made, as he wrote, " a pretty good slam" among these and discharged some for cowardice and others for fraud. Officers went off to their farms, taking privates with them to work, and drew pay for both. "Such a dirty, mercenary spirit pervades the whole, that I shall not be surprised at any disaster that may happen," was one of many such comments that the new commander wrote of those under him. Some of the higher officers, such as Major-General Schuyler, were so disgusted with the greed and selfish spirit manifested that they were restrained with difficulty by Washington from throwing up their commissions.

The militia, Washington wrote, could be depended on for only a few days at a time, when they would get tired, ungovernable, and slip off to their homes. By February, 1776, half the army had melted away. In time, he gathered a group of able officers, but throughout the war there was always the same difficulty with the troops. Wherever fighting occurred, the farmers could be counted on to swarm in from the countryside and take irregular part in the engagement, but it was extremely difficult to secure men to enlist, even with the offer of high bounties in cash. Not only have we always been a pacific and unmilitary people, but the scarcity of labor, the anxiety over the women and children left at home on the farms, the poor pay in rapidly depreciating paper money, the lack of supplies of all sorts in the army, all made the service extremely unpopular.

Given the general conditions of the time and the lack of public spirit on the part of most, of which Washington, John Adams, and other leaders constantly complained, all praise is due to the officers and the comparatively small band of Continental Regulars who stood by their commander throughout the duration of the war and under every discouragement. It was these men and not those who would occasionally run from their farms to take a pot-shot at the enemy or enlist for a month or two who saved the cause.

If the colonists generally did not support Washington, neither did the government give him efficient backing. Congress did not dare to tax the people, and all its decisions were made as the result of compromise among the representatives of thirteen jealous States, each thinking in terms of itself. Even the eight generals commissioned to serve under the commander-in-chief had to be chosen, like a modern President's Cabinet, to balance competing geographical sections and provincial jealousies rather than for their abilities.

There was no efficient War Department, and during most of the war the army was in straits for everything an army needs. There were scarcely any uniforms, and often only rags. The "Continental" uniform of portraits and popular pictures was mostly mythical. Shoes, food, ammunition, supplies for the sick, everything was always in arrears or never arrived at all. The Medical Department during the whole Revolution presents mostly a picture of quarrelling doctors and incompetency. Of the four Directors General, one was court-martialled and two were dismissed from the service. As Colonel Ashburn, the historian of our Army Medical Department, records, there is little or nothing in this aspect of the struggle in which we can take pride.

The point is not, however, our pride but the truth as to the sort of difficulties Washington had to overcome. What was true of the Medical Department was true also of almost every other. There were times when the troops nearly starved in the midst of rich farming districts. For lack of an adequate Commissariat, wherever the army marched or camped, it almost created famine in the neighborhood. Moreover, farmers and tradesmen, patriots as well as Tories, profiteered shamelessly at the expense of the soldiers. In the terrible winter at Valley Forge, Washington could scarcely get enough food to keep his men from starving, the farmers preferring to sell it for high prices in gold to the British in Philadelphia. Sometimes for weeks at a time his troops had no powder except what was in their cartridge boxes.

On the other hand, the British also had their difficulties. Although their troops far outnumbered ours, they had perforce to be broken up into several bodies. Almost all military supplies had to be transported three thousand miles across the ocean by uncertain sailing vessels. In

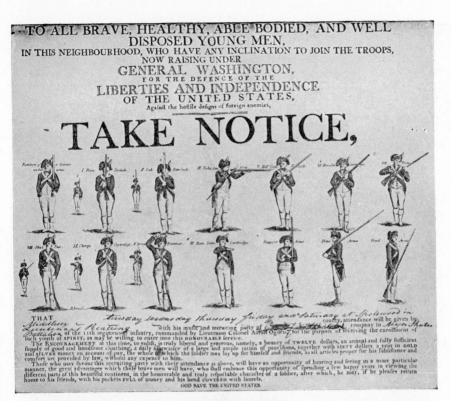

A RECRUITING POSTER

It reads in part: "The encouragement at this time to enlist, is truly liberal and generous, namely a bounty of twelve dollars, an annual and fully sufficient supply of good and handsome cloathing, a daily allowance of a large and ample ration of provisions, together with sixty dollars a year in Gold and Silver money on account of pay, the whole of which the soldier may lay up for himself and friends, as all articles proper for his subsistance and comfort are provided by law, without any expense to him. . . . Those . . . who shall embrace this opportunity of spending a few happy years in viewing the different parts of this beautiful continent, in the honorable and truly respectable character of a soldier, after which, he may, if he pleases return home to his friends, with his pockets full of money and his head covered with laurels.

From the original in the Pennsylvania Historical Society.

PROSPECT HILL.	BUNKER's HILL.
I. Seven Dollars a Month.	I. Three Pence a Day.
II. Fresh Provisions, and in Plenty.	II. Rotten Salt Pork.
III. Health.	III. The Scurvy.
IV. Freedom, Ease, Affluence and a good Farm.	IV. Slavery, Beggary and Want.

HANDBILL SENT AMONG THE BRITISH TROOPS ON BUNKER HILL
From the original owned by the Massachusetts Historical Society.

THE EVACUATION OF CHARLESTON BY THE BRITISH, DECEMBER, 1782

From the painting by Howard Pyle.

America, transporting large bodies of troops by land was almost impossible, and uncertain by water. The great valley of the Mississippi is bound together by the river that traverses it with its branches, but one of the factors which had kept the thirteen seaboard colonies separate and provincial was the fact that no rivers joined them. The short streams, which ran from mountain to sea, even such as the Hudson and Potomac, were inter-colonial barriers, not highways for those travelling up and down the coast.

Nor was there any one vital spot in America the possession of which would determine the conflict. As Chatham said, it was impossible to make war against a mere map. Nor, again, was the American army an objective. It was not Washington's forces, sometimes numbering only two or three thousand, but the swarms of country people ready to rise for a few days anywhere who were the real enemy. It was as though in the jungle one had been called upon to fight not a single specimen of big game but innumerable hosts of insects that were everywhere and nowhere, that would swarm and sting to death and then disappear.

The British had been badly misinformed about colonial sentiment by many of their governors and other officials. Everywhere in the eighteenth century the poorer people were thought of no importance, and a large proportion of the rich, with whom the governors came into contact, were in truth on the side of England in the controversy. This was particularly true in Boston, where such a wealthy patriot as John Hancock was an extreme exception. The jockeying for political advantage between the powerful families in New York led some of them to the patriot side, but the New York "aristocracy" was pretty solidly Tory. A larger proportion of rich and distinguished families went over to the American side in Virginia than in any other colony, but the British were right in believing that everywhere in America, even in recalcitrant Boston, they would be supported by a considerable part of the most important people, and others.

As we have seen, the number who joined the British fighting services was very large. The patriots greatly disliked to be called "rebels," believing, as the Southerners did in our later Civil War, that they were merely fighting for their legal rights, but on the other hand those Americans who espoused the British side of the argument and fight believed that they were on the side of law and order, of maintaining the established basis of society. They felt quite naturally toward those who were taking up arms against the English Government as today conservative people, rich or poor, even if they are "Sons" or "Daughters" of the American Revolution, feel toward Socialists and others who would alter the established social scheme. We must recall that although our Revolution was less bloody than most, nevertheless there was much mobbing and disorder, so that many even of those who believed that England was wrong dreaded a possible disastrous overturn of order in America by the lower classes more than temporary inconvenience or suffering from bad British laws.

But, although such people were numerous and in many cases individually powerful, they were not organized, and after the first bloodshed at Lexington the revolutionary committees all through the colonies took over control. Not only were freedom of speech and of the press entirely suppressed but those who were thought to be on the Tory side were threatened, persecuted, and disarmed. As the war went on and laws against them were passed in the heat of passion by the various States, in many cases Tories were imprisoned, tarred and feathered, gathered into concentration camps, ostracised socially or economically, and forced to cease carrying on their callings as lawyers, doctors, teachers or merchants, while their property was confiscated on a heavy scale.

In a number of States any one who acted or spoke against Congress could be imprisoned or fined, the fines sometimes running up to $20,000, and as half of them went to the informer, the way was open for vast injustice. Imprisonment was a far heavier punishment than the word suggests. All prisons were vile in those days, though few were so terrible as the almost incredible one in Connecticut far below ground in the shafts of the copper mine at Simsbury, where physical and moral conditions were indescribable.

Occasionally a Loyalist may have been a source of

danger to the patriot cause in his community but such cases were comparatively rare, and as the war went on and persecution became fiercer, and laws providing for confiscation of property more severe, they can be attributed mainly to the spirit of lawlessness, cruelty, and greed which revolution always breeds. A man would be accused of being a Loyalist by a prejudiced jury, and his property ordered confiscated. This would then be sold and would be bought, often for a small fraction of its value, by "patriots" who made large profits on it. Many of the finest estates in Massachusetts, including Governor Hutchinson's (which even under these conditions brought £98,000), as well as some of the largest in New York and other colonies, were thus seized.

The suffering was not confined to the rich, for a farmer who coveted his neighbor's acres or even a little straightening of boundaries, would find it convenient to obtain them in this way if any case, though of the flimsiest, could be made out against the owner. Such Loyalists alone as later turned in their claims to the British Government listed confiscated properties to the total amount of £10,000,000, of which the Claims Commission disallowed only £1,000,000. Many of the Tories were exiled penniless, a list of 300 in Boston including many of the families who had been most notable in the life of the colony from its very founding. In all, willingly or unwillingly, between sixty and a hundred thousand left America for Canada, the West Indies or England. 178

This aspect of the war, which brought bitterness and suffering to hundreds of thousands of those Americans who left and those who stayed, should not be forgotten. In almost every village, neighbor was divided against neighbor, and not seldom even the members of the same family against each other. In many communities it was the rich, educated, and conservative who remained loyal to the old order, so that the radicals were left more and more in control.

Opinion in England was also divided. Not only did America's defenders in Parliament stand by her, but the City of London showed its dislike of the war throughout. Many writers produced pamphlets upholding our actions, just as others, like Doctor Johnson, wrote in the pay of the Ministerial party against us. The English merchants were naturally opposed to war, as we owed them some £5,000,000 at its outbreak, of which the Virginians alone owed over £2,300,000. It was said in British newspapers of the day that one half of the English people had given their voices against their own country. The British landed interests were most strongly against us, and the merchants and common people for us. Of course as the war continued, the feeling developed among many that, right or wrong, England would have to see it through, a sentiment which grows in any nation in any war, whatever public opinion may have been at its outbreak.

SOME OF WASHINGTON'S DIFFICULTIES

We were, however, only at the beginning of all this when Washington was trying to organize an army actually in the face of the enemy at Boston. In September, 1775, he spoke of the situation as "inexpressibly distressing," the army without clothing or supplies, ready to melt homeward at the first touch of cold weather, and not a dollar in the pay-chest. However, an expedition against the British in Quebec met with the Commander's approval, and two small forces proceeded to try to make a joint attack, the one, under General Schuyler, advancing up the old route of Lakes George and Champlain, and the other through the Maine forests under command of Benedict Arnold, a capable and at that time wholly patriotic officer.

Owing to Schuyler's illness General Montgomery took his command, and although the difficulties of supplies, organization, and transport were almost insuperable, he captured Montreal with his forces November 12. Leaving detachments to garrison St. John's and Montreal, and losing a good part of the remainder of his troops who left him for home, he pressed on with only 300 men to join Arnold before Quebec. The joint assault was made in a heavy snowstorm on December 31, Montgomery, a gallant officer, being killed at the very beginning of the action, and Arnold wounded. The assault failed, and some months later the entire expedition had to be abandoned as a failure.

Apart from extremely bad organization, the lack of success was due to the rank and file of our troops. Montgomery complained that the New England soldiers were "the worst stuff imaginable," refusing to obey orders, and continually deserting because they were homesick. John Adams asserted that if they continued to run away as they had at Quebec and "the Cedars," the American cause would be lost. One of the objects of the expedition had been to unite the Canadians to ourselves but this also resulted in failure, in part on account of the conduct of our soldiers who were licentious and who pillaged houses and scoffed at the Catholic religion of the French. In spite of all, however, the expedition was to bear important fruit, as we shall see later, and happily success elsewhere was to encourage the Americans for the moment.

Washington managed to keep an army together through the winter, and in March he determined to drive the British from Boston. Seizing and fortifying Dorchester Heights, he commanded the British position by cannon dragged from Ticonderoga. At first the British thought of a counter attack, but a storm prevented this and then a complete evacuation was decided upon. It took ten days to make the preparations but finally on March 17 General Howe, who had succeeded Gage in command, sailed away in the British fleet, with about

11,000 British troops and 1000 Loyalist refugees. Washington took possession of the town, ordered the militia home, left five regiments to garrison the Massachusetts

Two favorite SONGS,

made on the Evacuation of the Town of BOSTON, ·

by the *British Troops*, on the 17th of March, 1776.

IN feventeen hundred and feventy fix,
  On March the eleventh, the time was prefix'd,
Our forces march'd on upon Dorchefter-neck,
Made fortifications againft an attack.
  The morning next following, as Howe did efpy,
The banks we caft up, were fo copious and high,
Said he in three months, all my men with their might,
Cou'd not make two fuch Forts as they've made in a night.
  Now we hear that their Admiral was very wroth,
And drawing his fword, he bids Howe to go forth,
And drive off the YANKEES from Dorchefter hill :
Or he'd leave the harbour and him to their will.
  Howe rallies his forces upon the next day,

IT was'nt our will that Bunker Hill
  From us fhould e,er be taken ;
We thought 'twould never be retook,
  But we find we are Miftaken.
The foldiers bid the hill farewell,
  Two images left fentreis,
This they had done all out of fun
  To the American Yankees.
A flag of truce was fent thereon,
  To fee if the hill was clear,
No living foul was found thereon,
  But thefe images ftood there.

ONE FORM OF POPULAR REACTION TO THE EVACUATION
From the original broadside in the Massachusetts Historical Society.

capital, and within three weeks was on his way to New York with the remainder of the army.

Meanwhile, the British, like the Americans in Canada, had tried a stroke at the extreme end of the colonies, hoping to capture an important town and rally to their side those who sympathized with them. In the beginning of 1776 a joint naval and land expedition was set on foot to capture Charleston, South Carolina, and to combine with the Tories to gain control of the far southern colonies. The land forces of British and Loyalists were defeated, however, at Moore's Creek, February 27, and the fleet, long delayed, failed in June in its attack on the little fort defending Charleston. This side expedition of the British had proved even less successful than the American one to Canada.

While all these acts of plain warfare had been occurring, the relations of the colonies to England were anomalous. It is true that Congress by declaring war, taking over the army, advising Massachusetts to resume its old form of government and to consider the "Intolerable Acts" as void, by making loans, issuing paper money, corresponding with foreign governments, fitting out war vesesls, and by other acts had obviously become a revolutionary body. On the other hand, it denied, and honestly, any thought of independence. Indeed, in July, 1775, the more conservative men in it secured the passage of another Petition to the King, which the Monarch declined to receive. Nevertheless, even as late as January, 1776, North Carolina, Maryland, Pennsylvania, New Jersey, and New York were instructing their delegates to have nothing to do with voting for independence, and men like Anthony Wayne and Washington had been violently protesting against it.

In that month came the news that Parliament had passed an Act prohibiting all nations from trading with the colonies, and making any ships engaged in such trade lawful prizes of war. Next came news of fighting in Virginia. Norfolk was strongly Tory and Governor Dunmore was using it as a base to spread British influence. Had he been a little wiser in action he might have come near succeeding in establishing a powerful British faction in the colony, but forced to take to sea by the more radical patriots he made the mistake of bombarding the town and setting fire to it before leaving, thus greatly strengthening the propaganda of the patriots.

A BOOK IS PUBLISHED

About this same time there appeared a book which perhaps more than any other, with the possible exception of *Uncle Tom's Cabin,* nearly a century later, has inflamed American public opinion. The literature of the Revolution was extensive, although thus far we have mentioned only James Otis and John Dickinson as having contributed notably to it. Both in the years of discussion leading up to the struggle and in those of the actual fighting, the presses were kept busy issuing books, pamphlets, and newspaper articles dealing with the controversy, while ministers, such as Jonathan Mayhew, Samuel Cooper, Charles Chauncey, George Duffield, and others, discoursed from their pulpits. To a great extent, the writings of the period dealt with the constitutional

COMMON SENSE;

ADDRESSED TO THE

INHABITANTS

OF

A M'E R I C A,

On the following interesting

S U B J E C T S.

I. Of the Origin and Design of Government in general, with concise Remarks on the English Constitution.

II. Of Monarchy and Hereditary Succession.

III. Thoughts on the present State of American Affairs.

IV. Of the present Ability of America, with some miscellaneous Reflections.

A NEW EDITION, with several Additions in the Body of the Work. To which is added an APPENDIX; together with an Address to the People called QUAKERS.

N. B. The New Addition here given increases the Work upwards of one Third.

Man knows no Master save creating HEAVEN,
Or those whom Choice and common Good ordain.
                                            THOMSON.

PHILADELPHIA PRINTED.

And sold by W. and T. BRADFORD.

FACSIMILE OF THE TITLE-PAGE OF PAINE'S *COMMON SENSE*
In the New York Public Library.

aspects of the problems which were splitting the empire.

In Massachusetts, for example, John Adams wrote out his views at length, while Daniel Leonard took the Tory standpoint, as Joseph Galloway did in Pennsylvania. In poetry, the revolutionary fervor and new patriotism found lyrical expression in the work of Francis Hopkinson and satirical in those of Philip Freneau and John Trumbull. Important as the writings of these and many others were in the intellectual discussion or emotional stimulation, they all paled before those of Thomas Paine.

Paine was a born revolutionist and was later to take part in the French Revolution. He had been dismissed from his small government post in England in 1774, and had come to Philadelphia, where he knew Franklin and other leaders. In January, 1776, his small volume entitled *Common Sense* was issued from the press, soon to run up to the then colossal sale of 100,000 copies. It was neither learned nor profound but its terse, vigorous style embodying the emotions that thousands were beginning to feel made it run like a prairie fire through the whole colonial mind from Maine to Georgia. Its sentences were to be the common-places in America for a century and to be recited by every schoolboy. "Of more worth is one honest soul to society, and in the sight of God, than all the crowned ruffians that ever lived." "Every spot of the old world is overrun with oppression. Freedom hath been hunted round the globe. Asia and

Africa have long expelled her. Europe regards her like a stranger; and England hath given her warning to depart. O! Receive the fugitive; and prepare in time an asylum for mankind."

To understand the full effect of such passages, we must recall the circumstances under which great numbers of the poorer colonists of recent years had then come to the colonies, as well as the general restlessness of the discontented classes we described earlier. America, he said, must always be secondary to the interest of England if tied to her. It was absurd to think of 3,000,000 people running to meet every ship in order "to know what portion of liberty they should enjoy." It was "madness and folly" to have further trust in Britain. England and America belonged to different systems, "England to Europe, America to herself!" American affairs were too complex, too important to be handled by ignorant men three thousand miles away. "The period of debate is closed. Arms, as the last resource, must decide the contest." "The last cord now is broken."

As compared with the best literature of the controversial period, Paine's book was superficial and crude, but it was incomparably written to reach the hearts of plain men and to stir them to action. It created a vast wave of feeling in favor of complete independence. It appealed to passion, but the overwhelming passion of the day, whether of Puritan patriot in Boston, of Virginia planter who wished to govern the "old Dominion" himself, or of the frontiersman smarting under the rule of the seaboard, was for liberty. To this the book was a flaming beacon.

Throughout the colonies, moreover, the control of events was fast slipping from the hands of the conservatives. In Pennsylvania, for example, the Assembly which had formerly defied the frontier had yielded step by step until it was taking its orders from the revolutionary Committee of Safety. In Virginia, although the Assembly sat, the real power had passed to the revolutionary Convention, which drew up a new constitution for the State, including a Declaration of Independence from England. In May, 1776, the Convention instructed the State's delegates to Congress to move a Resolution declaring the colonies "free and independent States."

THE DECLARATION OF INDEPENDENCE

The temper of Congress itself was becoming more radical, and in the same month, May, that body recommended to all the colonies that they form new governments for themselves. By June 7, Richard Henry Lee of Virginia introduced resolutions to declare the colonies independent, to negotiate foreign alliances, and to form a Confederation of the new States. There was still some struggling between the conservative and radical elements, the former from the Middle Colonies and South Carolina, but the latter won, and a committee was appointed to draft a Declaration of Independence, al-

though some good patriots, such as John Dickinson and
Robert Morris, still thought the action premature.

ARTICLES

OF

Confederation

AND

Perpetual Union

BETWEEN THE

STATES

OF

New Hampshire, Massachusetts Bay, Rhode Island, and Providence Plantations,
Connecticut, New York, New Jersey, Pennsylvania, Delaware, Maryland,
Virginia, North Carolina, South Carolina, and Georgia. .

WILLIAMSBURG:
Printed by ALEXANDER PURDIE.

From the original in the Library of Congress.

Written by Thomas Jefferson, with some minor
changes made by John Adams and Franklin, it was

brought up for debate on July 2. The day before, on a test vote, New York and Pennsylvania had been against making the Declaration, Delaware was divided, and South Carolina asked for time. On the 2d, however, all voted in favor, except New York, and on the 4th the draft made by the committee was accepted with certain alterations, and copies ordered to be sent to all the Assemblies and revolutionary Conventions and Committees. New York agreed on the 9th and the signatures of the members of Congress were appended, at various dates, to the engrossed copy which was not prepared until August 2.

The news of the passing of the Declaration was received with wild rejoicing throughout America. Bells were rung in the churches, bonfires blazed, and untold quantities of liquor were drunk to innumerable toasts. It is true that the Loyalists and many of the conservatives, who took the American side with heavy misgivings, believed the action rash and unjustified, and were deeply saddened at the severance of ties with the country from which they had sprung. But the die was now cast and such men, even if they remained in America, were to have no further influence.

Much of their criticism of the document itself was justified. It is not as easy as it was a century and a half ago to agree unqualifiedly with some of its most resounding statements, largely drawn from the philosopher Locke. In spite of all that can be said against it, it remains nevertheless one of the great milestones in the history of man. The greater part of the Declaration was taken up with a recital of the crimes of George the Third. Stupid and stubborn as the King was to prove, most of these were in reality merely the workings of the old Colonial System which the Americans had now outgrown, but the indictment had been made, and the trial was to take place,—trial by battle. We may have found that it is not so simple to resolve political questions by "the laws of nature and of Nature's God," but such phrases as "all men are created equal," "are endowed by their Creator with certain unalienable rights," that governments "derive their just powers from the consent of the governed," were dynamic forces which sent the world on a new course the end of which is not yet in sight.

WASHINGTON'S MOVEMENTS

As we have seen, Washington, appreciating the strategic position of New York, had gone there direct from Boston. He at once strengthened the lower defences of the city, and later built Forts Lee and Washington on either side of the Hudson about what is now 183d Street. Howe was also aware of the value of the city, and on June 25 arrived in the harbor with a fleet from Halifax. He was later joined by the troops returning from South Carolina and, August 12, by Lord Howe with fresh troops from England, including the first detachment of the hired Hessians from Germany. In all, the British landed about 32,000 troops on Staten Island. "On paper" Washington had about the same number, but in reality only slightly over 20,000 present for duty. Of his five divisions, one had been sent over to Brooklyn to intercept an approach of the British from Staten Island by that route which was to prove the one chosen.

On August 22, Howe ferried 15,000 troops over to Long Island, reinforced three days later by 5000 more, and camped about eight miles from the American lines, where Washington had 7000 of his men. General Greene, who was to have been in command, was ill, and the battle of August 27 was fought without a head, ending in disaster for the Americans, who lost about 1000 men, though Washington managed to rescue the remainder by a masterly retreat across the East River at night. The situation forced him to evacuate New York by September 12 and in the process, three days later, there was a disgraceful panic among the Americans as they were pursued by the British, Washington himself, while trying to rally his men, nearly being captured. In the battle of Harlem Heights, however, on the 16th, his troops gave an excellent account of themselves, and their morale was restored.

Little by little, however, the Americans were forced to give way. In the battle of White Plains, October 22, they met well a direct frontal attack, but again had to retreat, and Forts Lee and Washington, with over 2800 prisoners, soon fell into the hands of the British. Washington took up a temporary position at Newark, with only 6000 troops, but was forced southward by the British, who now believed the war almost over. Many of the New Jersey and Maryland militia marched off to their homes, and the American army dwindled to less than 3000 soldiers whose enlistment would be up in a month.

Washington then retreated across the Delaware, urging General Charles Lee to join him as rapidly as possible. Lee, however, who from jealousy was a traitor to Washington, moved with extreme slowness, and at Basking Ridge was taken prisoner by the British, whereupon he turned traitor also to the whole American cause. That cause, by this time, seemed almost hopelessly lost, but to Washington's surprise, Howe, instead of pursuing him, went into winter quarters in New York, leaving garrisons in Princeton and some other Jersey towns.

Determined to deliver a brilliant counter-stroke, the American Commander, on Christmas night, 1776, ferried his army across the ice-filled Delaware, and after a quick march to Trenton attacked the Hessians there, who had been celebrating Santa Claus with too deep potations and were mostly sound asleep. On the morning of December 26 they were driven from the town with heavy loss, and although they returned with reinforcements some days later, Washington eluded them by the trick of leaving his camp fires burning, and on January 3

made a surprise attack on Princeton. The terms of enlistment of all his men had expired on January 1 but he
had induced them to remain for another six weeks by
promising a bounty of ten dollars each above their
regular pay, and after Princeton, joined by the remnants
of Lee's army, he pushed on to Morristown, where, unmolested by the British, who evacuated all of New Jersey, he settled down for the winter. This unexpected
turning of the tables, at the very moment when all
seemed lost, was declared by Frederick the Great to be
the most brilliant operation in all military history. The
shattered morale of the Americans was restored, and
Washington's own prestige enormously and fortunately
strengthened.

The following year was to prove the most fateful of
the war. If throughout its duration Washington was to
be hampered by the interference of Congress, the British
also had their difficulties from the fact that military
operations were planned by men largely ignorant even
of American geography and terrain, 3000 miles from
where such plans were to be carried out. In war after war
the Hudson River-Lake Champlain route to Canada had
always figured, and the British now planned that General Burgoyne should lead an army along it southward
from Montreal to be met by Howe advancing northward from New York. Ever since the American attack
in Quebec, troops had been kept in Canada, whom it
was now proposed to use with heavy reinforcements

from abroad. The orders sent to Howe were conflicting, and, as we shall see, he did not attempt to carry out his part of the joint plan. It was, in any case, much too complicated a one for local conditions in America.

As spring came on, Washington, with a much augmented army, was watching to see what Howe would do in New York. There had been skirmishes which signified nothing when, on July 5, the British general unexpectedly embarked a large part of his troops on transports, and after being held by calms until the 23d, disappeared from view over the horizon. There was complete uncertainty as to where he would appear next, and meanwhile news came that Burgoyne, moving south with 7000 troops, nearly half of whom were hired Brunswickers, had captured Ticonderoga.

When Howe's fleet appeared in Delaware Bay, Washington at once moved to the defence of Philadelphia, but Howe again disappeared, and it was thought he had headed south for Charleston. The suspense was not for long, for the British fleet was next discovered in Chesapeake Bay, having been able to sail two hundred miles up that body of water without having been seen. After landing troops for the capture of Philadelphia, the ships once more cleared out to sea. On September 11, the Americans and British met at the Brandywine, where the former sustained a bad defeat, and after some additional fighting, notably at Germantown on October 4, Washington was obliged to abandon the capital city to

Howe and to take up winter quarters at Valley Forge while the British enjoyed themselves in Philadelphia. Had Howe followed up his advantage at the Brandy-wine with a few energetic blows, he might, instead of settling down comfortably for the cold weather, have ended the war completely and at once. He missed his opportunity, however, as he had at the battle of Long Island, with momentous effects on the history of the world.

BURGOYNE IS DEFEATED

Burgoyne had been meeting disaster in the North where his transport service in the wilderness had broken down. He was short of supplies, and the New Eng-landers, roused like angry hornets, were hanging on his flanks. While at Fort Edward he decided to send an expedition eastward to Bennington to capture stores which he understood had been collected there, but the Vermonters at once got wind of his intent. General John Stark hastily raised a force of about 2000 farmers and August 16 attacked Lieutenant-Colonel Baum and his Germans, capturing or killing the whole of them, the few British and Indians with them escaping. A second detachment, which had been sent to Baum's aid by Burgoyne, was met and defeated by Colonel Seth War-ner with more militia, and in all Burgoyne lost about 800 men out of the 6000 he had after leaving a necessary garrison at Ticonderoga.

The British commander had been ordered to count on help from Colonel St. Leger who was to advance along the Mohawk Valley to meet him, but this expedition had been defeated by the Americans under Benedict Arnold at Oriskany, and all hope was lost from that direction. He had also been told that Howe would meet him by way of the Hudson, but that officer had gone to Philadelphia. The army of the unfortunate Burgoyne was encumbered with about 300 women and an absurd amount of household stuff. The Americans felled trees and in other ways impeded both his advance and his lines of supply to the rear. By September there were about 20,000 Americans, chiefly short-term local militia. surrounding him, and his position was becoming desperate. His army was like a great clumsy antediluvian animal caught in a quagmire.

The American regulars were commanded by Gates and occupied high land, known as Bemis Heights, overlooking the Hudson, below which Burgoyne would have to pass. Believing that General Clinton in New York would be sent to his support by Howe, Burgoyne tried to push on, but suffered heavy losses in several engagements. His army was on half rations, but, although in spite of the difficulties, retreat was clearly the only course left to him, he now made no move.

It has been said that he temporarily lost his mind and it is impossible to explain his acts at this period. Finally the retreat was begun but his army was completely surrounded by the Americans and on October 17, after some days of negotiation, the British were surrendered at Saratoga with the loss of all their arms, although the troops were to be permitted to march to Boston and be

I George Washington. Commander en chief of the armies of the United States of America do acknowledge the UNITED STATES of AME-RICA, to be Free, Independent and Sovereign States, and declare that the people thereof owe no allegiance or obedience to George the Third, King of Great-Britain; and I re-nounce, refuse and abjure any allegiance or obedience to him; and I do *swear* _ _ that I will to the utmost of my power, support, maintain and defend the said United States, against the said King George the Third, his heirs and successors and his or their abettors, assistants and adherents, and will serve the said United States in the office of *Commander in chief as aforesaid*: which I now hold, with fidelity, according to the best of my skill and understanding.

Sworn before me
Camp at Valley Forge
May 12th 1778
Stirling Major Genl.

G. Washington Jr.

FACSIMILE OF WASHINGTON'S OATH OF ALLEGIANCE
In the War Department, Washington.

transported to England on condition of not serving again in the war. Gates had made a great blunder in not insisting, as he well could, on absolute surrender, but even as it was the disaster to the British had resounding consequences in Europe and for America.

France had been watching England's civil war with the colonies with intent interest. Smarting from the defeat of 1763 she had been longing for revenge. The situation was well understood in America, and Franklin had been sent to Paris to try to negotiate a treaty of alliance, but France, which had no interest in building up an American republic, was wary. Although a good many French officers had come to America, some merely to make money and a few like Lafayette, young and ardent, inspired by the dream of liberty, the French Government had only the thought of injuring England and of protecting her own West Indian islands, and no intention of committing itself until it should become evident that the old lion was going to be so heavily attacked by her cubs as to make it safe to join the fray. This was what the surrender of Burgoyne achieved.

When the Americans showed that they would be able to divert a large part of England's strength, France at once made two treaties with us, February 6, 1778, one of alliance and one of commerce. She recognized the independence of the United States of America, and agreed that if she and England should go to war she would serve as our ally until our independence had been acknowledged by England also. Neither America nor France was to make a separate peace.

For long we had been receiving surreptitious aid from Europe. Not only had such officers as the French De Kalb, the Pole Pulaski, and the Prussian Baron von Steuben proved highly useful, but we had been allowed to receive supplies from both France and Spain. The treaty of alliance, however, greatly changed the situation. England and France were at war, of course, within a few weeks of France's action, and although Spain did not join until 1779, and then as the ally of France only and not of us, the war was widening fast for England. It was no longer a matter of rebellious colonies but of a struggle for life against the second greatest naval power in the world.

It was well for us that France's selfish policy coincided with our needs, for these were almost hopelessly great when the treaties were signed. In spite of the victory at Saratoga, our most important cities were still in the hands of powerful British forces, while Washington at Valley Forge had an almost destitute army, half-naked, unshod, suffering severely and steadily dwindling. In all, at Newport, New York, and Philadelphia, the British had nearly 34,000 troops whereas the Americans had only 15,000, also scattered, which Washington hoped to be able to increase to 20,000.

When we recall that the number of Americans of military age was at least 300,000, we can understand the despair of those who were leading the revolt when only 15,000 of these could be induced to serve. Not only were men, supplies, and money lacking, but the old jealousies between colonies and individuals had broken out again. Most serious of all, efforts were being made, largely by New Englanders, to get rid of Washington and to put the incompetent Gates, who owed the victory at Saratoga mainly to Arnold, in his place. This intrigue, known as the Conway Cabal from one of its active instigators, General Conway, an Irishman who had come from France, was happily crushed, but the winter of 1778–9 was dark indeed for the American cause. In spite of all, however, when England sent commissioners to negotiate peace on any terms except the acknowledgment of American independence, all offers were spurned. Had it not been that the French alliance had been concluded, it would have been folly not to have accepted the olive branch.

From the entry of the French, although the war continued in America, England realized that that theatre was not the principal one for the events to come. Had General Howe had the energy of Washington he might easily have crushed him with greatly superior forces almost any time during the winter, but fortunately the British general found the life of Philadelphia too agreeable to bother, and in May, 1778, he was recalled to England, and succeeded by Clinton from New York.

Clinton had orders to send 8000 of his men to the new seat of war in the West Indies, and to move the remainder to New York. Marching from Philadelphia overland across New Jersey, with a baggage train twelve miles long, his slow progress offered a chance to Washington who attacked him at Monmouth. Charles Lee, whose treachery had not been known and who had been exchanged by the British, was given the post of senior major-general in the fight, and whether traitorously or not, acted so incomprehensibly as to rouse Washington to anger and to permit Clinton to escape. The "damned poltroon," as the Commander-in-Chief called Lee to his face, was later dismissed from the army.

Philadelphia, however, was once more in our possession, and there was to be no more fighting of consequence in the North. A minor affair, an attempted co-operative movement of the American troops and the French fleet under d'Estaing, against the British in Newport, failed of success and created some ill-feeling against the French on account of what was considered their unnecessary leaving of the Americans in the lurch. However, Newport was evacuated by the British in 1779, the troops being taken south for the operations in Carolina, and more of the New York troops were moved to the real seat of war, the West Indies.

Washington, however, did not feel strong enough to attack the British in our chief port. Each winter his army fell to only about 3000 men, and the fact is that we Americans were heartily sick of the struggle. The New England colonies as well as others were nearly bankrupt. Our Continental paper money was nearly worthless. The economic suffering had been great. For the most part our war, which had now developed into a tremendous struggle of England against France, Spain, and Holland, had been transferred to other parts of the world, mainly the high seas. We were, as even Washington admitted, at the end of our own rope. We had not achieved independence, and were waiting for the result of the conflict of greater forces than our own far from our shores.

THE PLOT OF BENEDICT ARNOLD

All fighting within our own limits, nevertheless, was not yet over. In the North there is little to record except the indecisive capture of Stony Point by the Americans, and the unhappy treason of Arnold. That officer had been one of the finest in our army. Wounded at Quebec, the conqueror of St. Leger, the real hero of the capture of Burgoyne, active and able in the American cause, he had been most ungenerously treated by both Gates and Congress. He also had a beautiful but extravagant wife to whom he was devoted. Finally after four years, he decided to change sides and betray his country. For £10,000 he offered to try to deliver West Point to the British, asking another £10,000 if he were successful and a commission as major-general in the British army. No definite terms appear to have been agreed to by the enemy, but negotiations were entered into.

The discovery and foiling of the plot was one of the dramatic incidents of the war and will always be recalled for the tragic fate of the young English officer who was used as go-between by Arnold and Howe. Major André was one of the most attractive of the younger men in the British service, a man of the highest honor and popular with all who knew him. After the negotiations had been proceeding for some time, he was sent up the Hudson in a small vessel to meet Arnold and arrange certain details in person.

Howe had ordered him not to wear a disguise nor to penetrate the American lines, but a change in Arnold's arrangements led to André's going ashore. While there, the vessel to which he expected to return was shot at and made to drop down stream, André being thus forced to attempt to make his return by land. With a pass signed by Arnold, he managed to fool an American sentry, but the following morning he was held up by four volunteers who had posted themselves near Tarry-town to prevent farmers from driving cattle toward New York for sale to the British. Their suspicions having been aroused, they forced André to undress in the bushes and discovered incriminating documents in his stockings. Turned over to the American military authorities, the fate of the young Englishman was sealed, and on October 2, 1780, he was hanged as a spy at Tappan. Although his doom provoked much sympathy even among his enemies, there was no question of his guilt, and he himself met his end with great fortitude, regretting only that he could not be shot instead of being hung like a criminal. Arnold escaped to the British and lived long and unhappily, despised by them and Americans alike. Apparently he was paid between £6000 and £7000 for his unsuccessful treachery.

There had been more or less fighting along the western frontier from the beginning of the war, the British from Detroit and other interior posts stirring up the Indians against us. We ourselves had used Indians against the French but their employment by the English aroused much resentment, and in 1778 Lieutenant-Colonel George Rogers Clark moved westward from Virginia and in a brilliant campaign, with less than 200 men under him, captured Cahokia and Vincennes. The territory north of the Ohio thus passed into American hands with the exception of Detroit, and the western, like the northern, phase of the war was over. The final scenes were to be enacted in the South.

The British had always believed the Loyalist element to be particularly strong there, and at the end of 1778 captured Savannah and overran Georgia, re-establishing the royal government. They next attacked South Carolina, the plan being to advance northward, conquering one colony after another. When this became evident, Washington despatched General Benjamin Lincoln to the new centre of operations. That officer was able to seize Charleston but failed in a joint attack with d'Estaing's fleet on Savannah, d'Estaing hurrying away from fear of the hurricane season.

The French fleet out of the way, Clinton sailed south with 7000 troops and recaptured Charleston, Lincoln having unwisely allowed himself to be shut up in that town instead of retreating. The surrender of that not very astute general with his entire force of 5000 was a serious blow, and left the South defenseless. Guerrilla leaders, such as Thomas Sumter, Francis Marion, and others, dealt swift and unexpected strokes against British forces but could make no great impression, and Clinton, believing South Carolina captured, returned to New York, leaving Lord Cornwallis and 5000 men to hold it.

Washington wisely wished to send a new army to the scene under General Greene, but was overruled by Congress, which sent its pet Gates instead. By August 14 Gates had reached a point about thirteen miles from Camden where Cornwallis lay with about 4000 men, of whom 800 were ill. Gates, almost incredibly, believed he himself had 7000, although he had in reality only a little over 3000 present and fit. On the night of the 15th both he and Cornwallis had each determined to make a surprise attack on the other, and at two o'clock on the morning of the 16th the armies came into contact, both getting a surprise.

The result was a complete disaster for the Americans. Gates's force, half of which was made up of raw militia, had been weakened by bad food the day before, and fled in a panic when attacked, throwing away their arms and fleeing in complete rout. De Kalb was killed and Gates himself did not stop his personal retreat until he had got 180 miles away, after having lost 2000 troops as against a loss of only 300 British. Washington now had his way, and Gates, who had become a laughing stock, was replaced by Greene, one of the ablest generals produced by the war. Before he reached the South, the British had received a severe check at King's Mountain from bands of North Carolina frontiersmen, who organized themselves under their own leaders.

Greene had at first only 2300 men when he reached that State and waited for reinforcements before entering upon a campaign against Cornwallis. In a minor action, however, a small part of his force under Daniel Morgan won a brilliant victory over the British Lieutenant-Colonel Tarleton at Cowpens, January 17, 1781. After Morgan rejoined Greene the combined forces amounted to about 5000 men, of whom less than 500 had ever been in action. Cornwallis had only 2250 but all were veterans. The American militia, although excellent for certain sorts of fighting, had nearly always proved weak in regular battle, and Cornwallis did not hesitate to attack the larger force at Guilford Court House on March 15.

Although he claimed the victory, his losses, nearly a third of his entire force, were so great that he immediately retreated to Wilmington where he might get in touch with a British fleet. Greene, in a masterly campaign, now operated against minor British bodies and cleared the Carolinas to near the coast. Meanwhile Cornwallis had marched northward to join Arnold with his 5000 troops in Virginia, where they had been harrying the country. Although the British pursued the American forces operating in that State under Lafayette, and even made their way as far as Charlottesville, nothing was gained, and in August Cornwallis made his base at Yorktown, which he fortified.

The end of the fighting in America was now approaching. Cornwallis had 7000 men of whom over 5000 had been sent from New York, cooped up behind his fortifications on the bank of the York River, an arm of Chesapeake Bay. Lafayette was watching him with 3500. Washington was waiting to strike at New York with an army of 7000 of whom 5000 were French and only 2000 Americans. Suddenly word came that the French Admiral de Grasse would be at the mouth of the Chesapeake about September 1 with a fleet and 3000 more French troops. Washington at once decided to make Cornwallis's army his objective, and marched rapidly southward across New Jersey.

It had been clear for some time that the great struggle between England and her foes would turn on sea power. The Americans had had a small navy and about 2000 privateers at sea, but although these inflicted much damage to commerce and in such fights as those between the *Bon Homme Richard* under Captain John Paul Jones and the English frigate *Serapis* brought glory to American sailors, they were in no way decisive of the final result. Jones was one of the most picturesque figures which emerged from the Revolution and although he was a properly commissioned officer of the American navy, having been made captain on May 9, 1777, the English persisted in regarding him as a mere privateersman and even a pirate.

On the two cruises in British waters which he made

first in the *Ranger* and later in the *Bon Homme Richard*
he affronted the pride of our enemy by daring to appear
and fight in waters which they considered peculiarly
their own. The romantic story of his having landed a
party at the mouth of the Dee to seize the Earl of Selkirk
as a hostage and having failed in this, due to the Earl's
absence, of his returning $500 worth of silver plate
which he found his men had carried off, appealed to
Americans, as did his capture of such ships superior to
his own as the *Drake* and the *Serapis*. The British, however, did not relish having him appear off Dublin, cruise
in their home waters, threaten to burn Leith in reprisal
for British burnings in America, and the other exploits
in which he indulged. Perhaps no other American was
so hated by them, and his name was a bogy with which
to frighten children. After the war, he took service with
Catherine of Russia, and added to the romance of his
life somewhat at the expense of his reputation.

If the doings of Jones were more romantic than influential, the French navy was an important factor in
the later struggle, and Cornwallis was lost unless the sea
could be kept clear between him and Clinton at New
York. A fleet under Admiral Graves had been sent to
the Chesapeake for that purpose by Rodney, but de
Grasse proved more energetic than d'Estaing, and having reached the Chesapeake first, at once sailed out to
give battle when Graves appeared. The English were
badly defeated and had to run for New York, leaving

Cornwallis helpless on his peninsula. Steadily the siege went on, the French and Americans almost equally divided in numbers, pressing their works closer day by day.

CORNWALLIS SURRENDERS

Finally, on October 19, 1781, Cornwallis surrendered his entire force, although a week before he had had word that Clinton was preparing to relieve him with Graves's fleet and 7000 more men. His case, though extremely serious, did not appear to be absolutely desperate, and it has remained a question whether he was justified or not in his sudden decision. In England, when Lord North was given the news, he threw up his arms and exclaimed, "It is all over."

Throughout the war, Washington had been most anxious to recapture New York, and when, as a result of his masterly combination with the French fleet, he had disposed of Cornwallis and his 7000 men, he urged de Grasse to combine with him for an attack on New York. The admiral, however, wished to return the French troops he had borrowed from Hayti as quickly as possible, and declined. Clinton thus remained unmolested for two more years while Washington was forced to remain inactive, but on guard.

Although the fighting in America was over, it continued elsewhere and by the end of 1781 England had lost all her West Indian possessions except Antigua,

Barbadoes, and Jamaica. The next year the Spaniards captured Minorca and were besieging Gibraltar. Ireland was in rebellion, and in India Sir Eyre Coote was struggling, successfully, against the Sultan of Mysore. The British fleet was much outnumbered by its combined opponents but in April, 1782, Rodney inflicted a severe defeat upon de Grasse. A powerful body of opinion in England, however, had long been opposed to the continuance of the war. It was realized that America was in any case lost to the empire, and nothing was to be gained by keeping up an aimless struggle against France, Spain, and Holland.

The North Ministry resigned in March, 1782, and under the new one, which included the Marquis of Rockingham, Fox, and Lord Shelburne, negotiations for peace were opened with the representatives we had had in Paris for that purpose, Franklin, John Adams, and John Jay. Franklin had been representing American interests in France since 1776. He had already spent sixteen years in England before the war, and without losing a whit of his racy Americanism, he knew Europe as did no other American of his day. Shrewd, humorous, a genuine child of the eighteenth-century philosophy, serene, imperturbable, realistic, infinitely curious, accepting life as it came in experience, one of the notable scientific investigators of his day, tolerant and mellow, unaffected, full of common sense, knowing how to make the best of every situation and of his peculiar qualities and characteristics, always Benjamin Franklin, whether carrying a loaf of bread under his arm in the streets of Philadelphia, talking with kings or being adored by French society, he had become the rage in Paris and done much to make the French idealize the life and character of his own new nation.

Both Adams and Jay we shall meet again, and it is unnecessary to follow in detail the negotiations of the three commissioners. The Treaty of Alliance with France had provided that neither nation should make a separate peace, but wisely the Americans did not trust the French minister Vergennes who, happily for us, having used the American war for his own purposes, had no wish to see the United States made any more powerful as an independent republic than he could help. In addition he was sympathetic toward the desires of Spain to strengthen herself in the New World, and had some thought of a possible future French empire in the Mississippi Valley.

In fact, although later the wily minister pretended to be offended because the Americans negotiated with the English more or less independently of him, he had wished that they might do so in order to have a free hand for himself to play off conflicting claims after the Treaty of Alliance had lapsed by the attainment of its American object, with the acknowledgment of our independence by England. Without the French we could not have won our independence, as Washington and other leaders admitted on various occasions. The men, money, and supplies that they sent direct to America and the weight of their power and Spain's were all necessary to us. A few distinguished individuals, like Lafayette, were genuinely on our side, as was a part of the French people. Without minimizing in the least the importance of the French aid or the generosity of individual Frenchmen, it is nevertheless unwise to wax sentimental over the Treaty of Alliance. The French are, and always have been, an extremely realistic race, and there was nothing sentimental on their side about the Treaty. Our revolt gave them the long desired opportunity to wipe off scores with England and they seized it. It was solely with self-interest in view and without the slightest desire to aid us in establishing a republic that the Bourbon government of France before its Revolution made its treaty with us.

Our negotiators, therefore, made their own peace with England, keeping strictly, however, to the terms of the Treaty with France by providing that the Peace Treaty with England should not become effective until peace had also been made by that country with our ally. In the preliminary treaty with England our complete independence was acknowledged and it was provided that our boundary line should run approximately up the St. Croix River, thence along the forty-fifth parallel to the St. Lawrence, passing from there along the middle of streams and lakes to the Lake of Woods, down the Mississippi to the thirty-first parallel, along that to the Chattahoochee River, down that to its confluence with the Flint, and so east to the Atlantic Ocean again.

Although Florida, the whole Gulf coast, and all west of the Mississippi remained in the possession of Spain, the Americans were given right of free navigation along the river. Thanks to John Adams's determination we also, against much British opposition, secured our accustomed right of fisheries on the Newfoundland and Canadian coasts. It was further agreed on our side that no impediment would be placed in the way of the just collection of debts owed by Americans to English, and that Congress should recommend to the several States repeal of the laws against Loyalists. These agreements were reached by the end of November, 1782, but it was not until nearly a year later, September 3, 1783, when a general peace was signed by all parties to the war, that the Anglo-American treaty also became operative.

Meanwhile the American army had been disbanded some months earlier but not without threat of a serious *coup d'etat*. As we shall see in the next chapter, the finances of the Confederation were in utter confusion. The army had long been unpaid, and both men and officers feared that if they went separately to their homes they would never receive their pay. There had also been much talk about a new government for the independent States and the advantages of a monarchy. In March, 1783, a paper was circulated among the officers at Newburg suggesting that they meet to consult as to the future and suggesting that they, unpaid, should not be the chief sufferers by the war. Hearing of this dangerous move, Washington issued an order against secret meetings and called a public one for the 15th. Gates, who had been one

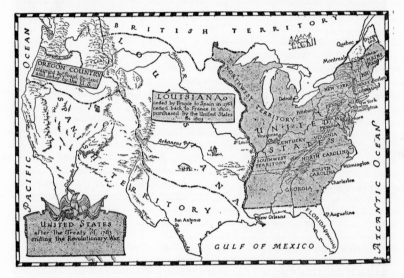

of the plotters, was asked to preside at this as senior officer and had taken the chair when to that officer's surprise Washington himself appeared.

The Commander-in-Chief advanced to the platform and began reading from a prepared address. After a few words, he paused, drew his spectacles from his pocket, and said that after growing gray in his country's service he now found himself growing blind. Continuing, he explained the difficulties of Congress, urged that on their honor the officers would express their detestation of any one who would destroy their country's liberty, promised that he would do his best to see justice done to them, and left the room. Immediately the officers passed resolutions of loyalty and denounced the secret circular. Congress voted full pay for five years, and with great difficulty gathered together enough for actual pay for three months, and soon after the proclamation of April 19, 1783, declaring the war at an end, the army was peaceably disbanded.

It would have been easy, with a devoted army at his back, for Washington to make himself dictator or even, possibly, as many wished, a king. Instead he kept a mere remnant of his troops until New York was at last evacuated by the British in November, on the 25th of which month he took his last leave of his officers in Fraunces' Tavern, and travelled to Annapolis to surrender his commission to Congress. Throughout the war he had declined all pay for his services, and returned to his beloved Mount Vernon with only the blessing of his country and the hope expressed by the President of Congress that God might give him that "reward which this world cannot give."

A century later one of the greatest historians of that English nation which Washington had fought was to write of him that "it was only as the weary fight went on that the colonists learned little by little the greatness of their leader, his clear judgment, his heroic endurance, his silence under difficulties, his calmness in the hour of danger or defeat, the patience with which he waited, the quickness and hardness with which he struck, the lofty and serene sense of duty that never swerved from its task through resentment or jealousy, that never through war or peace felt the touch of a meaner ambition, that knew no aim save that of guarding the freedom of his fellow countrymen, and no personal longing save that of returning to his own fireside when their freedom was secured. It was almost unconsciously that men learned to cling to Washington with a trust and faith such as few other men have won, and to regard him with a reverence which still hushes us in presence of his memory." To-day, his statue stands in the heart of London, the very centre of the British Empire, a gift graciously accepted by the British people from their oldest colony, Virginia.

CHAPTER VII

THE FEDERAL UNION FORMED

THE end of the war brought relief and rejoicing to the colonies. The eight years precisely, from the 19th of April, 1775, when the first really warlike engagement between Americans and the British had occurred at Lexington, to the 19th of April, 1783, when the formal announcement was made that the war was ended and independence won, had been years of suffering, anxiety, and turmoil. There had been so much passion spent over "slavery" and "liberty," that, liberty gained, the world seemed to open in endless vistas of prosperity and happiness. Nevertheless, although there was much truth in the belief that the American colonies when united as an independent nation had a future which would have been denied to them as outlying provinces of an European empire, the prospects of an immediate leap into the millennium were to be rudely shattered by actual conditions.

It has been claimed by some historians that America was prosperous in the last year or two of the war. It is true that after 1778 there was increasing importation of foreign goods and even luxuries. It is also true that, as compared with most wars of equal importance, the actual destruction of American property had been slight. Over ninety per cent of the population was engaged in agriculture, and even within the zones of actual military operations there had been little damage done to farm property. It has even been said that the great bulk of the population went on with their farming undisturbed by the fact of war. Such statements, however, do not appraise fairly the vast dislocation that occurred in the economic life of the people, and the false basis for even such prosperity as existed.

There was bred, of course, as in all wars, a class of new rich, of men who had been shrewd enough to take advantage of conditions for their private benefit, who had profited by army contracts, or had been lucky in speculation or privateering. The respectable firm of Otis & Andrews in Boston, for example, were charging the government 100 per cent profit, and at one time the United States owed them nearly £200,000 lawful money. Such families as the Derbys in Salem and the Cabots in Beverley grew rich from privateering. Sudden profits called for unwonted luxuries.

On the other hand, many firms were ruined. To a large extent the God of Chance had ruled. The loss of a ship or two to the enemy might cripple a merchant of standing whereas a capture of one or two enemy vessels might make some upstart rich. One of the most marked changes in Boston at the end of the war was the great alteration in the personnel of its "leading" citizens. If in that town after 1778 there was much dissipation and extravagance there was also much pinching poverty and economizing. What was true of Massachusetts was largely so also of the other colonies.

Apart from the influence of war on various occupations, such as the disastrous effect on the fisheries or the substitution of speculative privateering for the old substantial merchandise shipping, the factor that counted most in disturbing economic life was the colossal depreciation in the paper money, and the corresponding advance in prices.

Because of their fear of taxation, the colonies refused to grant to Congress any power to raise money by that means, and as they failed miserably in making voluntary grants to the central government, that body had to carry on the war by the simple but disastrous method of turning out paper money on the printing press. Over $240,-000,000 was thus issued by Congress and an equally large sum by the several colonies. The steady increase of the amounts outstanding, and the decreasing prospect of its ever being reduced as promised, naturally led to its decline in value as measured in coin or goods.

Over and over, the United States pledged its "sacred honor" that the bills would be redeemed at their face value. They were forced on the people at times regardless of depreciation. General Putnam issued an army order that any civilians declining to take the paper money at its face value in exchange for goods should be imprisoned and suffer forfeiture of their merchandise. The Council of Safety of Pennsylvania added banishment as the punishment. Yet the paper fell steadily until, like the German mark after the World War, it became practically worthless, and the Congress which had so often pledged our honor to its redemption finally redeemed it in new paper at one in forty after it had fallen to one in a hundred and twenty for coin.

THE RISE IN PRICES

The reverse of this movement was a fantastic rise in the prices of merchandise, farm produce, and all other goods, and in wages, though as usual wages did not rise in proportion to the cost of living. As we know well from our recent experiences, any such great readjustment in prices has very unequal effects on different classes and even individuals in a community. The rapid rise in prices gives the effect of a feverish prosperity, while many persons suffer and the whole community is on an unsound basis.

After a time, it became almost impossible to trade in terms of money, and barter was widely resorted to. The relations between debtors and creditors became impossible. If a man borrowed money or held up payment for purchases, all he had to do was to wait with the assurance that he could pay his debts for a half, a quarter or less than when he had contracted them. Creditors of all sorts, shop keepers with open accounts, lenders of money, mortgagees, persons whose property was held in trust, were often ruined. Even Washington refused to have his agent accept payments in the paper, declaring that although he would gladly sacrifice his entire estate in a common cause he would not consent to be ruined in such a dishonorable way while others were prospering. Bitterly did he complain that "idleness, dissipation, and extravagance," "speculation, peculation, and an insatiable thirst for riches seem to have got the better of every other consideration, and almost of every order of men."

Farmers who were getting high prices seemed on the one hand to themselves to be getting rich, yet on the other, their labor supply was greatly interfered with, and when the men were at the front it sometimes was almost impossible, even with the help of the women, to raise the crops. Moreover, the farmers paid equally high prices for such articles as they had to buy, and it must be recalled that the great mass of farmers did not raise their crops for sale but for their own consumption, so that they gained little or nothing on the high farm prices and lost on high merchandise ones, being at the same time under the psychological influence of the general extravagance engendered by the overturn of all the old standards of living.

Many States, wholly unsuccessfully of course, tried to fix prices by law, as had been done, so Pelatiah Webster said, from the beginning of the world, though such efforts never had had more effect than "sprinkling water on a blacksmith's forge." When the Continental money was at last funded in 1790 at the rate of one cent in the dollar, the wake of ruin that it left covered the whole country, a ruin of spiritual quite as much as of material values. The $200,000,000 of paper money issued by the several colonies had also heavily depreciated and in addition most of them had accumulated debts to an extent that could not be liquidated by ordinary taxation.

It is, I think, as unhistorical to speak of America as prosperous at the end of the war as of a man with nervous excitability and a high fever as being well. John Adams described the situation better when he said that the war was "immoderately gainful to some, and ruinous to others." The letters of his wife describing the hardships on their farm due to high prices and lack of labor give a very different picture from the account books of the privateering Derbys and Cabots, or the inventories of shops catering to the new rich or the foolishly extravagant.

There was, however, prosperity for certain classes, and with the return of peace all hoped to share in it. Rather naïvely, we expected the trade of the world to be open to us. We had hoped to negotiate with England a treaty of commerce as well as of peace, but England had declined. We had forced her to acknowledge our complete independence, and in her view we were, as in truth was the case, a foreign country. By our rebellion we had not only deprived her of the most important part of her empire but had become the ally of her immemorial enemy,

223

France. She saw no reason for giving us special privileges in her imperial trade, though Lord Shelburne and others had a wider vision and would have tried to unite the two nations closely in sentiment and commerce. Unhappily, narrower views, such as those advocated by Lord Shef-field in his *Observations of the Commerce of the American States,* were to prevail. In the war, England had found herself almost alone in a hostile world, with her fleet heavily outclassed, and she now determined to make no concessions which might build up American shipping at the expense of her own.

DIFFICULTIES FOR OUR COMMERCE

In 1783, by Orders in Council, she excluded our vessels absolutely from Canada and the West Indies, thus putting us on the same footing as any other nation, and she did the same when she allowed our vessels in her own ports precisely the same privileges as those of any European power. On the other hand she did admit free of duty all our raw materials, to be carried direct from America to England in either our vessels or her own, on the old basis of colonial days. This concession was an important one, but our exclusion from the West Indies played havoc with our old triangular trade routes. We were not, it should be noted, excluded from trading with the islands but from doing so in our own vessels. The owners of these were forced to hunt for new sources of trading and were rather unjustly irritated against the

British, who may have been narrow-minded but were certainly within their rights. Their policy, from the point of view of statesmanship, was unwise for the long run, but on the other hand we were rather illogical in demanding at once independence and those old special privileges in her trade which we had enjoyed as part of the empire.

France also reduced the privileges she had accorded us as allies in the war. In 1783 she excluded our vessels from her West Indies and although the following year she opened some of her ports there to us for certain articles, they had to be carried only in small vessels which were required to ply directly between the islands and our own ports. In so far as our triangular trade was concerned, therefore, she interfered with our shipping as much as England did. To a great extent, however, these foreign Orders in Council became dead letters and by 1785 we had begun to trade with the British West Indies much as we had been accustomed to do.

The Dutch and Danish islands had always been open to us, and Spain opened the ports of Santiago and Havana in Cuba. Our commerce returned to normal, and the economic life of the new States was also on a sounder basis from the rapid increase which had perforce taken place in manufacture during the non-importation periods and the war. Manufactories of firearms, iron works, textile mills, and other industries had been started and prospered, and these reduced to some extent the necessity of such imports, helped our trade balance, and gave greater variety to our occupations. There was a severe depression, as we shall note, in 1785, as usually happens two or three years after the close of a great war. Then there was increasing prosperity until our first national panic came in 1791.

OUR NEW FRONTIER

If our commerce gradually fell into the old grooves again, there had been one immense change wrought by the war, more momentous than any other save the fact of independence itself. That was the opening of what was then "the West." The old Proclamation Line of 1763 which the British had hoped would keep us from too rapid expansion and Indian complications had vanished. Even before the war its uselessness had become partially manifest. It could cause irritation but it could not prevent all emigration any more than the imaginary line of the equator affects the waves that flow across it. In 1769 pioneers had founded a small settlement on the Watauga in Tennessee, and the picturesque Daniel Boone had been several times across the mountains when, with a group of settlers, he built a fort and established Boonesboro in 1775. The following year Kentucky was made a county of Virginia, and gradually both Kentucky and Tennessee saw the pouring in of what may be considered our first great western movement, hordes of settlers tramping over the mountains through

Cumberland Gap and other passes from Pennsylvania, Virginia, and the Carolinas.

The boundaries and claims of the old colonies were vague, and the words "over the mountains" had deep significance. Restless, discontented, poor, and ambitious spirits had always been moving from older to new settlements further out, from the earliest days of colonization. There had been, as we have seen, jealousies and grievances on the part of new settlements against old. But this new frontier, "over the mountains," was isolated from the Eastern States as none of the old "frontiers" had been. The old frontiers had been merely rougher and rougher fringes of settlement on the advancing edges of a society that was based on the seaboard.

The new frontier over the mountains, by the enormous difficulties of transport, no longer looked to the eastward ocean ports but westward to the Mississippi. As the pioneers came through the passes or gaps in the mountains, the magnificent valley of the Father of Waters, 2000 miles wide, lay before them. Here was a vast new empire to be conquered, the outlet of which was not by way of Boston, New York, Philadelphia, or Charleston, but by way of the great river, Spanish New Orleans, and the Gulf. The interminable forests, infested with savages, covered "the dark and bloody ground" of Kentucky and stretched away to where Spanish America lay across the river, or down to the swamps and bayous of Louisiana.

The pioneers who had crossed the mountains before the war had been but the vanguard of the masses to follow. By 1790 there were probably about 150,000 people living in the land that looked westward. There had been land companies formed and men like Richard Henderson, one of the greatest of our land speculators, had tried to build new States. But for the most part the movement was one of individuals and families, who governed and defended themselves. In one year, 1788, over 18,000 men, women, and children went down the Ohio on rafts, and perhaps an equal number tramped over the southern passes. Various State organizations were proposed,—Transylvania, Westsylvania, Franklin, —but these came to nought in the uncertainty as to ownership under the conflicting claims of the older Eastern States derived from their colonial charters.

These claims on the part of some States also made for jealousy among the others, and Maryland, fearing Virginia's enormous western domain, refused to sign the Articles of Confederation in 1777, aimed at a closer and more effective union, unless the States with western claims should cede them to the Confederation for the common good. In 1780 and 1781, New York, Connecticut, Massachusetts, and, in part, Virginia consented to do so, so that when the Treaty of Peace was signed, it was the *United* States and not the *several* ones that became the sovereign of the West north of the Ohio. The new States later to be created there thus had a national origin and never looked to colonial charters as the basis of their liberties. The southern section of the West also passed to the Federal Government a few years later.

LAND CLAIMS OF THE THIRTEEN STATES

The West was to be national in another sense. The immigrants who so rapidly poured into it came from all the colonies, and commingled as did none of the populations "back East." A Connecticut Yankee and a South

Carolinian clearing the forest in adjoining patches felt themselves closely united as Americans and Westerners, and the old provincial jealousies of the East were largely sloughed off. On the other hand, the mountain barrier and the geographical unity of the great valley and river tended toward a new sectionalism, and the Westerners came to feel a corresponding unity in their interests as contrasted or even conflicting with those of both Northern and Southern sections in the East.

In part, the conflict of interests was to arise from the failure of both Americans and British to carry out the terms of the Treaty of Peace. America had fought through most of the war with scarcely anything that could be called a central government. Although a Confederation had been urged in 1776 it was not until May, 1779, that the States could agree upon its terms, and owing to the western land problem, Maryland did not join until 1781, so that it was not until March 1 of that year, scarcely more than six months before Yorktown, that Congress had authority as the representative body of the Confederated States.

The form of government then inaugurated was both clumsy and weak. There was no executive, the President of Congress being merely the presiding officer elected by that body, which itself sat as a single chamber. The Congress itself had no power of taxation, of regulating commerce, or of enforcing its measures on the several States. The acts it was allowed to perform, such as declaring peace and war, making treaties, sending and receiving ambassadors, determining boundary disputes, regulating Indian affairs and coinage, had to be agreed to by the representatives of nine States, each of the thirteen having a single vote. No amendments could be made to the Articles except by the unanimous consent of all.

When it came to carrying into effect terms of a Treaty which might be unpalatable to any State or its citizens, such a government was quite evidently helpless. In the Treaty with England there were two unpopular clauses, those relating to the Loyalists and to the payment of private debts to English merchants. Congress, as the Treaty demanded, did recommend to the States that they should restore confiscated Loyalist property and refrain from any further confiscations, but there being no means of coercion, the States to a considerable extent failed to take action. The Loyalists were heartily hated, and although much of their property had been unjustly seized, practically none was restored. This gave the British Government the chance to claim that the Treaty was being violated, though it is doubtful if the clause in it relating to Tories had been considered by the English Peace Commissioners as more than a gesture.

A much more legitimate grievance on the part of England was the disregard of the clear promise in the Treaty that no impediment would be placed in the way of the collection of just private debts by English creditors. This clause was unquestionably violated by some of our States, with Virginia in the lead. Nearly twenty years later, after endless litigation and negotiation, we admitted that we had been in the wrong, and the United States Government paid £600,000 to England as a compromise sum to settle the adjudicated debts.

However, in the years immediately following the peace in 1783, it was only too clear to foreign governments, and to our own ambassadors abroad, such as John Adams in London, that the so-called government of the United States under the Confederation was merely a rope of sand ostensibly binding together thirteen semi-independent small nations which did as they pleased and which, internationally, were wholly irresponsible.

Moreover, although the Confederation was to be brilliantly successful in inaugurating a national land policy, it failed, as the old colonies had, in an Indian policy, and proved itself powerless to prevent conflict between the lawless settlement by hordes of immigrants and the legitimate rights of the savages to their hunting grounds. By the Treaty we had come into possession of that immense territory north of the Ohio River which came to be known as the "Old Northwest," and in which, at the end of the war, there were practically no white inhabitants except Canadian fur traders, and a few French farmers about Detroit and the other military posts where, since 1763, there had been English garrisons for maintaining peace with the Indians.

All these posts were on the American side of the new boundary line. The very valuable fur trade was the only apparent asset in North America which England had saved from the war, and the Canadians, much chagrined to find where the boundary had been placed by the British negotiators in Paris, urged the government not to give up the posts, at least until they could get their merchandise out and reorganize the trade. Not to hold them, they pointed out, would be the ruin of Canada. The British Government, therefore, made no haste to recall their troops from American soil, and soon the obvious weakness of the Confederation, and the failure on our part to live up to the clauses in the Treaty about Loyalists and debts, gave the British an excuse for declining to carry out the clause about the evacuation of the posts until we had observed our part of the agreement.

Moreover, it began to look as though the United States might break up, and if it did, it was evidently to British interest to have grappling hooks on the great Northwest. We shall later notice events in the East which made even Washington fear that anarchy was coming, and consider here only the West. We need merely note that Vermont, which did not join the Union until 1791, was still intriguing with the British as an independent power. In the West, the British chance of detaching the new settlements from the Confederation was even brighter.

The interests of the new communities were, as we have pointed out, largely distinct from those of the East. The settlers rightly considered their future possibilities of development as boundless, but the barrier which separated them from the seaboard is shown clearly enough by the fact that it was easier to ship produce from the Ohio River to Philadelphia by way of New Orleans than it was direct by the few hundred miles of rough and rocky road which straggled over the mountains. Moreover, the East cared little or nothing about the new West. In fact, many conservatives on the seaboard intensely feared its growth, with the threat of radicalism and eventual shift in the balance of political power. In 1786 John Jay even proposed to Spain that we consent to the closing of the Mississippi for twenty-five years in exchange for new privileges in her ports in Europe. The West properly felt that its vital concerns were not safe in a government controlled by Easterners.

Both Spain and England realized the loose nature of the bonds which united the two sections of the new nation, and played for time until the West might become independent or fall into their several hands. Thus, while England retained military posts which should have been evacuated in the North, Spain likewise encroached on our territory from the south, maintaining garrisons at Natchez and elsewhere, and opening the river to the western traffic as a grace and not as a Treaty right. Many leading Westerners were in Spanish pay and were intriguing to secede from the United States with the thought, however, of founding an empire of their own which might come to include a good part of Spain's American possessions. The whole section was covered by a tangled net-work of intrigue in which no one trusted any one else, not even those in their own pay.

If conservative Easterners feared the West, they also had an ample supply of anxieties in the East itself. We have seen how as the Revolution advanced, control had fallen more and more to the radicals. The catch-words of the movement,—the talk about tyranny and slavery, the slogans about "no taxation without representation," the declaration that "all men are created equal," that "governments derive their just powers from the consent of the governed,"—had all, combined with the constant mobbing, the tarring and featherings, the Tory confiscations, and other war-time commotions, given a tremendous impetus to what were considered radical ideas, and the demands of the common man.

CONFLICT BETWEEN CONSERVATIVES AND RADICALS

The conflict between conservative and radical was well displayed in the drafting of the new State constitutions, some of which proved over-conservative, as in South Carolina, and others over-democratic and radical as in Pennsylvania. In the former, the large planters of the seaboard strongly entrenched themselves in control. The new constitution perpetuated the old under-representation of the western counties, and established a fifty-acre freehold as qualification for the suffrage, an estate of £2000 for election to the Senate, and £10,000 for election to the Council or Governorship. Pennsylvania went to the other extreme. All qualifications for the suffrage were abolished except payment of a State tax, thus giving the western counties control of the State, and there was no governor and no Upper House, in this new super-simplified democracy.

Although the new State constitutions thus varied greatly, in general there was a broadening of the suffrage and a democratizing of the fundamental laws in all of them. In Virginia, within a few years, primogeniture, entails, and the slave trade were abolished, and in Jefferson's Statute of Religious Liberty a complete separation was established between Church and State. What few relics remained of feudalism, such as quit-rents, were everywhere swept away. The strong feeling against anything resembling an aristocracy or class distinctions was evidenced in the violent opposition to giving the officers of the army half pay for life, and in the absurd alarm raised by their forming an association, the Cincinnati, to perpetuate the friendships and memories of their service. On the other hand, few or none in the upper classes had any confidence in the ability or honesty of the lower in political matters, and in a few years their worst anticipations seemed on the verge of fulfillment.

In Massachusetts, in spite of the wild talk of the radicals, such as Sam Adams, in the twenty years of controversy and war, the governing class had always insisted,
as far as possible, upon a narrow suffrage and the right
of the "wise, the rich, and the good," or in John Adams's
phrase the "well born" to rule. In the new constitution
adopted in 1780, the property qualification for the franchise had been doubled just when Vermont was abolish-
ing every restriction and New Hampshire was giving the
vote to every male over twenty-one who paid a poll tax.
Now that the war was won, "no taxation without representation" was considered radical doctrine, and the propertied classes were looking about for safety from the
possible attacks of the non-propertied ones. By 1786,
forty per cent of the entire taxation of the State was
being raised, with scandalous inequity, from the poll
tax alone.

Meanwhile, the feverish and unhealthy prosperity of
the end of the war had come to an end everywhere in
the colonies. The fictitious war-time prices for farm produce collapsed. The new manufacturing enterprises suffered from British competition. The currency was in
confusion. Enormous purchases had been made of British
goods, which it was impossible to find exchange to pay
for. The shoe was suddenly put on the other foot, and
the debtor class now found itself in unexpected difficulties. As ever under such conditions there was a strong
demand for "cheap," or paper money. The general crisis

was most clearly marked in Massachusetts, where the incoherent policy of the legislature did much to precipitate it.

The whole of the State appears to have been in trouble. In Groton every third or fourth man between 1784 and 1786 suffered from one to a dozen suits for debt, and in Worcester County there were 4000 suits in one year in a total population of 50,000. Farms could not be sold for enough to satisfy the owner's creditors. In 1785 the legislature laid no taxes; then the next year levied them so heavily that they could not be borne. In June the town meeting of Groton chose a "Committee of Correspondence" as in revolutionary days, and conventions were held in many counties to consider the grievances of the people.

A "reform" legislature, when elected, did nothing. Then open rebellion broke out under the lead of Captain Daniel Shays, who had had a good record in the war, and others of standing in their several communities, although the mass of revolters were farmers, mechanics, and laborers, numbering, it was reported, in the western part of the State one fifth of the population. Among other grievances, the various conventions reported that the rebels objected to the mode of taxation and of paying the State debt; the method of representation; the existence of the State Senate; lawyers and their high fees; and the lack of a circulating medium.

Nothing was done to remedy the real abuses and even

Sam Adams joined the reactionaries in Boston in denouncing the right of the people to voice their grievances! The court calendars were overflowing with suits
for debt which meant ejectment of the owners from their
farms or shops, and failing to obtain justice, the next
step of the "rebels" was to close the courts. This was
done by armed crowds in the autumn of 1786, at Northampton, Great Barrington, Worcester, Concord, and
elsewhere. Sam Adams, of all men, began to denounce
the mobs, and at a mass meeting in Faneuil Hall refused
to consider the demands of the people, claiming, with his
old fixed idea, that the trouble was caused by British
emissaries. Without touching the real troubles, the legislature temporarily suspended the sitting of the courts.

At Mount Vernon, Washington was deeply troubled
at the growing anarchy, but his advice to investigate the
grievances, and if they proved real to remedy them,
and if unreal, to put down the movement by force, was
not acted upon. The beginning of the next year the situation was worse. Convinced that neither the legislature
nor the "wise and good" would make any move to remedy the distress, the insurgents grew more violent, and
at last the legislature put a force under General Lincoln
in the field against them. Within a few weeks, "Shays's
rebellion," as it is called, was crushed, the leaders captured or fled, and, having had a thorough scare, the legislature at last took some action on the people's complaints.

Watching events in Massachusetts, multitudes besides

Washington had been profoundly alarmed for the foundations of society. Economic conditions were bad everywhere, and the grievances of the poor not limited to the Bay State. The rebels had shown how easily the old revolutionary machinery of committees and conventions could be initiated again, not against England, but against the newly established and unstable State governments. It was realized as never before that the central government of the Confederation was helpless and powerless. Our weakness in dealing with trade, commerce, and foreign nations had long been evident, but now that we had glimpsed alarming social revolution at home, the tide turned toward the possibility of a better union and a stronger government, there even being talk of a monarchy. Daniel Shays was in truth one of the chief fathers and begetters of our Federal Constitution.

There had already been many suggestions of the possibilities of strengthening the Confederation, but nothing had been attempted. Any action toward that end, in view of the attitude of the people and the jealousies of the States, had hitherto been outside the range of practical politics. These jealousies had been particularly manifested in the tariffs which the various States placed on the importation of foreign goods and even on goods imported from one State into another; and in questions arising between colonies as to navigation in waters, like New York Harbor and Chesapeake Bay, on which two or more States might border.

THE CONSTITUTIONAL CONVENTION

A dispute of the latter sort between Maryland and Virginia had been of long standing when, in 1786, Virginia, extending the range of the negotiations, suggested to all the States that they send delegates to a convention to be held at Annapolis to consider their relations to the trade of the United States. The meeting, held in September, was attended by delegates from only five States, but although there was little interest in it, the opportunity was seized by the more far-sighted among those, such as Washington, Alexander Hamilton, and James Madison, who were anxious for a stronger government. At Annapolis, Hamilton took the lead, and secured the passage of a resolution suggesting the holding of a convention, to be authorized by Congress and approved by the States, for the purpose of improving the form of government. Virginia at once endorsed the plan and chose delegates to the proposed convention. Other States followed her lead, and Congress forwarded an invitation to all of them to send delegates to the convention to be held in Philadelphia on May 14, 1787.

When the convention assembled in Independence Hall in that city as appointed, all the States were represented except Rhode Island, which had opposed the suggestion, and Vermont, which had not yet joined the Union. The fifty-five delegates formed as notable a gathering as had the first Continental Congress, but there were many changes to be observed. The more extreme radicals of the early days of the Revolution were now absent. Neither Sam Adams nor Christopher Gadsden had been chosen by their States to attend. Patrick Henry had been included in Virginia's delegation, but had declined to serve. John Adams was in England as our first minister to that country, and Jefferson was in France.

The work of the first Congress had been essentially destructive, that of the convention was to be constructive; and the temper of the members was essentially conservative. Their duty was not to sever political old ties but to find some instrument of government to preserve new ones. Much the ablest delegation was that from Virginia, consisting of Washington, James Madison, John Blair, George Wythe, George Mason, and Governor Edmund Randolph. Rufus King, then only twenty-two years old, although the youngest of the Massachusetts delegation, was the most important member on it. Connecticut sent excellent men in Roger Sherman, William S. Johnson (recently elected president of Columbia College in New York), and Oliver Ellsworth, while New York's leading delegate was Alexander Hamilton, just thirty but already possessing a national reputation. Among the seven from Pennsylvania were James Wilson, Robert Morris, Gouverneur Morris, and the aged Benjamin Franklin. The other more important

Northerners were John Dickinson from Delaware, William Paterson of New Jersey, and Luther Martin from Maryland, while South Carolina's delegation included two able representatives in John Rutledge and Charles Cotesworth Pinckney.

In running over the list of the total membership, one is struck happily with the evident calming down of the old passions of the war. Among the delegates, for example, there were Jared Ingersoll, who, as Stamp Distributor, had been subjected to personal violence by the Sons of Liberty; Dickinson, who had declined to sign the Declaration of Independence when in Congress; and Johnson who had been so lukewarm in the war as to have become unpopular. It is also interesting to note that of the fifty-five men who were to frame our Constitution, nine, or exactly one sixth of the total, were foreign born.

When the convention organized, Washington was made chairman, and although he took no part in the debates his influence throughout was great, quite aside from the occasional votes he cast. His influence was, indeed, notable from the very outset. The convention met in the same room in which, in 1776, the Continental Congress had voted the Declaration of Independence, and which had already become clothed with historic memories. The first meeting was informal, noticeable among the members being Madison, shy, small, and slender; Hamilton, also short but handsome, young, and distinguished in appearance; old Benjamin Franklin, with the benign face of the philosopher who had bewitched the ladies of the French Court; Washington, tall and dignified, receiving the natural deference of all the other members; the Scotch-born Wilson, and Rutledge, and the two Pinckneys from South Carolina.

There was some preliminary discussion of what sort of constitution would be acceptable to the people, and many voiced the fear that only half measures would win popular approval in view of the jealousies of the States, and the many opposing opinions on almost all points of the public at large. With unusual seriousness, Washington broke incisively into the discussion. In words which the politicians of today would do well to remember and act upon, he expressed his own independent view. Few speeches so brief have carried so much weight. "It is too probable," he said, "that no plan we propose will be adopted. Perhaps another dreadful conflict is to be sustained. If, to please the people, we offer what we ourselves disapprove, how can we afterward defend our work? Let us raise a standard to which the wise and the honest can repair; the event is in the hand of God." Although subsequent compromises had to be made, the temper of the meeting at once rose from the plane of politics to that of statesmanship.

The greatest difficulty which had to be overcome was the old jealousy of the States for one another and their pretensions to complete sovereignty individually. How to reconcile the sovereignty of the several States with the creation of a general government which should have genuine power would have been an almost insuperable problem to solve even had the States been all of the same size and power, but to this was added the fact that they differed greatly, and that the small ones feared placing themselves under control of the larger ones. The combined populations of Rhode Island, Delaware, New Jersey, and New Hampshire, for example, were only 453,000, which was but slightly larger than that of Pennsylvania alone, less than Massachusetts, and only somewhat more than half that of Virginia with its 747,000.

The latter State on May 29 submitted what came to be known as the Virginia Plan, and in introducing it Governor Randolph frankly said that it was intended to create not a "federal government" but a "strong *consolidated* union." It separated the executive, legislative, and judicial branches, and provided for a Congress of two Houses, the lower elected by the people of the several States, and the upper of persons nominated by the State legislatures, both in proportion to population or State tax quotas.

The Virginia Plan thus gave control to the larger States and around this point debate raged for a fortnight until Paterson of New Jersey introduced the "New Jersey Plan," which provided for equal representation in a one-chamber Congress by every State instead of resting it on the basis of population. Paterson's suggested Federal Government was in some ways an improvement over the old Confederation, especially in that it made the Acts of Congress and treaties negotiated by it the supreme law of the land and gave that body at least the theoretical right to coerce a State which did not pay its requisitions for taxes.

The chief difficulty, however, and the one which threatened to ruin the work of the convention, was that mentioned of how to provide for a fair balance of power in Congress between the big and little States. For weeks the wrangling went on, and as the weather became hot in July so did the tempers of the delegates. Franklin suggested praying to God for help and Hamilton is reported to have answered curtly that they needed no "foreign aid." It was not until the 16th that what is known as the "great compromise" of our Constitution was finally adopted, providing that representation in the lower branch of Congress should be according to free population plus three fifths of the slaves, and each State should have equal representation in the Upper House or Senate. There were several stages in reaching this fundamental compromise, and in connection with the slave apportionment neither South nor North was wholly satisfied.

Although the debates over representation had evolved from State jealousies, larger sectional cleavages also appeared. The East as a whole feared the West, and the possible development of large population and political power there. North and South split not only over the slavery question but also, as the former was becoming commercial and industrial and the latter was agricultural, over giving to the Federal Government the power to regulate commerce. This particular point was agreed to only after the South believed it had protected itself by the clause which prohibited Congress from passing any law placing an export duty on our produce. As a result of compromise after compromise, the Constitution gradually took form, and on September 17 it was signed by those present. According to the terms on which it had been drawn, however, before it could go in operation, the approval of at least nine of the States would have to be obtained.

THE CONSTITUTION

The new compact was an immense improvement over the old Confederation. An executive was provided for in the person of a President, who was to be elected for four years by electors specially chosen by each State as its legislature might direct, the number of electors of any State being equal to the total number of senators and representatives it sent to Congress. These electors were to meet in their own State and the person who received the greatest number of their votes in all the States was to be President, and the one receiving the next highest number to be Vice-President, provided that in each case the person voted for received a majority.

247

If two tied for the highest number of majority votes, the election for President went to the House of Representatives, where, for this purpose, each State should have only one vote, and in case of a tie for Vice-President, the election went to the Senate. If no one received a majority of all the votes in the Electoral College, the House of Representatives should choose a President from among those having the highest five votes. These provisions were altered later by the Twelfth Amendment, adopted in 1804, which was to provide that the President and Vice-President should be voted for separately by the electors, and if no one received a majority for President, then the choice should be made by the House of Representatives from among the highest three receiving the greatest number of electoral votes.

The President was made Commander-in-Chief of the Army and Navy; given the right to demand the advice of the heads of all departments of the government; the power to veto Acts of Congress, unless repassed by a two-thirds vote; the power "by and with the advice and consent of the Senate" to make treaties, provided two thirds of the senators concurred; to appoint ambassadors, judges of the Supreme Court and all other officers of the government, also with the advice and consent of the Senate; was required to give Congress information as to the state of the Union; to see that all the laws were executed; and the right to convene Congress in extraordinary session, and to adjourn it when he thought proper if there were a disagreement between the two Houses. He could be impeached and removed from office for treason, bribery or "other high crimes and misdemeanors."

The legislature was to consist of two Houses, the Senate and House of Representatives, the former to be composed of two senators elected by the legislature of each State for a term of six years, each senator having one vote. The Vice-President of the United States was to be President of the Senate until, on account of death, resignation or inability to perform his duties on the part of the President, he might succeed the latter in office.

The House of Representatives, in which all money bills had to be initiated, was to be composed of members chosen every second year directly by the people, the electors in each State having the same qualifications for voting as were required for electing the members of the lower House in the legislature of such State. The number of representatives was not to exceed one for every 30,000 inhabitants (excluding Indians and counting three fifths of the slaves), and although the Constitution did not require that a representative should be a resident of his particular district the growing habit of localism in American representation, which we noted earlier, received sanction in the requirement that he must be a resident of the State from which he was returned.

Numerous and varied powers were conferred upon the new legislature. It could lay and collect both direct and indirect taxes, provided these were uniform throughout the nation; it could borrow money on the nation's credit; regulate both foreign and interstate commerce; establish uniform laws as to naturalization and bankruptcy; coin money, regulate currency, and regulate weights and measures; establish post offices and post roads; provide for patents and copyrights; constitute courts inferior to the Supreme Court; declare war, raise and support an army and navy; call out the militia to execute the Federal laws, suppress insurrections and repel invasions; exercise complete jurisdiction over a tract ten miles square to be chosen as the location for the national Capital; dispose of or govern all territory belonging to the United States; admit new States to the Union; and make all laws necessary for carrying its powers into effect.

Certain things it was forbidden to do. It could not suspend the privilege of the writ of Habeas Corpus except in cases of rebellion or invasion when the public safety might demand it. It could not pass any bill of attainder or *ex post facto* law; could lay no direct tax except on the basis of population according to the census; could give no commercial preference to the ports of one State over those of another, nor oblige any vessel to enter, clear or pay duties in passing from one to another; nor could it grant any title of nobility. It was to guarantee a republican form of government to every State.

The judicial department of the central government

was to be vested in a Supreme Court, and such inferior courts as Congress might create. It was provided that the power of the Federal judiciary should "extend to all cases in law and equity arising under this Constitution, the laws of the United States, and treaties made, or which shall be made, under their authority;—to all cases affecting ambassadors, other public ministers or consuls;—to all cases of admiralty and maritime jurisdiction;—to controversies to which the United States shall be a party; —to controversies between two or more States;—between a State and citizens of another State;—between citizens of different States;—between citizens of the same State claiming lands under grants of different States, or the citizens thereof, and foreign States, citizens or subjects." This creation of a Federal judiciary with such wide jurisdiction and powers was, perhaps, the most daring of the moves made toward a strong nationalism in the Constitution, and from it was to arise the process of judicial review by the Supreme Court over the Acts of Congress itself.

Passing from the organization of the central government to the States, we may note that, on the one hand, each State was required to give full faith and credit to the public acts, records and judicial decisions of every other; that the citizens of each were to be entitled to all the privileges and immunities of those in all the others; and that a criminal fleeing from one to another was to be given up to the jurisdiction of the first, and that a person "held to service or labor" (such as slaves) under the laws of one State and escaping to another should be returned to his owner. On the other hand, no State was to be permitted to make any foreign treaty or alliance; to coin money or emit bills of credit; to make anything but gold and silver legal tender; to pass any *ex post facto* laws, bills of attainder, laws impairing the obligation of contracts, or to confer titles of nobility; nor in general to lay any duties on imports or exports.

At the end of the Constitution were added the provisions for amending it which are still in force.

Such was the extraordinary document to which the delegates appended their signatures in September, 1787. Many had contributed their ideas to it and worked for final harmony, but unquestionably the master spirit had been James Madison, who combined great constitutional knowledge with a firm grasp upon the actualities of the situation. It was in the latter point particularly that Hamilton, whose great work was to be done later, was lacking, and during the later sittings he was not even present. Next to Madison, it was either Wilson or possibly Washington who had the greatest influence in bringing about the final result, which was at once forwarded to the Congress of the old Confederation in New York. By that body it was transmitted to the several States so that it could be everywhere submitted to conventions for ratification or rejection, the latter appearing all too likely.

Meanwhile, the old Congress had itself been engaged in momentous legislation, ending what was to prove its final session with one of the most statesmanlike measures which have ever been enacted. The members had been struggling with the problem of the western lands for many years, and in 1785 had passed an ordinance providing for a survey and the division of the territory into townships six miles square, made up of sections of 640 acres each, one section in each being reserved for a school fund and four for the Federal Government.

Believing that the land should be made a source of revenue, it was arranged that it should be sold at not less than one dollar an acre. This had proved too costly for most pioneers, but speculators, such as those forming the Ohio Company, had purchased tracts as large as 1,500,-000 acres, the price for such wholesale transactions being reduced by the government, and the companies had undertaken to plant settlers. Rapid development, however, called for administration, and in July, 1787, while the Federal Convention was sweltering in Philadelphia over a new organic law for the nation, the old Congress was also drafting one for the Northwest Territory.

This "Ordinance of 1787," passed in New York on the 13th, organized the Northwest into a district to be administered by a governor and judges appointed by Congress, but provided that when it should have 5000 free male inhabitants over twenty years of age, they could elect a legislature of their own, and send a delegate, without vote, to Congress. The territorial government thus provided for followed somewhat closely the old colonial governments as devised by England. It was to have a popularly elected assembly as the lower House of the legislature, but the governor was to be appointed by Congress, which body also made selection of the councillors, or members of the upper House, from names submitted by the lower.

The whole territory was eventually to be cut into not less than three or more than five States, which were severally to be admitted to the Union, when any one had a population of 60,000, "on an equal footing with the original States in all respects whatever," except that slavery was forever forbidden. The way was thus wisely opened for an expansion of our people westward with no permanent loss of political rights. There was to be no colonial status or subordination, and the easy transition from wilderness through territorial government to full Statehood was made possible by the old Confederation, which had otherwise been growing weaker and less competent each year.

The plan was not one which would work well for an empire scattered in all parts of the world and made up of diverse races. Close geographical contiguity, indeed, seems essential for its success, since it has not proved satisfactory even in Alaska, but it solved our continental problem extremely well as we moved westward until the original States became forty-eight and their citizens had come to share the benefits and responsibilities of the Federal Government from the Atlantic to the Pacific.

The wisdom of the measure has deserved all the praise bestowed upon it, but it is only fair to point out as we have suggested, that it was not a general solution of the "colonial problem." So long as any portion of our national domain has remained in a territorial or dependent status, as Alaska, Hawaii, the Philippines, Porto Rico, and other portions yet do, we have found ourselves forced to govern much as England did in the eighteenth century. We have declined, as England did, to accord complete self-government, have appointed officials, legislated for and even taxed the inhabitants without their consent, and done many if not most of the things for which we so heavily blamed England. The fact is that the colonial problem, like that of racial or other minorities, has not yet found a theoretically perfect solution at the hands of any government, our own no more than others. As in many situations in life when seemingly legitimate interests of different groups conflict, the best that can be hoped for is a moderately satisfactory working compromise.

THE CONSTITUTION IS RATIFIED: WASHINGTON IS CHOSEN PRESIDENT

When the suggested framework for a new Federal Government was offered to the people of the old thirteen States in 1787, by the Constitutional Convention, it was far from certain that they would accept it. Throughout the country, newspapers and pamphlets voiced the opposing views of those who were soon called "Federalists" and "Anti-Federalists," according as they approved or disliked the suggested plan of union. There was much appeal to prejudice but on the whole the debate was carried on upon a high and serious plane. From 1763 the people had been arguing constitutional problems, and perhaps no other nation was ever so well prepared to consider so important a question. The preparation had been so long and thorough that it is certainly questionable whether we would be as competent today to consider such a matter as our ancestors were in 1787. Then as now, however, many did not care to bend their minds to serious discussion, and for such there were innumerable squibs published in which the question was brought down to the level of their mental laziness or incapacity.

The lack of a Bill of Rights was one of the most influential arguments against the Constitution on all sides, and one of the more humorous pamphlets complained, its author thought only in jest, that we were not guaranteed the right to drink. Washington and the other delegates, sipping their port and Madeira, could hardly have foreseen the need for that. The best controversial articles in the whole discussion were those written by the New Yorkers Hamilton and Jay and the Virginian Madison, which were published together in the volume called *The Federalist,* which has become an American classic. That none of these were New Englanders is but another evidence of the loss of that section's former intellectual predominance.

When we study the proposed form of government and contrast it with the niggardly grant of power to the old Confederation, recalling the jealousies of the States and their long training in opposition to authority from outside as hitherto represented by King and Parliament, it appears remarkable that there was any chance of ratification. Some of the small States ratified promptly, Delaware December 7, New Jersey December 17, 1787, Georgia January 2, and Connecticut on the 9th, 1788. Meanwhile there was a great struggle going on in some of the most important ones.

In Pennsylvania the majority of the people were probably opposed to the suggested Constitution, but those in favor of it rushed a call for a convention through the assembly before their opponents had time to organize, and ratification was announced December 12, 1787. In the convention in Massachusetts the Anti-Federalists were in a majority, and ratification, after much anxiety, was attained only by a sharp political deal with John Hancock, the presiding officer, who was inveigled into thinking he might be the first Vice-President if the new government were formed, and by gaining over other delegates by appropriate means. Sam Adams, provincially minded as ever, was also opposed, but in February the Massachusetts convention by a very narrow margin voted for ratification provided that certain amendments might be offered to the other States for adoption.

Just as the revolutionary Adams opposed the Constitution in Massachusetts, so did Patrick Henry in Virginia, and the contest in that most important State of all was prolonged and bitter. He who in Stamp Act days had proclaimed that there should be no Virginians or New Yorkers, but only Americans, now declaimed as violently against the preamble of the Constitution because it began, "We, the people of the United States" instead of "We, the States." Like many, he feared a "consolidated" government, and the loss of State's rights. Not only Henry but much abler men, such as Mason, Benjamin Harrison, Monroe, and R. H. Lee, were also opposed and debated with Madison, John Marshall, Wythe, and others in what was the most acute discussion of the question carried on anywhere.

As in all the colonies, the richer tidewater section was on the whole overwhelmingly in favor of a strong government. Shays's Rebellion was still fresh in mind, and the proposed Constitution protected property. In Virginia, however, the far western section, looking to problems of interstate trade and the enforcement of the Treaty with England, was also, for different reasons, in favor of ratification. Won in Massachusetts by only 19 votes out of 355, approval was won in Virginia, even with the west in favor, by only 10 votes in 168, June 25, 1788. In New York the opposition between the small, rich group on the coast and the interior farmers had no make-weight as in Virginia, and New York City had to threaten to secede and enter the Union without the rest of the State before a favorable vote could be secured, and then by only 3 votes in 57.

By that time all the other States, except North Carolina and Rhode Island, had ratified, and there remained no question as to the establishment of the new government. The last of the Southern States came in on November 21, 1789, and of the Northern May 29, 1790. Owing to the way in which the conventions were held, the great opposition manifested everywhere, and the management required to secure the barest of majorities for ratification, it seems impossible to avoid the conclusion that the greater part of the people were opposed to the Constitution.

It was not submitted to the people directly, and in those days of generally limited suffrage, even those who voted for delegates to the State conventions were mostly of the propertied class, although the amount of property called for may have been slight. No one can question that, had the Constitution not been ratified, the old Confederation would have broken down, and the States become a quarrelling lot of small independent sovereignties. Had the America of 1787 been a pure democracy based on manhood suffrage, such a breakdown would seem to have been inevitable.

Nevertheless, the sharp corner had been turned. It

was announced by the old Congress that the new form of government had been ratified, and the States proceeded to the choice of electors. The unanimous vote of these in all States was for Washington as President, and, by a lesser number of votes, John Adams was chosen Vice-President. New York was picked for the temporary capital, and the government was to be started on March 4, 1789. Whether "we, the people of the United States" had really wished it or not, all acquiesced, and the most momentous step since the Declaration of Independence had been taken in peace.

CHAPTER VIII

THE NEW NATION GETS UNDER WAY

IT was with genuine regret that Washington felt obliged once more to obey the call to his country's service. The eight years of war had placed a terrific strain upon him, and although only fifty-seven he spoke of himself as already "in the evening of life." He loved, as a large planter, to manage his beautiful estate over-looking one of the most peaceful and lovely stretches of the Potomac, and might well feel that he had done his duty and that the task of statesmanship might now be taken up by others. Throughout the war his thoughts had ever turned to his beloved "Mount Vernon," and his one ambition, second only to that of serving his country, had been to return thither and take up again the life of country gentleman, interested in all which had to do with his farms and the affairs of the neighborhood. He had, indeed, become a world figure, and so many guests were to claim his hospitality that he at times, somewhat regretfully, spoke of his home as "an inn," but it was around that home that his affections centred. Unallured by the glamour of high office or the glare of publicity, he would have infinitely preferred to remain the Virginia planter than to accept the election to the Presidency.

WASHINGTON IS INAUGURATED

He was, however, indispensable as the head of the new and untried government, the establishment of which had been opposed by probably a majority of the citizens. No one else commanded the universal trust and reverence which he did in 1789, and as always in a crisis the people turned instinctively to a strong leader. Others, however able, were sectional. Washington alone held the confidence of the entire nation, and him only would the people follow in the dangerous work of establishing a government that would be honeycombed with local jealousies, and which might be saved only by belief in the even-minded justice of the man at its head. Wearily, and prompted only by a compelling sense of duty, Washington started on his journey to New York.

The whole trip was one long ovation. Cannon roared salutes, children sang by the roadsides, bridges were festooned with flowers, there were banquets at every halting place. The roads were still bad, and the members of the new government assembled but slowly in New York. Instead of March 4, the inauguration could not take place until April 30, on which day Washington, standing on the balcony in front of Federal Hall at the corner of Broad and Wall Streets, took the oath of office in full sight of the crowds.

The procession which had accompanied him from his house in Cherry Street, along what is now Pearl Street, to Broad, and thus up to the yet unfinished Hall where the Sub-Treasury now stands, had passed along the

THE TRIUMPHAL ARCH WHICH GREETED WASHINGTON ON HIS ENTRY
INTO TRENTON ON APRIL 21, 1789
*From "The Columbian Magazine" of May, 1789, in the Historical
Society of Pennsylvania.*

narrow winding streets, lined with sight-seers, offering a strong contrast to the inaugural parades of today. The crowd which watched the Chancellor of New York administer the oath to him on the balcony was full of the color of the gay clothes of men as well as women. Artisans were there in their yellow buckskin breeches, checked shirts, and red flannel jackets; while the richer gentlemen were notable in their three-cornered cocked hats, heavy with lace, their bright-colored long coats, with lace at the cuffs, their striped stockings, short breeches, and silver-buckled shoes. Unlike the artisans, their long hair was tied in a cue and heavily powdered. Their ladies were gorgeous in brocades and taffetas, high hats with tall feathers rising from them, and their skirts puffed out nearly a couple of feet on either side. As Washington took the oath, shouts rose from the crowd of "Long live George Washington, President of the United States," while the guns of the Battery roared their salute. The brief ceremony over, the new President retired to the Senate Chamber to deliver his first inaugural address.

There were at that time no political parties. At the beginning of the war, people had divided into Whigs and Tories, or Patriots and Loyalists, but the result of the struggle had left only the Whigs. During the discussion and ratification of the new Constitution there had been Federalists and Anti-Federalists, but the adoption of that instrument seemed to end the reason for the existence of the latter. Nevertheless, there was an ample supply of groups and of cleavages from which parties might in time arise. There were the frontier and old sections; the rich and the poor; the agricultural and the commercial classes; the men whose property was in land and those who owned securities; those who believed in a strong central government and those who stood for the fullest possible sovereignty of the component States;

those who believed the Constitution should be interpreted as strictly as might be and those who wished to give its clauses the widest possible interpretation. But on the 30th of April, 1789, there were no party organizations nor, as yet, clearly defined parties. Washington thus had a clear field from which to make his appointments, and he also believed that the Presidency should not be a partisan office.

If there were no parties, there was also at first scarcely any government. Everything had to be organized. During its first session Congress passed the Judiciary Act, which gave form to the Supreme Court; approved sixteen amendments to the Constitution, ten of which, after being accepted by the States, were declared operative in 1791; and, in addition to much other legislation, created the four departments of State, Treasury, War, and Justice. War seemed remote, our international relations were slight, but our fiscal problems were pressing, so that the most important post was easily that of Secretary of the Treasury. Washington appointed to it Alexander Hamilton of New York, making Jefferson Secretary of State, General Knox, of Massachusetts, Secretary of War, and Edmund Randolph, of Virginia, Attorney-General. Two of these, Hamilton and Jefferson, were not only so important in their own day but their ideas and policies have continued so to dominate American thought that we must consider them in some detail.

HAMILTON AND JEFFERSON

Hamilton, at that time thirty-two years of age, was the illegitimate son of a Scotch planter and a French woman of the Island of Nevis, his mother being unable under the laws of that day to secure a divorce in order to legalize her union with Hamilton's father. He had come to New York for his education, and as a youngster had eagerly espoused the cause of the Revolution. Handsome and brilliant, he had secured a place on Washington's staff and although his career as a soldier was not distinguished in the field, he had won the affection and respect of the Commander who employed him as aide and had led one of the storming parties at Yorktown. Less than a year before that episode he had married the daughter of General Philip Schuyler, and so had become allied to one of the most powerful families, socially and politically, in New York, where, at the end of the war, he became one of the leading lawyers.

New York political life was notoriously sordid, and the cleavage between the rich families who endeavored to rule and the general mass of the people, of whom a larger proportion were city dwellers than in any other State, made politics more "aristocratic" than anywhere else except perhaps South Carolina. Hamilton, who had reached America as a poor boy, with a blot on his birth, and who by his own abilities had risen to high position and become a member of the ruling caste, became, as often happens in such cases, more of an "aristocrat" than the "aristocrats" themselves, if that were possible, in his views as to government.

Those views of Hamilton are of great importance, for he is one of the half dozen or so of men who have most conspicuously moulded not only the nation of his own day but that of our own. His fundamental thesis was that most men are not good and wise but vicious and not to be trusted. Government cannot rely upon their good qualities but must depend upon careful manipulation of their passions. Each class, he believed, had its faults, but those of the rich were less likely to prove inimical to prosperity and sound government than those of the poor. The latter might sometimes mean well but they could not reason rightly as to how to secure good ends. He denied totally that the voice of the people was the voice of God. This, he said, was opposed to the real facts, which were that "the people are turbulent and changing; they seldom judge right or determine right." The people constantly needed to be checked.

For these reasons, he believed in the necessity of a strong central government, which should have power to control both the people and the States, which should be kept as far from democracy as possible, and which should derive its strength from the rich. Basing government on men's passions, he found the two most influential ones to be ambition and self-interest. Give men a large financial stake in the maintenance of a form of government, he thought, and they can be counted upon to support it. Ownership of government securities would be one such incentive. The larger the moneyed class would become, the more stable the government. The farmer, with no interests outside his own acres, or the town artisan, might easily be led to revolt. Not so the owner of government bonds, the manufacturer, the banker, and all those who in one way or another received special favors from government. A tariff, for example, would not only build up the moneyed class by developing manufactures but would also create a body of citizens dependent upon government for special privilege. A privilege of any sort binds a man closely to the conferrer of it.

Hamilton was not an orator and his style was diffuse, but his mind was brilliantly clear and his thought more impeccably logical than that of any other statesman we have had. Based upon propositions that seemed to him self-evident,—that democracy had always failed, that the people were incapable of self-government, that they must be governed, that for this a strong government was essential, that strength must be derived from those with heavy stakes of self-interest,—his system led straight, as it has ever since, to the final use of special privileges as the strongest ties between the individual and government or party.

Jefferson's views were the antitheses of these. Born in 1743, in the Blue Ridge section of Virginia, he had been brought up among the best and soundest of the frontier yeomanry of that State. Married at twenty-seven to a beautiful and rich young widow, he built Monticello on its hill top near Charlottesville, and no one can visit that delightful estate without realizing that, whatever his political views might be, its owner was, in the best sense, an aristocrat to his finger tips.

Jefferson, however, unlike his New York opponent, had a deep and abiding faith in the ability to govern himself inherent in the common man, or, rather, the common man as Jefferson then found him in the America of his day. Jefferson knew London and Paris and some of the other cities of Europe. He had no faith in the common man when living under such crowded and unsatisfactory conditions, "steeped in the vices" which such situations bred. If we also should come to have manufacturing, great, crowded cities, and to approximate to European social and economic conditions, our electorate, Jefferson believed, would also become corrupt and incapable of self-government. But American conditions, he considered entirely different, and so long as we could keep the simplicity of our life, the door of opportunity wide for every man to own his own home, and the chance to make a comfortable living in a wholesome way, he believed the American common men could safely be trusted to govern themselves and others. Looking westward, he thought he saw sufficient free land for the maintenance of such conditions for a thousand years ahead.

269

This then was Jefferson's major premise,—belief in
the common man. From it he deduced his views on
government. He wished as little of it as possible. Later,
in his first inaugural as President he was to define what
he considered "the sum of good government," as "a
wise and frugal government that shall restrain men from
injuring one another, shall leave them otherwise free to
regulate their own pursuits of industry and improvement, and shall not take from the mouth of labor the
bread it has earned." He feared the power of wealth,
the change from agriculture to manufactures, the creation of a strong central government. He would keep all
matters of government, even the selection of those who
should administer justice, as close to the people as
possible.

Hamilton thought from the Federal Government
downward; Jefferson from the parish or county upward.
Jefferson was for free trade and no special privileges for
any one, and although we may call him an idealist as
contrasted with the realist Hamilton, there is no question but what he incarnated the dream that we Americans have always dreamed as Hamilton did not. Hamilton's mind, more powerful and coherently logical than
Jefferson's, might have worked out its syllogisms and
system of government as readily in any historic period
and any Old World country as in the America of 1789.
Jefferson voiced the peculiar hope and aspiration of the
people of that time and place as he had done in the

Declaration of Independence. For Hamilton that document was war-time propaganda; for Jefferson it was still a living faith. Today we pay lip homage to Jefferson but time and men's daily passions and desires have been on the side of the realist Hamilton who believed in the innate corruptibility of all of us.

The America of today, with its prohibitive tariffs, its special privileges, with its constant demand for more and more gifts and interference from "government," has developed from the Hamiltonian formulæ. We must not get too far ahead of our story, and have taken a glance forward merely to indicate the lasting nature of the conflict which was to arise in Washington's Cabinet, and the magnitude of the two men who were to lead the parties soon to be formed. Beside the two giants, Hamilton and Jefferson, the other two officials, Knox and Randolph, assume mere antiquarian interest.

Congress had had many things to attend to before organizing the Departments. The new government had got going more or less piecemeal, for although Washington was not inaugurated until April 30 enough members of the House had arrived by April 1 to permit of organizing that body, and the Senate was able to do so on the 6th. As the old Continental Congress had expired on March 4, the nation was without a Federal government of any sort for more than a month, but as soon as the new one had been started it set itself to the most immediately pressing task of all, that of providing money.

James Madison at once proposed a tariff, which he wished to have for revenue only, and the discordant interests of sections and occupations were quickly disclosed.

New England wanted a low rate on molasses and a high rate on the rum they made from it. Pennsylvania wanted its rum free and a duty on steel, which it had begun to manufacture. New England and South Carolina wanted no duty on steel, which would increase the cost to them of ship-building and of agricultural implements. South Carolina asked a duty on hemp which was opposed by Pennsylvania and New England because it would increase the cost of rigging ships.

So it went. The process, with which we have since become so familiar, of "log-rolling," that is of each congressman voting for a duty not wanted in his district if a vote could thereby be obtained for a duty that was wanted, began within the very first week of the national government. It was made evident at once that a tariff, even for revenue only, would be involved in sectional and class interests, and was bound to be regarded in the light of protection and special privilege, and to bring about bargaining and lobbying.

OUR NATIONAL FINANCES

It was only later in the year that Congress could organize the Departments, and Washington could appoint the Secretaries and create his Cabinet. Hamilton,

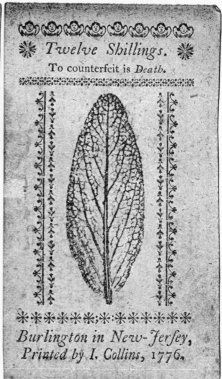

OBVERSE (TURNED) AND REVERSE OF TWELVE–SHILLING NOTE OF THE
COLONY OF NEW JERSEY, MARCH 25, 1776
From the collection of George R. D. Schieffelin.

PAPER MONEY ISSUED BY CONGRESS IN 1779
From the American Numismatic Society Collection.

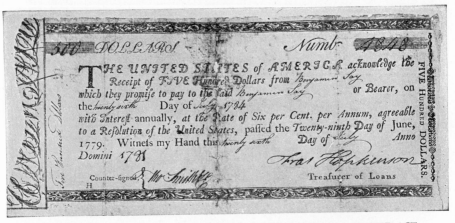

A PENNSYLVANIA LOAN OFFICE CERTIFICATE REDEEMED BY THE ACT
OF AUGUST 4, 1790

According to the records of the Pennsylvania Loan Office now filed in the Treasury Department, the original of the certificate, issued in favor of Benjamin Say, remains outstanding.

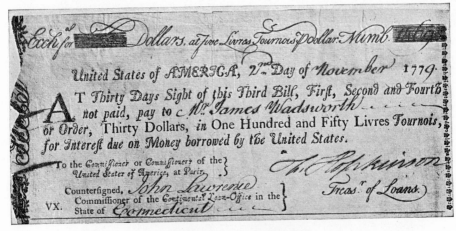

A THIRD BILL OF EXCHANGE

Issued by the Connecticut Loan Office under authority of an Act of Continental Congress of September 9, 1777, in payment of interest due on Loan Office Certificates representing money borrowed by the United States at Paris from funds advanced by the French Government. The bills were issued in sets of four, and the first one of any set to be paid automatically voided the rest.

From the Chase Bank Collection of Moneys of the World.

who took office on the 2nd of September, 1789, was at once asked by Congress to report a plan for the support of the public credit, and set to work. Jefferson did not take his desk at the State Department until the following March, so slowly as a whole did the government get under way.

By January, 1790, Hamilton was able to report to Congress and it was at once evident that this young Secretary of the new Treasury could rival any Finance Minister of the Old World in the daring and scope of his proposals. Our foreign debt was about $11,710,000 including the unpaid interest; the domestic debt about $42,400,000; and the debts of the individual States about $25,000,000. Hamilton proposed to pay the first in full, to fund the second in new bonds, dollar for dollar without any consideration of their depreciated value or the price they were selling at, and to have the Federal Government assume the full payment of the State debts.

No objections were made to the meeting of our foreign obligations but the other two suggestions aroused a storm of protest. We had repudiated the old Continental currency almost entirely, and the Loan Certificates for the debt had fallen to below twenty per cent in 1786 and were quoted at only forty per cent in 1789. They had been sold and resold and it was uncertain how many were in the hands of the original lenders to the government. When Hamilton's unexpected plan was made public, shrewd men sent agents on fast ships to the

South or on horseback through the country to buy up Certificates for as low as twenty which Hamilton was proposing to refund at one hundred. His suggeston was a wise and far-sighted one for the re-establishment of the fallen credit of the United States but to most it looked like a deal to allow speculators to feed at the public trough.

The assumption of the State debts was also bitterly opposed by some of the States. Massachusetts and South Carolina had the largest debts, and were well satisfied, but Virginia had paid off nearly all of hers and did not see why she should be now taxed again to help pay off those of less thrifty commonwealths. As usual, it came down to a question of self-interest on the part of each. The intrigue by which Virginia's opposition was overcome and enough votes secured to pass the measure has never been fully explained. Jefferson, apparently innocently, was mixed up in it. In any case, Virginia finally voted in favor of the assumption of the debts, and Congress voted to locate the new national capital, which had been a bone of contention, on the banks of the Potomac River. Although not quite in the way he had proposed them, all of the Secretary's measures eventually passed, and by the following summer U. S. Government six per cent bonds were selling at a premium in Europe, a notable triumph for the new nation.

Hamilton had to a great extent followed English precedent in his funding measures, and he wished to facili-

274

tate yet further the building up of the moneyed interests by the establishment of a bank similar to the Bank of England. In December, 1790, he offered a report on the subject, and, against much opposition, the bill creating the Bank of the United States was passed by both Houses, and sent to Washington for approval. So much criticism had been aroused, however, that the President hesitated, and asked for opinions as to the constitutionality of the measure.

The conflict between Jefferson and Hamilton now clearly emerged. The former claimed that according to the Tenth Amendment to the Constitution, "all powers not delegated to the United States by the Constitution, nor prohibited by it to the States, are reserved to the States respectively or to the people," and that the power to charter a bank had not been expressly given to the Federal Government in any of its clauses.

On the other hand, Hamilton defended his position, claimed that the Federal Government was "sovereign," that the power to create corporations is an attribute of sovereignty, and that the clause authorizing Congress "to make all laws necessary and proper for carrying into execution the enumerated powers" would cover the case. In other words, he invoked the doctrine that there existed "implied" as well as "enumerated" powers.

Opinion will always differ as to the merits of the two sides of this controversy, which has run throughout our national history. There would seem to be no doubt, however, that Jefferson expressed the will of the people, and that, dubious as the ratification of the Constitution had been in any case, it could never have been brought about had the Hamiltonian doctrine of implied powers been put forward as the way in which the Constitution would be interpreted if adopted. Washington was convinced, nevertheless, and signed the bill.

In December, 1791, Hamilton went a step further and presented to Congress his celebrated Report on Manufactures. It contained practically every argument which has since been used in favor of a high protective tariff, and its author's purpose was clearly expressed. This was in part to protect "infant industries," but such infants have a way of never growing up in the opinion of their parents who inevitably continue to demand more and not less favors at the public expense the bigger and stronger their infants become. The copper, steel and certain other industries are assuredly far from being infants today, yet the demand for pap has also far from diminished. It is impossible to say what Hamilton would think of the development of his theory in practice, although an opinion may be ventured that he would not be greatly shocked, for he had, in fact, a political quite as much as an economic end in view in his tariff policy. That was chiefly to gain another large body of citizens who would be linked to the new government by the strongest ties of economic self-interest, but Hamilton was, as yet, a little ahead of his time.

The Secretary's vigorous handling of the national finances, and the rapid rise in the price of government stocks, had induced a period of wild speculation. There was as yet no organized stock market but people everywhere sold government scrip from hand to hand, and its enormous advance, with the attendant easy profits, soon led the speculation into other channels, notably land. Business in general had been getting better since about 1786 and this, with the speculation in national securities, probably helped greatly to float the new government safely, and recovery from the temporary crisis of 1791-2, our first panic under the Constitution, was rapid.

The differences between Hamilton and Jefferson, and the schools of thought they represented, were, however, becoming more marked as the Secretary of the Treasury rapidly pushed his policies. Hamilton, young, brilliant and successful, self-confident and conceited, took little pains to explain his views or to conciliate Jefferson and the opposition whose convictions were derived from quite different political bases. Jefferson, Madison, and many others felt that Hamilton was twisting the new government into a shape that had never been contemplated, and not only did they disagree with him on fundamental constitutional interpretation, but the sectionalism and class favoritism of his policies also repelled and alarmed them.

Both manufacturing and the ownership of liquid capital in government or other securities were for the most part concentrated in the northern seaboard communities. The South and the frontier West were agricultural, and began to dread the rapid rise of a powerful Northern moneyed interest which might control banks, manufacturing, tariffs, and the form of taxation. Moreover, although Hamilton was personally honest, he was surrounded by men who were not, and there was no lack of scandal in the advantages taken by congressmen to profit personally by advance knowledge. Hamilton himself took no pains to hide his belief in the necessity of corruption, and in the advantage of a monarchical form of government, though he admitted the impracticability of the latter in America. His cynical view of the art of governing may have been the correct one, and Jefferson's an impossible dream, but Jefferson did represent the hope and belief of the common man and many who were far above his level, and these began to see little difference between government as advocated by Hamilton and that of George the Third with his bought Parliamentary seats. Before the end of Washington's first administration the rift in his Cabinet had become dangerously wide.

During that period the work of the State Department was complicated but less spectacular and important than that of the Treasury. Our impotence at the end of the old Confederation was well known in Europe and we were treated with the contempt meted out to a tenth-rate nation. France, indeed, went so far as to give her consuls in the United States extra-territorial powers similar to those that foreign consuls have had in such countries as China and Siam, and the French Vice-Consul in Norfolk did not scruple to seize a ship captain, put him into irons, and was only at the last moment prevented from shipping him to France for trial.

Spain owned at this time not only Florida and the Gulf coast but practically all the country between the Mississippi and the Pacific, and when war was threatened between her and England over the right to trade in furs at Nootka Sound in Vancouver Island, we became alarmed at the possibility of this vast territory passing into British hands and finding ourselves hemmed in, not by the waning power of Spain but the rising one of the British Empire. The latter still held the northern posts in her military control, and Spain took advantage of the situation to occupy two more on our side of the Mississippi. The war cloud blew over but in the tangled negotiations and in our continuous efforts to secure from Spain the rights of navigation of the great river and of deposit at New Orleans, Jefferson had come to realize the full importance of the West.

New parties had not yet taken definite shape, but it was evident that Hamilton would lead the commercial and financial interests of the North, whereas Jefferson stood for the inchoate mass of men everywhere, though more particularly in the South and West, who objected to a too powerful central government, and to the rise of Hamilton's money power. The strongest group of anti-Hamiltonian men in the North, not only artisans and other city workers but the families who had always contended with those allied to the Schuylers and their crowd, was in New York. Jefferson's party, when it might be formed, would thus find itself in alliance with these.

In 1792, however, the situation had not crystallized, and both Jefferson and Hamilton urged Washington, much against his will, to run for another term. He was unanimously elected, and John Adams again became Vice-President, although the "Republicans," as those opposed to the Hamiltonian theory of the State were beginning to be called, tried to defeat Adams and elect George Clinton of New York in his place. Affairs in Europe were soon, as always, to have sharp repercussions on our side of the water, and in this case to bring about the sharp alignment of the developing political parties.

OUR TROUBLES WITH FRANCE AND ENGLAND

The French Revolution had broken out in 1789, and at first we all followed its course with enthusiasm. It was easy to get drunk on abstract liberty in the eighteenth century, and the French people seemed to be only following in our footsteps. Washington had been in office but a few weeks in his second term when news arrived that caused a revulsion of sentiment among a large part of the Americans. The increasing bloodshed and brutal violence of the French movement had culminated in cutting off the head of the King after the Declaration of a Republic, and France had declared war on England

THE CONTRAST

A cartoon comparing American and French liberty in 1789.
From C. C. Coffin's "Building the Nation," New York, 1882.

and Spain. Not content with putting her own house in order, she had, like modern Soviet Russia, called on the people everywhere to rise against their monarchs,—practically a declaration of war against every European state. These events killed the sympathy of many Americans, as did the news that the revolutionists had forced Lafayette to fly from Paris. There was, nevertheless, a large body of American opinion still in favor of the Revolution, an opinion shared by Jefferson.

The position of our government was extremely deli-

281

cate. Under the Treaty of Alliance we had guaranteed France possession of her West Indian Islands, which would undoubtedly soon be attacked, and had also, somewhat vaguely, agreed that in case France was involved in war we would not give shelter to privateers of other nations. England, believing we would attack her on the side of France, as perhaps most Americans in an outburst of emotion wished to do, began to impress seamen from our vessels and enlarged the list of contraband by declaring that all food stuffs destined for French ports could be seized. In the course of the war hundreds of our vessels, particularly those trading to the French West Indies, were destined to be captured, although the profits of the trade must have been great or the risks would not have been taken.

The immediate problem which faced Washington on receipt of the news in April, and the further notification that the Revolutionary government was despatching a French minister to us, was whether to enter the struggle or to remain neutral. Hamilton urged strongly that the Treaty of 1778 had been made with the government of the Bourbon monarchy, and that that monarchy having been overthrown, we were in no way bound to carry out the treaty provisions in favor of an entirely different government. This would seem to have been a reasonable interpretation, for assuredly no one today would feel obliged to carry out with the Russian Soviet government treaty obligations incurred with the old Czarist régime.

Washington, however, adopted Jefferson's view that the treaty was not dead but merely suspended, and on April 22, 1793, issued a Proclamation of neutrality. Three weeks later the French minister, Edmond Charles Genêt, arrived in Philadelphia by way of Charleston, South Carolina.

Genêt was the Frenchman at his worst. Vain, impractical, puffed to bursting with the presumed importance of France, ignorant of other nations, he at once entered upon the most absurd and fantastic career which any foreign diplomat has displayed for our amusement or annoyance. At Charleston he formed a Jacobin Club, fitted out a privateer, and from that city satiated his vanity to the full by receiving the plaudits of the partisans of France all the way up the coast.

The President and members of the government in Philadelphia, even Jefferson, realizing his character, treated him with cool civility. Genêt, however, attempted to use American ports as bases for attacks on British commerce, to organize an expedition in the West to attack Spain, and in general to act as though America were French soil and we had never declared our neutrality. Finding himself rebuffed by the government, he lost his head completely, if he ever had any, and tried to appeal directly to the people through letters to Congress as though the President and the Cabinet did not exist. In August, by a unanimous Cabinet vote, France was requested to recall him immediately, which was done.

The comic opera minister, however, who had no desire to return to Paris to lose his head literally and not metaphorically, married a daughter of Governor Clinton of New York, and settled down on the banks of the Hudson.

Meanwhile, we were also having trouble with England. Not only was that country seizing our ships, impressing our seamen, and in general disregarding the somewhat vague rights of neutrals which she had never recognized, but the question of the Northwest was also becoming acute. The first British minister to be accredited to us, George Hammond, was a painstaking but not very tactful youth of twenty-seven, who arrived at his American post in 1791. As we have noted, neither the British nor ourselves had fully carried out the terms of the Treaty of 1783, and the new minister started to thresh out the old straw, with new grievances. Jefferson turned on him with demands for the evacuation of the western posts and compensation for the slaves the British had carried away at the end of the Revolution.

The fact was that the British were anxious to use our own derelictions in carrying out the Treaty as an excuse for altering the boundary line on the North. There was talk of creating a great neutral Indian Territory embracing the lands north of the Ohio River, and Lieutenant-Governor Simcoe of Canada was intriguing with the Indians against us. The seat of the Canadian Government had actually been transferred to our own side of the boundary and additional posts had been established on American soil. Our West was restless, loosely attached to the United States, pinched between British and Spanish encroachments, and there were vaguely known but certain conspiracies being hatched up among its people.

The situation was becoming intolerable. John Adams's prediction in 1785 had come true. If we did not carry out the Treaty in every particular, England, he had said, would not either and would probably use the excuse to infringe it further. We had not carried it out but England was becoming the worse offender. It began to look as though she had no intention of ever giving up the posts and the Northwest to us, and her depredations on our commerce were serious. Jefferson, Madison, and the gradually forming Republican Party were for measures of retaliation of a commercial sort. On the other hand, in New England the important mercantile class which formed the backbone of the Federalist Party was against any such measure. Hamilton pointed out that our imports from Great Britain in 1792 had been over $15,250,000 and from France only a little over $2,000,000, and that three fourths of all our trade was with the former country.

During all the time that these war clouds had been gathering, there had been war within the Cabinet itself. Under a party system two such diverse statesmen as Hamilton and Jefferson could never have been expected to act together, for their differences, as we have said, were not merely of judgment on particular courses of action but of fundamental political philosophy. Hamilton, who regarded himself somewhat in the light of an English Prime Minister and not merely the ranking member of the President's Cabinet, interfered in all the other departments instead of confining himself to his own sphere of the Treasury. It must be admitted that with all his dazzling qualities, he had a taste for low intrigue, and he had for long been attacking Jefferson in the public press in articles which he signed with assumed names or initials. Washington did his best to bridge the widening breach between his highest two officials, but finally, December 31, 1793, Jefferson, who had long wished to do so, resigned his office and retired to Monticello.

Washington had frequently taken his advice as against Hamilton's but the latter Secretary was more and more attempting to force himself into all departments of the government, and to dictate the foreign as well as the fiscal policy. His services had been very great but he was beginning to make the mistake of thinking that his was the master-mind which must control the nation, a mistake that in a few years was to ruin his party and bring him to his own death.

The difficulties with England demanded settlement if war were to be avoided, and in April, 1794, the President appointed John Jay as Special Envoy to proceed to London and arrange all matters in dispute. The envoy was a man of high patriotism, unblemished character, and wide experience, but as the English Foreign Minister was advised in a confidential report on his psychology, "Mr. Jay's weak spot is Mr. Jay." Lord Grenville undoubtedly made the most of this weak spot. It is only fair, however, in considering the treaty made by Jay, execrated at the time and much criticized since, to admit that even if he allowed himself to be somewhat outplayed by his English opponent it was imperative that he make some treaty and not return empty-handed.

Jefferson's successor in the State Department, Edmund Randolph, did not count, and Hamilton was running that Department, as well as his own. He was at the height of his power, and he had explained to Washington that the very life of the United States depended on avoiding war with England. Moreover, he carelessly destroyed one of Jay's strongest weapons,—the possibility of the United States joining Sweden and Denmark in an Armed Neutrality,—by telling Hammond that such a move would be against our policy. It is true that England, for good and sufficient reasons, did not want war with us either, but whereas it might have been impolitic for her, it would, in the opinion of the Federalists who had sent Jay, have been fatal for us. The envoy was not a strong negotiator but he was thus sent to the enemy with his hands partly tied, and in the midst of the negotiations, word of what Hamilton had said to Hammond snatched his best weapon from him.

By the terms of the Treaty England agreed to turn over the Northwest posts to the United States by June 1, 1796, although Grenville refused to agree that both nations should not influence the Indians of the other, or to promise that in event of war the savages should not be used as allies. The old colonial debts, certain boundary disputes, and compensation for such captures made at sea as might have been unlawful, were to be settled by commissions. Nothing was said either of compensation for slaves taken in the Revolution or of impressment of seamen. There was to be complete freedom of trade between British ports in Europe and the United States, as well as in the East Indies.

The West Indies were to be opened to our vessels, if not over seventy tons, but in exchange for this Jay, who evidently overlooked, even if he knew of, our growing production of cotton, agreed that while the West Indies were open to us we would not export in American vessels any cotton, sugar, coffee, and cocoa. As a matter of fact, England did not know either that we were beginning to raise cotton, and the enumerated articles were all supposed to be foreign products as far as the United States was concerned. This last article in the Treaty was struck out by the American Senate, and West Indian ports were kept open just the same until the War of 1812, for, if the commerce were essential to us, so also fortunately was it to the Islands.

Although Jay had secured the return of the Western

posts, which were duly surrendered to us, it was considered that he had ransomed what rightly was ours by surrendering our interests in other quarters. The West gained much by the Treaty but the mercantile East felt that far greater concessions should have been won for trade. In weighing Jay's work it must be recalled that since 1783 England had treated us with disdain as an insignificant power, which in truth we were, and it was only in 1791 that she had even consented to send a minister to us. That she had now made a Treaty with the United States was, as Admiral Mahan has pointed out, a matter of epochal significance.

The Americans, however, did not so regard it. A howl of rage went up when the terms became known. Jay was burned in effigy and was execrated in the press and public speeches. The Treaty, with the West India clause excluded, barely passed the Senate by the requisite two-thirds vote, but the President, who felt that it sacrificed American interests and would bring down a storm of obloquy on himself, signed it after mature consideration as preferable to war. "If this country is preserved in tranquillity twenty years longer," he wrote, "it may bid defiance in a just cause to any power whatever," but he knew far better than the public that that time had not yet come.

The Treaty also helped to clear our relations with Spain, and the following year, 1795, that nation recognized the 31st parallel as our southern boundary and accorded us the right of deposit at New Orleans as well as that of navigating her section of the Mississippi. It took her three years more to make a leisurely evacuation

BURNING OF JOHN JAY IN EFFIGY
From a drawing by Darley.

of her posts on our soil, but by 1798 both Spanish and English had left us in possession of our own territory.

Western affairs were clearing, and the West was developing. Kentucky had been admitted as a State in

1792 and Tennessee was to follow in 1796. While the English had been in possession of the posts, trouble had broken out with the Indians, and Governor St. Clair of the Northwest Territory had suffered a terrible defeat November 4, 1791. This had been retrieved by General Wayne who crushed the natives at the battle of Fallen Timbers in August, 1794, just before Jay's Treaty was signed. The subsequent Treaty with the Indians, negotiated at Greenville August 3 the following year, gave the United States all the territory below a new boundary line, including about two thirds of Ohio, and certain localities, such as those where Chicago and Detroit are located. The opening up of these new lands to settlement gave another great impetus to the westward movement, and after Cincinnati, which had been settled in 1788, came Dayton and Chillicothe in 1795 and Cleveland in 1796.

At the very moment when we were fighting the savages, the militia of four States, under Federal orders, was also putting down a rebellion of our own people. In 1791, as part of his general fiscal policy, Hamilton had secured the imposition of an excise tax on whiskey. An excise was considered by Americans as the most odious form of all taxation, and the Continental Congress had declared it to be "the horror of all free States." In 1793 the gross return from the whiskey excise was only $422,-000, and allowing for drawbacks and the cost of collection this was reduced to only about $100,000 net, and in subsequent years it dwindled to much less. From various bits of evidence it had apparently been Hamilton's idea in part that its unpopularity might result in a minor insurrection somewhere, which could be put down by the Federal Government, thus helping to make clear its strength and paramount authority.

This is precisely what occurred, and in 1794 the people of the western counties of Pennsylvania held meetings, appointed a committee of safety, and attacked both sheriff and excisemen. But as an English pamphleteer had written, an excise "hath an army in its belly," and Hamilton was ready for his opportunity. He induced Washington to call out State militia and quell the revolt by force.

Although the rebellion itself was unimportant, the effect of the prompt suppression of resistance to the execution of Federal laws was lasting and wholesome. From the utter weakness and prostration of the old Confederation in 1789 to a treaty with England, an energetic war against the Indians in the Northwest, and a putting down of a popular uprising by the President of the United States with troops under Federal orders, all in 1794, the advance had been almost miraculous considering the hopelessness of the prospect in the earlier year. Most of the credit for the extraordinary success and vigor of the new government must be given to Washington and Hamilton.

When the government had been inaugurated, its cost

had been much dreaded by the people, who complained loudly about senators and congressmen receiving such a huge sum as six dollars a day while attending to their duties. The Secretary of the Treasury had been given a salary of only $3500, and Hamilton, who was not rich though he lived with the rich, resigned his office January 31, 1795, as innumerable public men have been forced to ever since because they could not continue to serve the public for what the public was willing to pay. So great, however, had been his influence that he continued, from his law office in New York, to be the real leader of the Federal Party until the split with John Adams, which we shall soon reach. Jefferson, at Monticello, had been quietly but most efficiently gathering together the elements, North, South, and West, which were to form the "Republican" Party, a name which must not be confused with that of the present Republican Party formed in 1854.

Party spirit was beginning to run high, and the various acts of the government in its first eight years,—its fiscal policies, the excise, the Jay Treaty, the refusal to befriend France, and the apparent desire to placate England,—had all roused furious antagonism among a large part of the people. Republics are notoriously ungrateful, and peoples tire of their greatest men. A violent partisan press had also come into being, and no President, not even Roosevelt or Wilson, has been more bitterly assailed than was Washington in his second term.

The man who had served throughout the Revolution without pay was denounced as avaricious. His character was declared to be false and he was compared to the British tyrants. Immediately after his retirement from office, Franklin's grandson, B. F. Bache, in *The Aurora* wrote that every heart should beat with happiness to think that "the man who is the source of all the misfortunes of our country, is this day reduced to a level with his fellow citizens" and that "the name of *Washington* from this day ceases to give a currency to political iniquity, and to legalize corruption." Tom Paine called him either "an apostate or an imposter," "treacherous in private friendship, and a hypocrite in public life." Such was the reward meted out by a considerable part of the electorate to the man who had done more than any other to win independence for them and to establish their new nation.

WASHINGTON DECLINES TO BE A CANDIDATE

Sixty-five years old, thoroughly weary of public life, Washington wisely declined to allow his name to be used again as a candidate, and so laid the first stone in the valuable tradition limiting the Presidency to two terms, a limitation not mentioned in the Constitution.

On September 17, 1796, shortly before the election of that year, he issued what has come to be known as his "Farewell Address" in which he summed up the political wisdom garnered from his experience. He stressed the immense value of the national Union to every citizen, and the danger of setting local politics above it or of forming parties based on sectional interests, "Northern and Southern—Atlantic and Western." He urged the importance of the division of governmental powers and warned against the encroachment of any one division upon the spheres of the others. Religion and morality, he noted, were indispensable supports to government, and added that national morality could not prevail if religious principles were destroyed.

Looking abroad to the Europe of his day, he pointed out that that continent had a set of primary interests with which America had nothing to do, and that it would be unwise for us to entangle ourselves politically by alliance or otherwise in the Old World system. "Permanent, inveterate antipathies against particular nations and passionate attachments for others," he continued, "should be excluded" and "there can be no greater error than to expect or calculate upon real favors from nation to nation."

He was clearly thinking of England and France, and the advice to make use of our geographical isolation to develop peacefully into maturity and strength was urgently needed by those numerous citizens whose emotional sympathies for or against one or the other of those two countries would have led us into European entanglements. We must consider the Address, as later the Monroe Doctrine, against the background of the circumstances of the time, but for generations both were to prove the soundest of policies for the development of the New World, even if no policy can be literally adhered to through centuries of infinite changes. Nor was Washington's advice, wisest of all for his own day, followed by the people,—as events were soon to prove.

For one thing, the sectionalism that the President warned against was made evident in the election a few weeks later. It was the first which was fought on a party basis, and the Republicans decided to have their electors vote for Jefferson and Aaron Burr. The latter was a grandson of Jonathan Edwards and son of the president of Princeton; and at the time was a prominent lawyer in New York and a bitter political foe of Hamilton, with nothing as yet having occurred to smirch his public career. The Federalists decided upon John Adams and Thomas Pinckney, to balance, like the Republicans, the North and South.

There were no "tickets" in the modern sense, and although the party leaders might agree among themselves whom they wished for President and Vice-President, the system, which we have noted, provided that the man receiving the largest number of votes in the Electoral College should receive the first office and the next highest the second. Attempts were made to have votes cast in such a way as to ensure the election of Adams and Pinckney but when they were counted it was found that Adams had received seventy-one and Jefferson sixty-eight. The Presidency was thus filled by Adams, a Federalist, and the Vice-Presidency by Jefferson, a Republican. If the administration was curiously mixed, the geographical alignment was clear. Every State from Virginia southward had gone Republican and every one from Maryland northward Federalist.

ADAMS IS CHOSEN PRESIDENT

Adams had been a distinguished patriot in the Revolution and was to found the most notable family in American annals. Sprung from simple farming ancestors, he had graduated from Harvard and after becoming a lawyer in Boston had taken prominent part in the controversies leading to the rupture with England. He had been a member of the Continental Congress, a member of the committee to draft the Declaration of Independence, Minister to Holland, where he had rendered valuable service, a member of the commission to negotiate peace with England, and the first minister to that country from America.

These were but the more important offices he had filled, and his voluminous writings on controversial and constitutional questions had been of considerable influence. He was rather vain and somewhat fussy about etiquette but of strong mind and character and, like his descendants, of extreme independence in thought and action. His views on government naturally affiliated him with the Federalists but no Adams could be a party man in the strict sense of the word for he would always have to insist upon the integrity of his own mind when in conflict with party policies.

Such was the man who at sixty-two years of age succeeded Washington as our first party President, March 4, 1797. Hoping to continue Washington's policies, Adams made the disastrous error of continuing his Cabinet in office. There was not a man of outstanding ability in it, and several of them, including Timothy Pickering of Massachusetts, and Oliver Wolcott of Connecticut, were to prove traitors to the President, taking their orders from Hamilton and acting as his spies, Hamilton insisting upon being the actual, and regarding Adams as merely the titular, head of the government.

When Adams took charge, relations with France were difficult. The guillotine had been fast at work in Paris, and the Directory of five who were governing the country had dropped all the earlier idealism of the Revolution and had adopted the policy of military supremacy in Europe which is always at the back of the French mind. Washington had recalled our minister in 1796 and the Directory had refused to accept C. C. Pinckney as his successor. We were thus unrepresented at the French capital, where our Treaty with England was regarded as an offence which called for retaliation. By the summer of 1797 France had captured over 300 of our vessels and was far out-distancing any injuries the English had done us, besides employing a tone toward us which was indecently offensive.

Adams thought of sending Jefferson as envoy but Jefferson declined, wisely, as the office was not compatible with his duties as Vice-President. France was over-running her neighboring states, and the war with England continued. Adams, like most of the Federalists at this time, was bent on remaining neutral in spite of great provocation, and the Republicans still maintained their traditional French friendship. Although the Directory refused to accept an American minister until their so-called grievances were redressed, Adams despatched a mission of three to see what could be gained by diplomacy, while to some extent preparing for war.

The envoys, C. C. Pinckney, Elbridge Gerry, and John Marshall could make no headway in Paris, the Directory insultingly declining to receive them at all. Hamilton and a large part of the Federalists began to believe that the only solution was to join England and to declare war against the French, who had conquered their other victims. Meanwhile, in Paris the American envoys were approached by mysterious go-betweens who, with threats as to what would happen to the United States if their demands were not complied with, asked for a loan of $10,000,000 and a personal gift to Talleyrand of $250,-000 as a preliminary to negotiations. On receiving word of this, Adams announced to Congress that he "would never send another minister to France without assurances that he will be received, respected, and honored as the representative of a great, free, powerful, and independent nation."

The Republicans demanded proof of the need for such

CONGRESSIONAL PUGILISTS
During a session of Congress in Philadelphia in February, 1798.
From the Library of Congress.

language, and early in 1798 the President sent the damning despatches from the envoys to Congress complete, except that the letters X, Y, and Z had been substituted for the names of the go-betweens. Talleyrand became the laughing stock of Europe, and the French party in

America was completely broken. The excitement throughout America was intense; "Millions for defence but not one cent for tribute" became a rallying cry; and war seemed inevitable.

The French Treaties of 1778 were declared at an end; a Navy Department was created; fourteen American men-of-war put to sea, as did a couple of hundred privateers; the U.S.S. *Constellation* captured the French frigate *L'Insurgente;* 10,000 volunteers were called for a term of three years; and war with France apparently had come. The New England Federalists were delighted, and Hamilton was dreaming marvellous dreams of heading an army which should co-operate with the British fleet and capture all the Spanish possessions in North America, including Mexico. Indeed we were so near to war that the usual squabbling had begun as to chief command of the forces, involving Hamilton and Adams in an irritable controversy. The Hamiltonian Federalists completely ignored Washington's advice to keep out of European broils if possible with honor, but Adams believed in it, and was working hard toward that end, knowing, however, that he could no longer trust either his party or his highest officials. The French bluff had been called. France had no wish to add us to her enemies at sea, and it was intimated to Adams that if we sent a minister he would be honorably received.

By this time the President had learned that he could not trust his Cabinet which was disloyal to himself while supplying his enemy Hamilton with information of the most confidential sort. The situation was one of the most disgraceful in our history. No one with the instinct of a gentleman could have remained in the Cabinet, pretending to serve the head of the government with fidelity in a confidential post while in reality acting as a spy for an outsider. It must also be considered a blot on the nature of Hamilton that he was willing to be served in such fashion and to endeavor to secure his ends by a system of moral debauchery which if more than an isolated incident in our history would prevent any President from being able to trust his most intimate advisers as provided for him in the Constitution.

With characteristic courage, Adams acted without consulting any one. The Federalists, happy in the thought of war, were debating their plans in Congress when, like a thunderbolt, they received a message from the President enclosing the offer of peace from Talleyrand, and the nomination of William Vans Murray as American minister. The Federalists could not take the responsibility of plunging the country into war when a clear road to peace had been opened, but Hamilton and all the leaders were furious. Adams alone had saved the nation and carried out Washington's wise policy. The treachery toward him justified him in acting without consultation, but he knew he was thwarting the wishes of the party leaders. It was an act of high courage on which he justly prided himself the remainder of his life.

Every difficulty was thrown in his way. The suggested single minister was replaced by a commission of three, and Pickering, by mean subterfuges, managed to hold up even the sailing of these for some weeks in the hope that something would turn up to defeat his chief. Arriving in France early in 1800, the envoys were received by Napoleon, and after seven months made a treaty of commerce with him. The following day, however, unknown to us, he forced Spain to cede to France the whole of the Louisiana Territory, so that our West once more faced a first-class European power across the Mississippi, and New Orleans became an outpost of the most dangerous nation of the Old World.

The war excitement had as usual brought a crop of hysterical legislation. In 1798 a new Naturalization Act was passed prolonging the required term of residence from five to fourteen years before citizenship could be obtained, and placing all foreign residents under surveillance. An Alien Act gave the President the power to expel from the country any alien whom he might judge dangerous to our peace and safety. A Sedition Act, in almost the precise wording of the law we passed in the World War, made any person punishable by fine or imprisonment who should speak or write against the President or Congress with "the intent to defame" or "bring them into contempt or disrepute."

No action was taken under the Alien Act but a few Republican editors were got out of the way under the

303

Sedition Act. Among them was Thomas Cooper, later to become president of the University of South Carolina, who was fined $400 and jailed for six months. Although the persecutions and the infringement of the right to freedom of speech guaranteed by the Constitution were comically mild as compared with what went on during the Civil War and even more during the World War, our ancestors cared more about liberty than we do, and there was much opposition to these legislative Acts of the Federalists. The State of Kentucky passed a set of Resolves, written by Jefferson, which declared that, if Congress transcended its powers, each State had the right to determine for itself both the wrong and the mode of redress. Virginia also passed a set, drawn up by Madison, which similarly suggested the compact theory of the Federal Government and the doctrine of States' Rights.

No other State took action, but the Kentucky and Virginia Resolves marked another step forward in the crystallization of a section of public opinion as to the nature of the Federal Government which was diametrically opposed to the Federalist theory. It is worth noting that Madison, in his later life, explained why he and Jefferson had split with Hamilton by saying it was because the latter was deliberately trying to turn the government into "a thing totally different from that which he and I both knew perfectly well had been understood and intended by the Convention who framed it, and by the People adopting it."

304

IT is with the deepest grief that we announce to the public the death of our *most distinguished* fellow-citizen *Lieut. General George Washington.* He died at Mount Vernon on Saturday evening, the 13th inst. of an inflammatory affection of the throat, which put a period to his existence in 23 hours.

The grief which we suffer on this truly mournful occasion, would be in some degree alleviated, if we possessed abilities to do justice to the merits of this *illustrious benefactor of mankind*; but, conscious of our inferiority, we shrink from the sublimity of the subject. To the impar-

For the Gazette.

tial and eloquent historian, therefore, we consign the high and grateful office of exhibiting the life of *George Washington* to the present age, and to generations yet unborn, as a perfect model of all that is *virtuous, noble, great,* and *dignified* in man. Our feelings, however, will not permit us to forbear observing, that the very disinterest d and important services rendered by *George Washington* to these United States, both in the Field and in the Cabinet, have erected in the hearts of his countrymen, monuments of sincere and unbounded gratitude, which the mouldering hand of Time cannot deface; and that in every quarter of the Globe, where a free Government is ranked amongst the choicest blessings of Providence, and *virtue, morality, religion,* and *patriotism* are respected, THE NAME of WASHINGTON WILL BE HELD IN *veneration.*

And as along the stream of TIME, his name
Expanded flies, and gathers all its fame,
Oh! may our little bark attendant sail,
Pursue the triumph, and partake the gale!
While Statesmen, Heroes, Kings, in dust repose,
Whose sons shall blush their fathers were his foes!

ANNOUNCEMENT OF WASHINGTON'S DEATH

From "The New York Gazette and General Advertiser," December 21, 1799, in the New York Historical Society.

No one had a deeper understanding or wider knowledge of what went on in the convention which adopted the Constitution than Madison, to whose painstaking notes, made day by day, we owe the most of what we know ourselves. It is only reasonable, therefore, to lay great stress upon his opinion, and when we are inclined to think of the Constitution as something immutable, it is well to recall that it has been gradually twisted and altered far from its original intention through a century and a half, notably by Hamilton in its first decade.

The election of 1800 was to bring on the first serious contest between the Federalist and the Republican points of view. The old harmony was gone, and America was entering upon a new era. As if to mark the passing of the old, Washington, the one symbol of unity, sickened and died after a few days' illness, on the 14th of December, 1799. Everywhere there was mourning. Shops and offices closed, bells tolled all day, and memorial services were held in village after village as the news reached them. In Congress, Henry Lee uttered the now hackneyed words, "first in war, first in peace, first in the hearts of his countrymen." But it was noted that although the Federalist newspapers had heavy black borders and columns, the Republican journals used only a narrow band and that merely around the notice of his death.

Our country is rich in the men and women who have risen to distinction as workers and leaders. Our country is rich in natural scenes of beauty and grandeur. Our country is rich in buildings which have expressed the courage, tenacity, and imagination of our people.

The final pages of each volume of this edition of James Truslow Adams's *History of the United States* present in attractive form some of these outstanding personalities, some of the most thrilling moments of our history, some of our most beautiful natural scenes, some of the most conspicuous representations of our architectural imagination—a veritable panorama of American life.

GEORGE WASHINGTON

A great American painter, Gilbert Stuart, had the good fortune to be chosen to paint the picture of George Washington. Although our first great President was the subject of many fine paintings, perhaps no one is more famous and no one gives a better impression of the stately bearing of the man who was "first in the hearts of his countrymen" than does this painting by Gilbert Stuart, reproduced on the opposite page.

There is probably no subject which could be looked at and studied with greater profit than the likeness of this man who did so much to make our country what it is today. The characteristics of that man as they have been woven into the structure of our country have ever been a more steady influence toward fine accomplishments and permanency of ideals than the work of any other man who has lived in our nation's history.

BENJAMIN FRANKLIN

There is probably no face that is more familiar to Americans than that of Benjamin Franklin. From childhood we have read of the thrilling incidents of his active life—as a mere boy, knowing what it was to work for a living, using his ingenuity in devising ways to make himself useful to his employer and helpful to his neighbors; later, applying prodigious imagination and his inventive skill in hundreds of ways for the betterment of mankind; and, finally, using his social and intellectual accomplishments as the representative of the United States in countries abroad.

In a marked degree we think of him as a real and typical American, ready to be a pioneer when pioneering was needed, ready to persuade his fellow citizens in ways of diplomacy when diplomacy was needed, and ready with a sober mind when sober judgment was needed. It has been truly said that there is no greater heritage for a country than its noble men and women, and among them Benjamin Franklin will always be numbered.

The painting which is reproduced on the opposite page is by Duplessis, 1778, and now hangs in the Pennsylvania Academy of Fine Arts.

ALEXANDER HAMILTON

Alexander Hamilton was not an orator and his style was diffuse, but his mind was brilliantly clear. Hamilton was the antithesis of Jefferson. Hamilton thought from the Federal Government downward; Jefferson from the parish or county upward. Jefferson was for free trade and no special privileges for any one, and although we may call him an idealist as contrasted with the realist Hamilton, there is no question but that he incarnated the dream that we Americans have always dreamed as Hamilton did not.

Hamilton thought that the Declaration of Independence was a war-time propaganda. For Jefferson it was still a living faith.

This portrait, painted by Trumbull, is in the Essex Institute, Salem, Massachusetts.

JAMES MADISON

Madison was a scholar. When his fellow delegate to the Constitutional Convention, William Pierce, described him as a "profound politician" the word was used in the sense of statesman or student of the art of governing. Modest and shy, short in stature, slight in figure, his presence was not distinguished, but no other man has come to the Presidency with a wider knowledge of all that concerned the United States combined with so deep an insight and understanding of that Constitution of which he has properly been called the "father." He had less ability in the management of practical politics than had either Jefferson or Madison's own successor in office, James Monroe, but he far exceeded the latter in brilliancy and solidity of intellect.

This portrait of him was painted by Gilbert Stuart.

JAMES MONROE

Monroe, the last of the Virginia dynasty, which had been broken only by the one term of John Adams, was in many ways a mediocre man, but, like many other such, had made a most useful President, reaching his own judgments deliberately and shouldering responsibility while displaying a fair-minded generosity toward all men and a magnanimity and tolerance which his Secretary of State, John Quincy Adams, felt that he carried to the extent of weakness. He was, however, a worthy successor of the preceding Virginians.

It is a bit of the irony of history that Monroe should have his name associated with one of the most famous documents ever issued, although the actual inspiration of the Monroe Doctrine came very largely from his Secretary of State.

The portrait of him reproduced on the opposite page is by Sully and now hangs in the United States Military Academy at West Point.

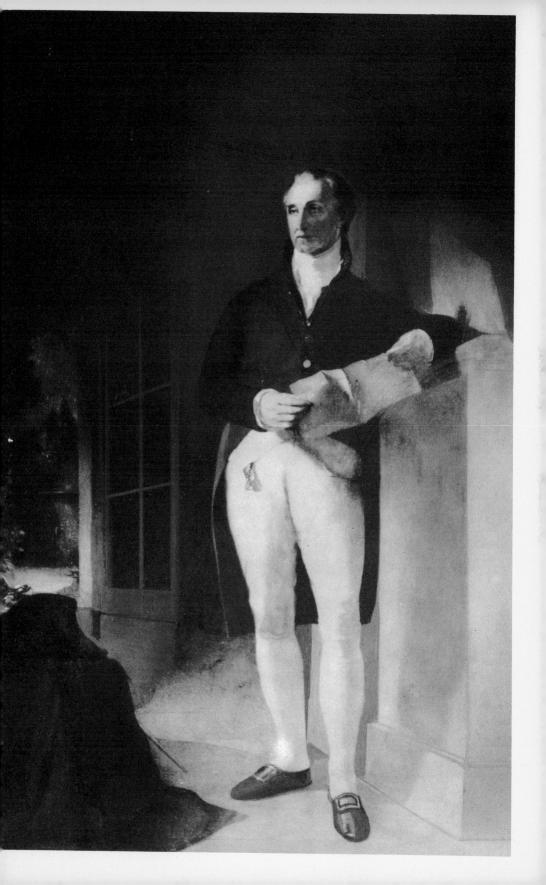

ANDREW JACKSON

"Old Hickory," as a swashbuckling fighter, had endeared himself to the West from the days of his famous fight at New Orleans and his lurid adventures with the Creek Indians in Florida. In him the West found a leader to its taste and by placing him in the Presidency did much to change the course of history.

The old picture of Jackson as an illiterate radical has long since passed from history. Although his knowledge of books was slight, he was far from illiterate, and his judgment was firm and quick. He possessed not only courage and strength, but, on the whole, sound judgment, tenacity of purpose, and inflexible honesty, together with what was to prove a surprising independence of opinion and character. Completely sincere, he believed in democracy to an extent that no other President has yet done with the exception of Jefferson, and even Jefferson had had mental reservations on the subject denied to Jackson.

Vanderlyn painted this portrait of him which is now in the City Hall, New York City.

ABRAHAM LINCOLN

A photograph by Alexander Gardner, taken April 10, 1865

Nature, they say, doth dote,
And cannot make a man
Save on some worn-out plan,
Repeating us by rote:
For him her Old-World moulds aside she threw,
And, choosing sweet clay from the breast
Of the unexhausted West,
With stuff untainted shaped a hero new,
Wise, steadfast in the strength of God, and true.
How beautiful to see
Once more a shepherd of mankind indeed,
Who loved his charge, but never loved to lead;
One whose meek flock the people joyed to be,
Not lured by any cheat of birth,
But by his clear-grained human worth,
And brave old wisdom of sincerity!

JAMES RUSSELL LOWELL.

GROVER CLEVELAND

Grover Cleveland was a self-made Buffalo lawyer, who had risen with clean hands through the political offices of sheriff of the county and Mayor of Buffalo to the governorship of the State.

The reputation of Grover Cleveland, like that of few of our Presidents, has increased with the years. During his lifetime he was often regarded as a very stolid and unyielding character without many of the human qualities that endear a leader to his people. As time has gone on, Cleveland stands out not only from his own time, but among all the statesmen of our country for his independence, common sense, and courage.

THEODORE ROOSEVELT

In many respects there has been no other figure in American public life to compare with Theodore Roosevelt. After a rather sickly youth he had become a man of almost incomparably abounding physical as well as mental vigor. Never a profound and often not a logical thinker, the range of his intellectual interests was wide and his memory unusual. Standing firmly for the ideals, which he was fond of preaching, of the ordinary clean, honest American, he also delighted to describe himself as a "very practical man," a combination which sometimes brought him into strange combinations with political bosses. He was essentially pragmatic, and believed in working with what tools one had.

Of his patriotism, ideals, and ability both in politics and statesmanship, there can be no doubt. He had an extraordinary capacity also for making himself popular, which he used as an actor does, but apart from this, there were genuine qualities in the man himself which enormously interested people of the most varied sorts. No other American, if any statesman anywhere, has ever aroused the world-wide interest in himself and his doings which attended Roosevelt in the fifteen years after the Spanish War.

WOODROW WILSON

Wilson was an idealist, perhaps the greatest idealist in the history of the world who has held the post of a responsible statesman of such surpassing importance in any crisis of world history. Had he been called upon to deal only with American affairs, as he hoped he would, during his terms of office, his idealism would have been wholesomely kept in touch with practicality by his knowledge of the psychology and history of his own countrymen.

Wilson had a profound belief in morality, and also believed that a government could not govern usefully or efficiently unless its acts were moral. He believed, again, profoundly in democracy, and in the ability of the ordinary human being to govern himself wisely.

STONE STREET LOOKING TOWARD WHITEHALL, 1659

From the miniature group in The Museum of the City of New York, modelled by Ned J. Burns.

Brouwer Street, the present Stone Street, was one of the first to be paved in New Amsterdam. In the background can be seen the Dutch fort, which stood on the present site of the Custom House. Its eastern side, half of which may be seen, faced Stone Street and fronted on Matckvelt (now Whitehall Street).

The smaller house on the right side of Stone Street was the residence of Surgeon Varrevanger. It had formerly been the Wooden Horse Tavern. The stone building beside it was erected in 1658 to 1659 by the carpenter Frederick Philipse.

During the Dutch occupation of New Amsterdam, pigs and other domestic animals roamed at large through the streets, often damaging the gardens. The many fences seen in the group were erected in order to prevent this destruction.

THE EXPULSION OF THE QUAKERS FROM
MASSACHUSETTS, 1660

Painted by Edwin Austin Abbey.

The first Quaker missionaries came to America in 1656. They did not believe in consecrated churches, ordained ministers, or set forms of worship, refused to take oaths, to recognize titles in their speech, and would remove their hats to no one. As a result they were feared by the authorities and treated very harshly, particularly in the New England colonies where the Quaker denunciations struck at the foundations of the Puritan life. Accordingly they were banished by the Massachusetts authorities. Despite drastic punishment they persisted in returning as fast as they were deported so that finally a law was passed, by a narrow margin, punishing by death any who returned. Later, because of public feeling against the hangings, and a more conciliatory attitude on the part of the Quakers, this law was succeeded by the Cart and Whip Act, which provided that the offenders be tied to the end of a cart and whipped through successive towns until out of the jurisdiction of the colony. In 1677 these whippings were terminated.

A MODEL OF THE OVERSHOT WATER WHEEL IN THE
JOHN WINTHROP MILL, NEW LONDON, CONNECTICUT

By courtesy of the New York Museum of Science and Industry.

Built in 1690 by Governor John Winthrop, this old town mill still grinds grain into flour. In this type of wheel the water is directed overhead, and, by its own weight as it falls, turns the wheel round. In order to give the water the necessary force and height, the stream must be dammed above the mill and the water led on to the wheel by a wooden trough or pipe.

THE SURRENDER OF FORT WILLIAM HENRY TO
MONTCALM IN 1757

*From the painting by J. L. G. Ferris, copyright by the Glens Falls Insurance Company,
Glens Falls, New York, and used by their permission.*

On August 4, 1757, Montcalm, with a force of eight thousand French and
Indians, appeared at the head of Lake George in a descent upon Fort William
Henry, commanded by Lieutenant-Colonel Monro with two thousand one
hundred and forty men. Monro, without reinforcements, held out for five days
but at the end of that time surrendered. Under the terms of surrender the English were to march out with their personal belongings and proceed to Fort Edward under French escort. As they marched out, the Indians in the French
command, athirst for blood, fell upon them. Montcalm and his French regulars
threw themselves into the defense of their enemies, but despite their efforts,
fifty English were tomahawked and scalped.

THE BURNING OF THE *PRUDENT* AND CAPTURE OF
THE *BIENFAISANT* IN LOUISBOURGH HARBOR,
JULY 26, 1758

*Large folio line engraving by P. C. Canot after the painting by R. Paton. Published by
John Boydell, London, 1771. Courtesy of the Mabel Brady Garvan Institute of American
Arts & Crafts, Yale University.*

The artist's dedication as given on the engraving is:

For the Captains & Seamen, who with a detachment of Boats from the Fleet
commanded by Admiral Boscawene, Burnt the *Prudent* & Took the *Bienfaisant*
in Louisbourgh Harbour, about 1 o'clock in the morning of the 26th July 1758
—In Memory of that Singular & Brave Action This Representation is Humbly
Inscribed by Their Most Obedient Servant—Rich'd Paton.

and the description:

Capt.ⁿ Laforey with 25 Boats attacked and took the *Prudent* of 74
Guns but finding her aground was
obliged to burn her.

Capt.ⁿ Balfour with 25 boats attacked, took, and towed off the *Bienfaisant* of 64 guns into the N.E. Harbour then in possession of the British
Troops.

ABERCROMBIE'S ARMY EMBARKING AT THE HEAD OF
LAKE GEORGE IN AN EXPEDITION AGAINST
TICONDEROGA, JULY, 1758

From a painting by F. C. Yohn. By courtesy of the Glens Falls Insurance Company,
Glens Falls, New York.

Six thousand redcoats and nine thousand provincial troops landed the next day and proceeded on foot to Ticonderoga through heavy woods. The first disaster befell the party when Lord Howe, the second in command and an officer outstanding in his knowledge and ability to adapt himself to the mode of French and Indian warfare, was killed in a chance encounter with a French ranging party.

Arriving at Ticonderoga, Abercrombie, despite his vastly superior numbers, decided to storm the fortress. The British advanced in three columns; under orders not to fire until they were within the lines. The three thousand French regulars waited from behind their nine-foot embankment, and then opened fire at the same time as the guns from the fort, riddling the British ranks. As each regiment fell back in face of the terrific fire, another advanced to take its place. This lasted for four hours. Sixteen hundred regulars and three hundred and fifty provincials were killed when Abercrombie ordered the retreat. Montcalm lost only four hundred.

THE COLLEGE OF PHILADELPHIA BEFORE THE
REVOLUTION

From a painting by Lefferts. By courtesy of the University of Pennsylvania.

In 1751, a group of citizens of Philadelphia, with Benjamin Franklin as president, opened an academy in the building which had been erected as an auditorium for George Whitefield, the English evangelist. This had been the first building in this country intended for the use of an itinerant preacher-evangelist.

In 1753, the institution was chartered as the "College, Academy and Charitable School of Philadelphia." The picture shows the first buildings on Fourth Street.

BRUTON PARISH CHURCH, WILLIAMSBURG, VIRGINIA

This church was built in 1715 and is still in use.
The painting by A. Wordsworth Thompson, now in the Metropolitan Museum of Art, New York, was made during the time that Lord Dunmore, the last colonial governor of Virginia, appointed in 1771, was in power.

THE PARLOR OF THE POWELL HOUSE IN PHILADELPHIA

AS REBUILT IN THE AMERICAN WING OF THE METROPOLITAN MUSEUM OF ART

A room famous for its association with many events in the artistic, social, and political life just prior to the Revolution, and considered one of the finest interiors in the colonies.

The furniture is of mahogany of Chippendale influence, designed and carved in Philadelphia. Beautifully moulded panelling distinguishes the fireplace wall, while the others are covered with a Chinese paper showing mountains, pagodas, and mandarins painted in water-color. From the ceiling hangs a handsome cut-glass lustre.

A DINING ROOM OF THE EARLY REPUBLICAN PERIOD OF WASHINGTON AND BALTIMORE

AS RECONSTRUCTED IN THE AMERICAN WING OF THE METROPOLITAN MUSEUM OF ART

The cornice is an exact reproduction of one in "The Octagon," the brick house built in Washington for John Tayloe between 1798 and 1800. The arched openings are original woodwork from a house in Baltimore built about 1810. The furniture is of Sheraton type showing a transition into Directory and Empire styles, much of it coming from the workshop of Duncan Phyfe. The large pedestal dining-table of the extension type is surrounded by side-chairs with lyre motif on the backs.

THE EVENING MAIL—TRAVEL BY STAGECOACH ON
THE BOSTON POST ROAD

Painted by Stanley M. Arthurs.

As far back as 1772 there was a stage running from Boston to New York, but these early coaches were not entrusted with the mail. Long before that time a monthly service had been established between these points, and the first postman to arrive from Boston had appeared on horseback in the little Dutch burgh of Haarlem in 1692, following a road no better than an axe-blazed trail.

In 1704, Madame Sarah Knight, a Boston schoolmistress, journeyed with the post to New York. She was probably the first woman to travel overland on the Boston Post Road.

In 1806, daily stages left both New York and Boston, the more rapid mail coaches making the run in three days. Later in connection with the Sound steamboats, New York and Boston were brought within less than thirty hours of each other. In 1832, there were one hundred and six stage lines running regularly from Boston to various destinations.

OTIS PROTESTING THE WRITS OF ASSISTANCE

From the painting by Robert Reid in the State House, Boston.

James Otis was an outstanding figure and popular leader in the fight for freedom in the days preceding the Revolution. In 1761 he was advocate-general of Massachusetts, which position he resigned to become counsel for the merchants protesting the Writs of Assistance. These Writs of Assistance, part of the old Act of Trade, were search warrants, authorized by an Act of Parliament and issued by local courts, which enabled the officers of the crown to enter and search storehouses at will.

Otis argued his case with fiery eloquence before the Supreme Court in Boston, disdaining the technicalities involved, and stating that the writs were "the worst instrument of arbitrary power, the most destructive of English liberty and the fundamental principles of law that ever was found in an English law-book. . . . Reason and constitution are both against this writ. Let us see what authority there is for it. Not more than one instance can be found in all our law-books; and that was in the zenith of arbitrary power, in the reign of Charles II. . . . But had this writ been in any book whatsoever, it would have been illegal. All precedents are under the control of the principles of law. . . . No acts of parliament can establish such a writ. . . . An act against the constitution is void."

PAUL REVERE

From the painting by N. C. Wyeth.

General Gage, Commander-in-Chief of the British force in America, spent the winter of 1774–75 in Boston where his efforts to seize Sam Adams and John Hancock and send them to England for trial had proved fruitless.

On April 19, 1775, he decided to try and capture stores which he understood had been gathered at Concord. Although the British regulars started before daybreak, the alarm was at once given and Paul Revere and two others rode through the country spreading the news so that by the time the thousand advancing British reached Lexington, they found about fifty colonials blocking the way. Most of the stores at Concord had been removed and when the British began their return march they were shot at by minutemen from behind rocks and trees all along the way, so that their retreat became a rout and, despite reinforcements, they reached Boston only with difficulty and a loss of more than two hundred and seventy men.

WINTER AT VALLEY FORGE

THE RELIEF

From the painting by F. C. Yohn.

When General Howe retired to Philadelphia to pass the winter in comfort, entertained by theatrical performances, balls, and dances, Washington selected Valley Forge for his winter camp. From a military standpoint it was an excellent site, being both central and easily defended. There the Continental forces waited throughout the long winter for Howe's next move. It was not easy for Washington to maintain the life and strength of his army without resources or equipment, and with an inefficient and carping Congress for his only resort. Streets were laid out and huts built—the men had shelter, but that was about all. Blankets and coverings were few and even straw to lie upon was hard to get. At night the men huddled about fires to keep from freezing. Many soldiers were without shoes and waded through the snow with naked feet. Provisions were scarce—there was barely any meat and bread, the diet being largely flour mixed with water and baked into cakes. By January some three thousand men were unfit for duty—frostbitten, sick, and hungry. Had it not been for the fine influence of the officers and the patient courage, warm sympathy, and indomitable spirit of the Commander-in-Chief, the winter of cold, hunger, and disease might easily have resulted in mutiny and general desertion. As it was, the courage and endurance of the men were marvellous. It is a proof of the devotion and patriotism of the American soldier that he bore these sufferings and came through them loyally and victoriously.

F C YOHN

HAMILTON SURRENDERING TO GEORGE
ROGERS CLARK AT VINCENNES

*From a painting by F. C. Yohn, reproduced by courtesy of the
Historical Society of Indiana.*

Colonel Hamilton, hearing that Vincennes had deserted British allegiance and accepted the rule of the United States, left his headquarters at Detroit, and, with a strong force of five hundred English, French, and Indians, descended on Fort Sackville on December 17, 1778, and reoccupied the fort. Thereupon the French inhabitants deserted the American Commandant and went over to Hamilton. The latter decided to keep only one hundred of his men with him, winter in the fort, and in the spring reassemble his forces and attack Clark at Fort Kaskaskia. To prevent this Clark determined to attack first. With one hundred and seventy men he struggled through the flooded wilderness to Vincennes. Fearing that a surprise attack might force the French and Indians to unite with the British, while if given time for a choice they might remain neutral or desert, Clark announced his approach. As he had expected, the French retired into their houses in terror and the Indians remained aloof. Clark then opened fire on the fort, and, under cover of the night, threw up an intrenchment, from which the Americans poured a deadly fire into every port hole that their adversaries opened and silenced the British guns. Hamilton, with but seventy-nine loyal men left, was forced to surrender. By this victory Clark broke up the English campaign in the West.

BENJAMIN FRANKLIN AND RICHARD OS-
WALD, BRITISH REPRESENTATIVE, DISCUSS-
ING THE TREATY OF PEACE AT PARIS

Painted by Howard Pyle.

In 1782 negotiations for peace were opened with the representatives we had sent to Paris for that purpose: Franklin, John
Adams, and John Jay. Franklin had been representing American
interests in France since 1776. He had already spent sixteen
years in England before the war, and without losing a whit of
his racy Americanism, he knew Europe as did no other American of his day. Shrewd, humorous, a genuine child of the eighteenth-century philosophy, serene, imperturbable, realistic, infinitely curious, accepting life as it came in experience, one of
the notable scientific investigators of his day, tolerant and mellow, unaffected, full of common sense, knowing how to make
the best of every situation and of his peculiar qualities and characteristics, always Benjamin Franklin, whether carrying a loaf
of bread under his arm in the streets of Philadelphia, talking
with kings or being adored by French society, he had become
the rage in Paris and done much to make the French idealize
the life and character of his own new nation.

THE SIGNING OF THE CONSTITUTION IN
INDEPENDENCE HALL, PHILADELPHIA, 1787

*From the mural painting by Albert Herter, in the Supreme Court, State Capitol,
Madison, Wisconsin.*

The convention at Philadelphia included many of the able men of the day. Prominent among them were Robert and Gouverneur Morris, Roger Sherman, George Clymer, James Wilson, Luther Martin, Charles Pinckney, Alexander Hamilton, and James Madison: representatives of law, finance, and students of government. They had come with instructions to change the Articles of Confederation, but it was apparent to them that a new constitution was necessary for the new government, and this they proceeded to draft. On September 15 the Constitution was accepted by the delegates of all the States represented, and on September 17 it was signed. Of the members present three refused to sign. On September 28 the Constitution was sent to the States for ratification.

WASHINGTON ARRIVING AT THE BATTERY, NEW YORK, PRIOR TO HIS INAUGURATION

Painted by Ernest Peixotto for the Seamen's Bank for Savings, New York City.

Having accepted the Presidency offered him by the unanimous vote of the Electoral College, Washington left Mount Vernon on the 16th of April, 1789, to begin his journey to New York. It was a triumphal procession. All along his route people turned out to do him honor. Towns were decorated, troops of cavalry and citizens' committees greeted him everywhere, young girls strewed flowers in the road over which he passed. At Elizabethtown Point, Washington embarked for New York on a special barge manned by thirteen masters of vessels and followed by other barges filled with public officials and distinguished citizens. On all sides bells rang, flags waved and cannons roared. A throng awaited him at Murray's Wharf where Governor Clinton welcomed him and accompanied him to his house on Cherry Street.

WASHINGTON TAKING THE OATH OF OF-FICE AS FIRST PRESIDENT OF THE UNITED STATES

Painted by Harry Ogden.

The inauguration took place at Federal Hall on the 13th of April, 1789. Washington was received in the Senate Chamber and then escorted to the balcony where the oath of office was administered by the Chancellor of the State, Robert Livingston, in full view of the eager spectators who thronged the streets and crowded the windows and roofs of the nearby buildings. Grouped around Washington were the Vice-President and many of the Revolutionary generals. At the conclusion of the ceremony Livingston stepped to the balcony railing and cried "Long live George Washington, President of the United States." The Stars and Stripes were raised on the staff above the balcony, a storm of cheers broke from the crowd, and harbor cannon announced the new President.

CONNECTICUT SETTLERS ENTERING THE
WESTERN RESERVE

From the painting by Howard Pyle.

From earliest times the little Yankee Colony of Connecticut seemed possessed of a restless spirit of pioneering and colonizing. Her people were acquisitive, and endeavored strenuously to realize her early dreams of territorial expansion. In 1662, Charles II had granted Connecticut a charter, combining former charters and deeds and conveying to that colony all the territory of the present State and all *of the lands west of it, to the extent of its breadth from sea to sea.* Connecticut was anxious to realize this—axes rang out in the wildernesses and log cabins went up—her expansion in the eighteenth century was the most remarkable example of internal colonization in the history of our entire country. Many of her sons looked with longing to Wyoming, envisioning the rich reward that awaited them in what was to become the "Connecticut Western Reserve." However it required fifty years of struggle and warfare, during which her people were seven times evicted and twice massacred, before she secured clear title to the three hundred acres of this Western land, and the beautiful valley, which she coveted.

DANIEL BOONE LEADING A GROUP OF PIONEERS
THROUGH THE CUMBERLAND GAP

From a painting by George C. Bingham, the property of Washington University,
St. Louis, Missouri.

As the pioneers came through the passes or gaps in the mountains, the magnificent valley of the Father of Waters, two thousand miles wide, lay before them. Here was a vast new empire to be conquered, the outlet of which was not by way of Boston, New York, Philadelphia, or Charleston, but by way of the great river, Spanish New Orleans, and the Gulf.

Daniel Boone, with a group of settlers, built a fort and established Boonesboro in 1775. The following year Kentucky was made a county of Virginia, and gradually both Kentucky and Tennessee saw the pouring in of what may be considered our first great western movement, hordes of settlers tramping over the mountains through Cumberland Gap and other passes from Pennsylvania, Virginia, and the Carolinas.